W9-BKS-946

# SPANISH IS FUN

BOOK 2

# SPANISH IS FUN
## BOOK 2

***Lively Lessons for Advancing Students***

Heywood Wald, PhD

Former Assistant Principal
Foreign Language Department
Martin Van Buren High School
New York City

When ordering this book, please specify *either* **R 483 H**
*or* SPANISH IS FUN, BOOK 2, HARDBOUND EDITION

AMSCO

**AMSCO SCHOOL PUBLICATIONS, INC.**
**315 Hudson Street/New York, N.Y. 10013**

ISBN 0-87720-542-6



Printed in the United States of America

# Preface

If Spanish is fun, more Spanish is more fun. That is the premise on which this book is based.

SPANISH IS FUN, BOOK 2 continues the natural, personalized, enjoyable, and rewarding program of language acquisition begun in the first course. BOOK 2 provides all the elements for a full second course and prepares students for their first formal proficiency testing.

SPANISH IS FUN, BOOK 2 is designed to broaden the student's level of achievement in basic skills, with special emphasis on communication. Through the topical contexts, students will also expand their acquisition of vocabulary, their control of structure, and their ability to communicate about their daily lives, express their opinions, and supply real information.

SPANISH IS FUN, BOOK 2 consists of four parts. Each part contains five lessons followed by a *Repaso* unit, in which structure and vocabulary are recapitulated and practiced through various *actividades.* These *actividades* include games and puzzles as well as more conventional exercises. Repaso II and Repaso IV are followed by an Achievement Test. A concluding Proficiency Test provides an opportunity for evaluating student performance in speaking, listening comprehension, reading comprehension, and writing.

Each lesson includes a step-by-step sequence of learning elements designed to make the materials directly accessible to students:

### Vocabulary

Each lesson begins by presenting the topical and thematically related vocabulary through sets of drawings that convey the meanings of new words and expressions in Spanish without recourse to English. This device, sometimes in individual vignettes, sometimes in composite scenes, enables students to make a direct and vivid association between the Spanish terms and their meanings. The *actividades* that follow directly also use pictures to help students practice words and expressions.

### Structure

SPANISH IS FUN, BOOK 2 introduces new structural elements in small learning components—one at a time, followed directly by appropriate *actividades,* many of them personalized and presented in a communicative framework. By following this simple, straightforward, guided presentation, students make their own discoveries and formulate their own conclusion and in the process gain a feeling of accomplishment and success.

### Conversation

To encourage students to use Spanish for communication and self-expression, each lesson includes a dialog exercise designed to stimulate creative speaking. All dialogs are illustrated in cartoon-strip fashion, with students completing empty "balloons" with appropriate bits of original dialog. Students should have fun with these dramatizations.

### Reading

Each lesson contains a short narrative or playlet that features the new structures and vocabulary and reinforces previously acquired vocabulary. Each reading selection is not only a vehicle for the presentation of these elements but also deals with a topic of intrinsic interest related to the real, everyday experiences of today's students: social relationships, humorous science-fiction, school experiences, human-interest material, and so on. Cognates and near-cognates are used extensively to permit a much greater range of vocabulary.

### Personal Information

A major goal of the entire program is to enable students to personalize language by relating the situation in the lesson to their own lives. In this activity, students are asked easy-to-answer, open-ended questions that require them to respond with information from their own experiences.

### Composition

Guided writing practice affords students the opportunity to express themselves creatively about a variety of situations related to the theme and topic of the lesson.

### Culture

Each lesson is followed by a *Cápsula cultural.* These twenty *cápsulas,* most of them illustrated, offer students a picturesque view of the vast mosaic of Hispanic culture.

### Testing

The two Achievement Tests (after Repaso II and Repaso IV) are designed to give ALL students a sense of accomplishment. The tests use various techniques through which mastery of structure and vocabulary and comprehension of contextual material may be evaluated. The final Proficiency Test evaluates student performance in all basic language skills—speaking, listening comprehension, reading comprehension, and writing.

### Teacher's Manual and Key

A separate *Teacher's Manual and Key* includes suggestions for teaching all elements in the book, additional oral practice, and a complete key for all exercises and puzzles.

H.W.

# *Contents*

## Primera Parte



## Segunda Parte

## Tercera Parte

## Cuarta Parte

# Primera Parte

# 1 Comidas típicas

## Interrogative Words; **conocer** and **saber**

## Vocabulario

Restaurante «Su Casa Española»

MENÚ

ESPECIALIDADES DEL DÍA

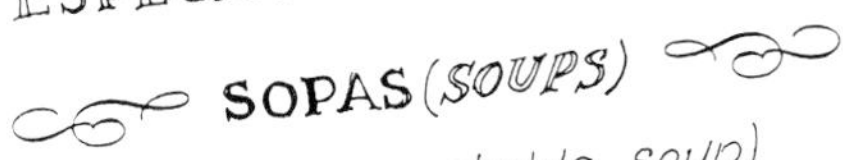

SOPAS (SOUPS)

Gazpacho (Cold, fresh vegetable soup)
Sopa de ajo (Garlic soup)
Fabada (Bean soup with sausages)
Caldo gallego (White bean, turnip, and potato soup)

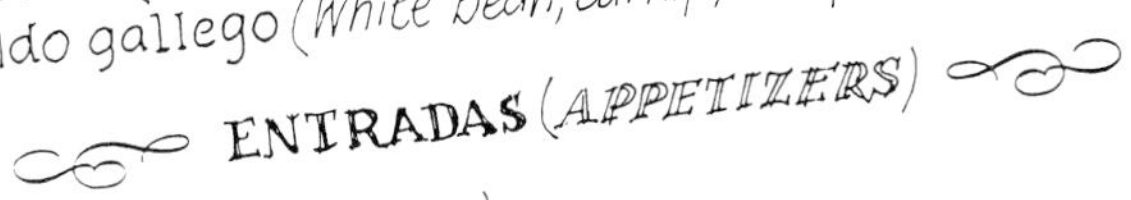

ENTRADAS (APPETIZERS)

Empanada (Meat pie)
Camarones al ajillo (Shrimp in garlic sauce)
Tortilla de patatas (Potato omelette)

PLATOS PRINCIPALES (MAIN DISHES)

Paella (Saffron rice with meat, seafood, and vegetables)
Calamares en su tinta (Squid in its own ink)
Arroz con pollo (Rice with chicken)
Ternera a la sevillana (Veal, Sevillian style with sherry and green olives)
Zarzuela de mariscos (Shellfish stew)

POSTRES (DESSERTS)

Brazo de gitano (Gipsy's arm, sponge-cake roll with rum cream filling)
Natilla (Soft custard)
Flan (Caramel custard)
Arroz con leche (Rice pudding)

## ACTIVIDADES

**A.** You are a waiter in a Spanish restaurant. A tourist comes in and asks for a "comida típica." What would you recommend?

1. la sopa: ____________________

2. la entrada: ____________________

3. el plato principal: ____________________

4. el postre: ____________________

**B.** Your school is planning a Spanish food festival. Each student has to prepare one dish. What does each of these students prepare?

| | SOPAS | ENTRADAS | PLATOS PRINCIPALES | POSTRES |
|---|---|---|---|---|
| Silvia | | | | |
| Margarita | | | | |
| Roberto | | | | |
| Ana | | | | |
| Carlos | | | | |
| Pablo | | | | |
| Carmen | | | | |
| Andrés | | | | |

**2** Sra. López talks to her students about their plans for the Hispanic food festival. Read the dialog, paying special attention to the questions:

¿Qué platos van a preparar para la fiesta?
Vamos a preparar platos típicos de España e Hispanoamérica. ¿Cuáles son fáciles de preparar?

**3** Which question words did you notice in the conversation? __________ and __________. Right. **¿Qué?** means *what?* or *which?* and **¿cuál?** means *which one?* but it also means *what?* or *which?* How do you know when to use **¿qué?** and when to use **¿cuál?** It's very simple: **¿Qué?** is used before the verb **ser** when asking for a definition. You use **¿cuál?** instead of **¿qué?** before the verb **ser** when a choice is asked for:

| | |
|---|---|
| **¿*Qué* es una paella?** | *What is a paella?* |
| **¿*Cuál* es su comida preferida?** | *Which is your favorite food?* |

**¿Qué?** doesn't change, but **¿cuál?** has a plural form, **¿cuáles?**, if you are referring to more than one. Let's look at some examples:

| | |
|---|---|
| **¿*Qué* pasa?** | *What's going on?* |
| **¿*Qué* cosa dice Ud.?** | *What are you saying?* |
| **¿*Qué* libro quiere leer?** | *Which book do you want to read?* |
| **¿*Qué* es la Casa Blanca?** | *What is the White House?* |
| **¿*Cuál* es la Casa Blanca?** | *Which (one) is the White House?* |
| **¿*Cuáles* son sus libros?** | *Which (ones) are your books?* |
| **¿*Cuál* es la fecha de hoy?** | *What is today's date?* |

## ACTIVIDADES

**C.** Complete with the missing Spanish word for *which* or *what:*

1. ¿__________ postres le gustan a Ud.?
2. ¿__________ es su postre favorito?
3. ¿__________ es un diccionario?
4. ¿__________ es la capital de España?
5. ¿__________ son los ingredientes del flan?

**D.** Your school wants to make some changes in the cafeteria menu. A student questionnaire is being circulated. Can you think of five questions you'd like to ask? Use **¿qué?** and the forms of **¿cuál?**:

1. ______________________________
2. ______________________________
3. ______________________________
4. ______________________________
5. ______________________________

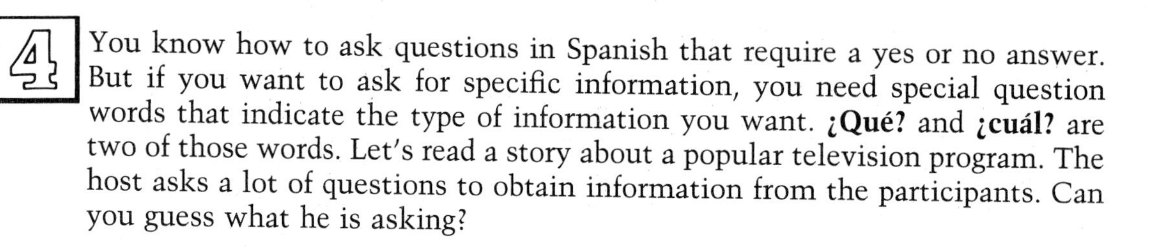

You know how to ask questions in Spanish that require a yes or no answer. But if you want to ask for specific information, you need special question words that indicate the type of information you want. **¿Qué?** and **¿cuál?** are two of those words. Let's read a story about a popular television program. The host asks a lot of questions to obtain information from the participants. Can you guess what he is asking?

## 5 Un programa de televisión

Buenas noches, amables televidentes. Yo soy su maestro de ceremonias, Baldomero Bocagrande. Bienvenidos a nuestro programa «¿Conoce Ud. a su marido?» Las reglas del concurso son fáciles. Hacemos diez preguntas a una mujer. Ya sabemos las

**el/la televidente** *TV viewer*
**el maestro** *master*
**bienvenido** *welcome*
**el marido** *husband*
**el concurso** *contest, show*

respuestas de su marido. Si las respuestas de los dos son iguales, el matrimonio puede ganar hasta un total de mil dólares, cien dólares por cada respuesta correcta.

**los dos** *both (of them)*
**igual** *similar*
**el matrimonio** *married couple*

Y ahora, vamos a comenzar con nuestra primera concursante, María López. ¿Cómo está Ud., María? Tenemos una serie de preguntas para Ud. La primera pregunta es: ¿Sabe Ud. cuál es la comida preferida de su marido?

**el/la concursante** *contestant*

MARÍA: Sí, él prefiere la comida mexicana.
M. de C.: Muy interesante. ¿Por qué?
MARÍA: Porque le gusta la comida picante.
M. de C.: ¿Cuáles son algunos de sus platos favoritos?
MARÍA: A él le gusta comer tacos de pollo, tamales, enchiladas verdes, chile con carne, guacamole, arroz con frijoles refritos—y todo con tortillas y mucha salsa.
M. de C.: ¿Adónde van Uds. para comer una comida típica mexicana?
MARÍA: Vamos al restaurante El Rancho Grande.
M. de C.: ¿Dónde queda el restaurante?
MARÍA: En la parte vieja de la ciudad.
M. de C.: ¿Cuánto cuesta una cena, más o menos?
MARÍA: Seis o siete dólares.
M. de C.: ¿Cuántas veces al mes comen Uds. afuera?
MARÍA: Dos o tres.
M. de C.: ¿Cuándo van a comer afuera?
MARÍA: Los fines de semana.
M. de C.: ¿Quién va con Uds., generalmente?
MARÍA: Nuestros hijos.
M. de C.: ¿Qué hacen después de comer?
MARÍA: Vamos al cine o regresamos a casa para mirar la televisión.
M. de C.: Damas y caballeros, esto es fantástico, sensacional. ¡Un aplauso para María! Sus diez respuestas son exactamente iguales a las de su marido. Felicitaciones, Uds. son un matrimonio perfecto. De veras, María, Ud. conoce muy bien a su marido, Manuel López.
MARÍA: ¿Cómo? Manuel López no es mi marido. Es el marido de la otra concursante.

**porque** *because*
**picante** *hot*
**el frijol** *bean* **refrito** *refried*
**la salsa** *sauce*
**quedar** *to be (located)*
**más o menos** *more or less*
**comer afuera** *to eat out*
**damas y caballeros** *ladies and gentlemen*
**felicitaciones** *congratulations*
**de veras** *really*
**¿cómo?** *eh? what was that?*

## ACTIVIDAD

**E.** Conteste en frases completas:

1. ¿Quién es Baldomero Bocagrande?

______________________________

2. ¿Qué tipo de programa es «Conoce Ud. a su marido»?

______________________________

3. ¿Cuántas preguntas tiene que contestar María?

______________________________

4. ¿Cuánto dinero pueden ganar los concursantes?

______________________________

5. ¿Por qué le gusta la comida mexicana al marido de María?

______________________________

6. ¿Cuál es el restaurante mexicano favorito de los López?

______________________________

7. ¿Dónde queda?

______________________________

8. ¿Cuándo salen a comer afuera?

______________________________

9. ¿Adónde van después de comer en el restaurante?

______________________________

10. ¿Quién es Manuel López?

______________________________

**6** What do all the above question words have in common? ______________
If you answered an accent mark, you are correct. All question words in Spanish have an accent mark. **¿Qué?, ¿por qué?, ¿cómo?, ¿cuándo?, ¿adónde?,** and **¿dónde?** never change. **¿Quién?** has a plural form **¿quiénes?** to ask about more than one person. **¿Cuánto?** functions as an adjective and thus agrees in gender and number when a noun follows:

| | |
|---|---|
| **¿*Cuánto* dinero tienes?** | *How much money do you have?* |
| **¿*Cuánta* carne quieres?** | *How much meat do you want?* |
| **¿*Cuántos* libros lees?** | *How many books are you reading?* |
| **¿*Cuántas* respuestas sabes?** | *How many answers do you know?* |

## ACTIVIDADES

**F.** Circle the word that completes each question correctly:

**1.** ¿(Cuántas, Cuánto) casas hay en la avenida?
**2.** ¿(Cuál, Qué) de los dos quiere comprar Ud.?
**3.** ¿(Cuál, Qué) es un circo?
**4.** ¿(Cómo, Por qué) está su papá?
**5.** ¿(Dónde, Cuántos) hace mucho calor?
**6.** ¿(Adónde, Dónde) van los autobuses?
**7.** ¿(Cuánta, Cuántas) personas viven en California?
**8.** ¿(Qué, Por qué) dice Ud. eso?
**9.** ¿(Cuándo, Cuánto) vas al cine?
**10.** ¿(Quién, Cuál) quiere mirar el programa?

**G.** You are preparing a series of questions for a TV program. Complete the questions in Spanish:

**1.** ¿_______________ es el maestro de ceremonias? (who)

**2.** ¿_______________ quiere ir Ud.? (where)

**3.** ¿_______________ no come Ud. afuera? (why)

**4.** ¿_______________ dinero tiene en el banco? (how much)

**5.** ¿_______________ es un diccionario? (what)

**6.** ¿_______________ van a salir? (when)

**7.** ¿_______________ hijos tiene Ud.? (how many)

**8.** ¿_______________ trabajan los sábados? (who)

**9.** ¿_______________ es la capital de Puerto Rico? (what)

**10.** ¿_______________ queda su restaurante favorito? (where)

Two other expressions to obtain information are formed with the word **quién(es): ¿a quién?** (*whom?*) and **¿de quién?** (*whose?*). Look at these examples:

| | |
|---|---|
| **¿*A quién* ves?** | *Whom do you see?* |
| **Veo *a* Juan.** | *I see John.* |

| | |
|---|---|
| **¿*De quién* es el libro?** | *Whose book is it?* |
| **El libro es *de* Carlos.** | *It is Charles' book.* |

If you respond to the question **¿a quién(es)?, a** must come after the verb in your answer. If you respond to the question **¿de quién(es)?, de** must come after the verb **ser** in your answer.

## ACTIVIDAD

**H.** Tell us about yourself by answering the following questions in Spanish:

1. ¿Quién prepara la comida en su casa?

_______________

2. ¿Quiénes son sus actores favoritos?

_______________

3. ¿De quién es la casa donde vive Ud.?

_______________

4. ¿A quién visita Ud. en las vacaciones?

_______________

5. ¿A quiénes va a invitar a su fiesta de cumpleaños?

_______________

6. ¿De quién es Ud. amigo en su clase?

_______________

**8** The TV show you read about is called **¿*Conoce* Ud. a su marido?** (*Do you know your husband?*) One of the questions was **¿*Sabe* Ud. cuál es su comida favorita?** (*Do you know which is his favorite food?*) Both verbs, **conocer** and **saber,** mean *to know*. Both have an irregular **yo** form in the present tense:

| | | |
|---|---|---|
| **yo** | ***conozco*** | ***sé*** |
| **tú** | **conoces** | **sabes** |
| **Ud., él, ella** | **conoce** | **sabe** |
| **nosotros** | **conocemos** | **sabemos** |
| **Uds., ellos, ellas** | **conocen** | **saben** |

When do you use **conocer** and when do you use **saber?** Let's look at some examples:

***Conozco* a Miguel, pero no *sé* dónde vive.**
*I know (am acquainted with) Michael, but I don't know where he lives.*

***¿Conoces* ese restaurante? *¿Sabes* si es caro?**
*Do you know (are familiar with) that restaurant? Do you know if it's expensive?*

Can you see the difference? **Conocer** is always used in the sense of *to be acquainted with, to be familiar with* (something or somebody). **Saber** means *to know facts, to have knowledge or information about something.* **Saber** can not be used with nouns that refer to people or places. When **saber** is followed by an infinitive, it means *to know how to:*

***¿Sabes* preparar comida mexicana?**
*Do you know how to prepare Mexican food?*

## ACTIVIDADES

**I.** Complete the following sentences with the correct form of **saber** or **conocer:**

1. Yo ________________ que su mamá no está en casa.
2. ¿________________ Uds. a Felipe?
3. ¿________________ Ud. dónde vive el presidente?
4. Yo no ________________ contestar la pregunta.
5. Yo ________________ bien esta ciudad.
6. ¿________________ Ud. al señor Pérez?
7. ¿________________ Uds. a qué hora termina la clase?
8. Yo no ________________ cómo se llama el profesor nuevo.
9. Nosotros no ________________ esa novela.
10. ¿________________ tú si la puerta está cerrada?

## *PREGUNTAS PERSONALES*

1. ¿Cuál es tu programa de televisión favorito? ¿Por qué?

________________________________________

2. ¿Cuándo vas al cine?

___

3. ¿Qué tipo de comida te gusta?

___

4. ¿Cuáles son tus restaurantes preferidos?

___

5. Generalmente, ¿adónde vas los veranos?

___

## INFORMACIÓN PERSONAL

You have just been selected to serve as "maestro de ceremonias" for your class' TV quiz show. Prepare five questions you would ask one of the contestants:

1. ___
2. ___
3. ___
4. ___
5. ___

## COMPOSICIÓN

You have just met a new friend in your class. Ask him/her for the following information:

1. name

___

2. address

___

3. phone number

___

4. favorite class

___

5. number of brothers and sisters

___

## DIÁLOGO

You are an investigator getting information from a client. Can you ask the right questions for the answers you are given?

# CÁPSULA CULTURAL

## Platos típicos

Students from several Spanish-speaking countries have prepared dishes for a school food festival. Which ones would you try?

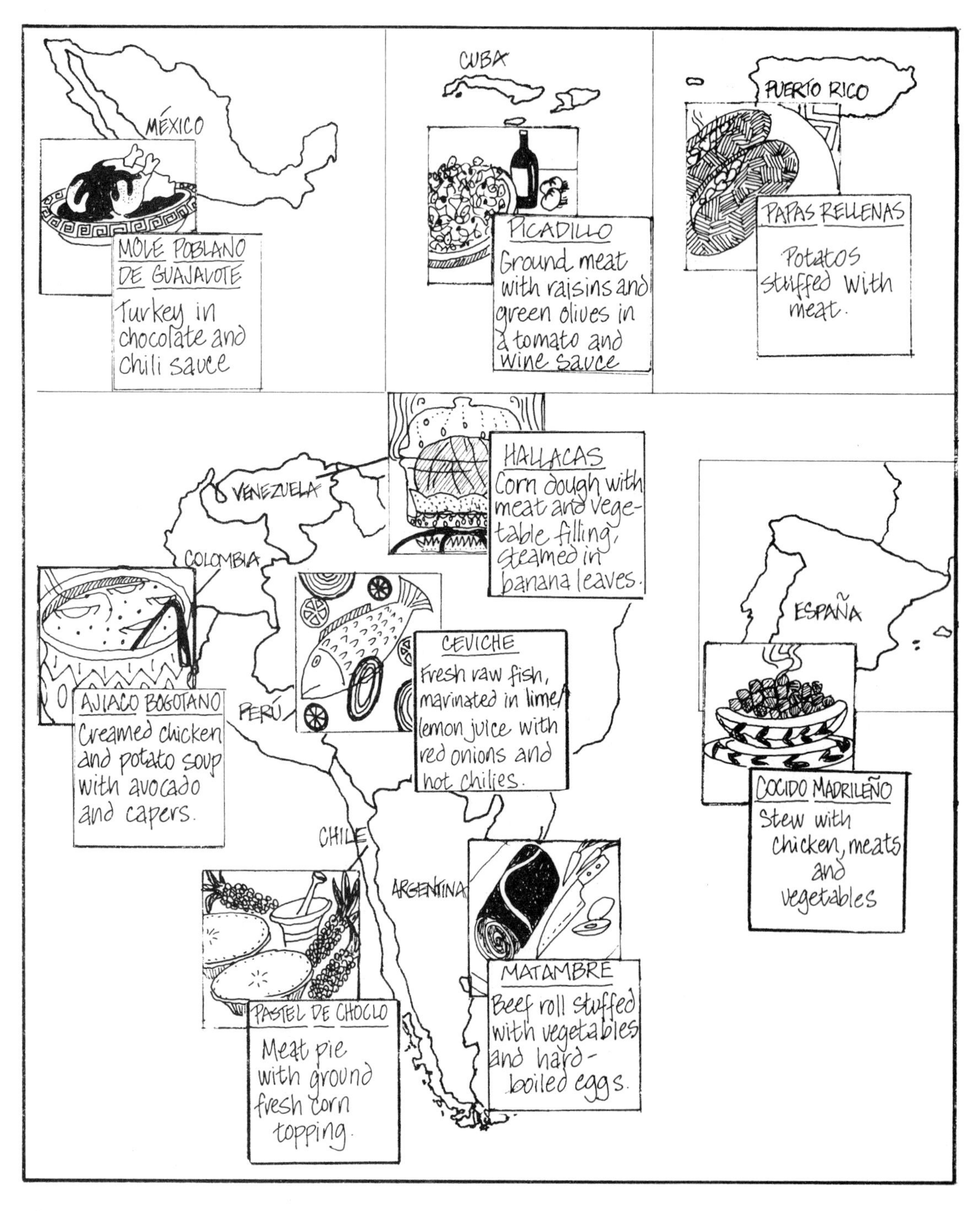

MÉXICO
MOLE POBLANO DE GUAJAVOTE
Turkey in chocolate and chili sauce
CUBA
PICADILLO
Ground meat with raisins and green olives in a tomato and wine sauce
PUERTO RICO
PAPAS RELLENAS
Potatos stuffed with meat.
VENEZUELA
HALLACAS
Corn dough with meat and vegetable filling, steamed in banana leaves.
COLOMBIA
AJIACO BOGOTANO
Creamed chicken and potato soup with avocado and capers.
PERÚ
CEVICHE
Fresh raw fish, marinated in lime/lemon juice with red onions and hot chilies.
ESPAÑA
COCIDO MADRILEÑO
Stew with chicken, meats and vegetables
CHILE
PASTEL DE CHOCLO
Meat pie with ground fresh corn topping.
ARGENTINA
MATAMBRE
Beef roll stuffed with vegetables and hard-boiled eggs.

# 2 En la playa

## Stem-Changing Verbs

### 1 Vocabulario

## ACTIVIDADES

**A.** Here's a happy beach scene. But there's been a nasty rumor that "Jaws" has been seen in the vicinity. You've been sent by the local newspaper to report on the situation. Tell what you see:

EXAMPLE: **Una muchacha toma el sol.**

**B.** Make a list of the ten most important things you would take to the beach, in order of importance (1, most important, to 10, least important):

1. ______________________ 6. ______________________

2. ______________________ 7. ______________________

3. ______________________ 8. ______________________

4. ______________________ 9. ______________________

5. ______________________ 10. ______________________

**2** You are at the beach with a group of your friends. Read the dialog and see if you can find all forms of the verbs **querer** (*to want*) and **poder** (*to be able to, can*). The forms look slightly different from the infinitives:

**3** Can you fill in the correct forms of the verbs **querer** and **poder** in the box below?

| | querer | poder |
|---|---|---|
| **yo** | ________ | ________ |
| **tú** | ________ | ________ |
| **Ud., él, ella** | ________ | ________ |
| **nosotros** | ________ | ________ |
| **Uds., ellos, ellas** | ________ | ________ |

What happened to the stem of the verb **querer**? The **e** changed to ______ in all forms except for **nosotros**. What happened to the stem of the verb **poder**? The **o** changed to ______ in all forms except for **nosotros**.

**4** There are other verbs that undergo the same changes. We identify them in the vocabulary at the end of the book like this: **empezar (ie)** (*to begin*), **mover (ue)** (*to move*). Now let's see some more examples. Can you complete the boxes below?

| **e** to **ie** | **pensar** (*to think*) | **perder** (*to lose*) | **mentir** (*to lie*) |
|---|---|---|---|
| **yo** | **p*ie*nso** | ________ | ________ |
| **tú** | **p*ie*nsas** | ________ | ________ |
| **Ud., él, ella** | **p*ie*nsa** | ________ | ________ |
| **nosotros** | **pensamos** | ________ | ________ |
| **Uds., ellos, ellas** | **p*ie*nsan** | ________ | ________ |

| **o** to **ue** | **almorzar** (*to have lunch*) | **volver** (*to come back*) | **dormir** (*to sleep*) |
|---|---|---|---|
| **yo** | **alm*ue*rzo** | ________ | ________ |
| **tú** | **alm*ue*rzas** | ________ | ________ |
| **Ud., él, ella** | **alm*ue*rza** | ________ | ________ |
| **nosotros** | **almorzamos** | ________ | ________ |
| **Uds., ellos, ellas** | **alm*ue*rzan** | ________ | ________ |

## ACTIVIDADES

**C.** What do the students in the class prefer?

EXAMPLE: **Carlos *prefiere* nadar.**

1. Yo ________________ dormir.
2. Tú ________________ ir al cine.
3. Ellos ________________ comer.
4. Miguel y yo ________________ salir.
5. Uds. ________________ cantar.
6. Julia ________________ estudiar.

**D.** You are observing some children playing on the beach. What do they find?

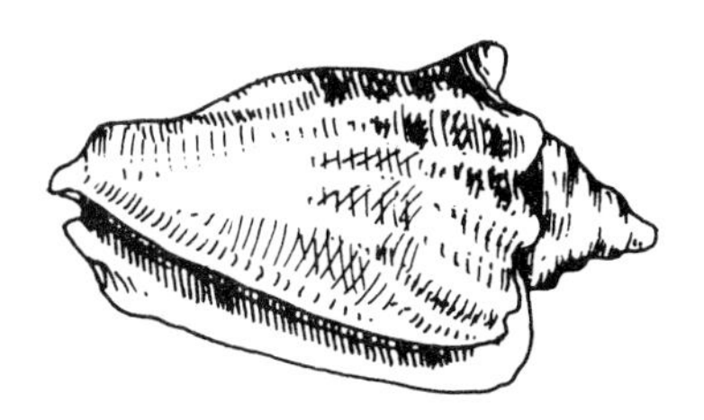

EXAMPLE: **Ellos *encuentran* una concha.**

1. Carlos ________________________

2. Yo ________________________

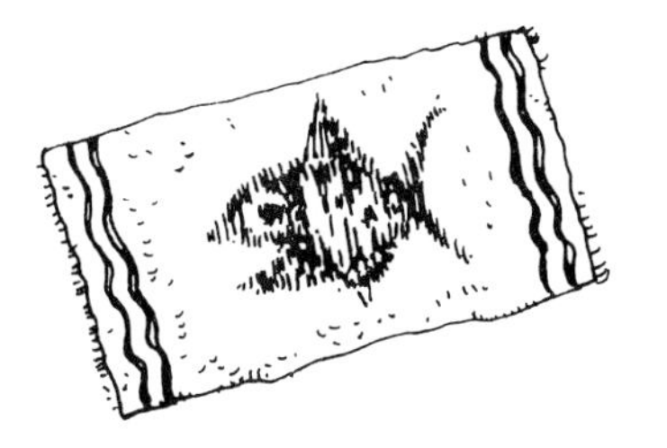

3. Ud. ________________________

4. Uds. ________________________

5. Nosotros ________________________

6. Tú ________________________

**5** There is one more important verb that has a similar change in the stem: In **jugar**, the **u** changes to **ue** in all forms except for **nosotros**.

## ACTIVIDADES

**E.** Several students are discussing plans for the summer vacation. Can you help them complete their thoughts with the correct form of the verb in parentheses?

1. (jugar) ¿Qué juegos ________________ Uds. en el campamento de verano?
2. (querer) Mis padres ________________ ir a Venezuela.
3. (preferir) Yo ________________ ir al Perú.
4. (pensar) ¿Dónde ________________ (tú) pasar las vacaciones?
5. (almorzar) ¿A qué hora ________________ los mexicanos?
6. (llover) ¿________________ mucho en el verano?
7. (poder) Nosotros no ________________ viajar este verano.
8. (perder) (encontrar) Mi madre ________________ la paciencia cuando no ________________ información sobre excursiones interesantes.
9. (costar) ¿Cuánto ________________ viajar a España?
10. (volver) ¿Cuándo ________________ tú de Europa?

**F.** Each of the following sentences has a verb in bold type. Can you figure out the infinitive of the verb?

1. Los soldados **defienden** su país. ________________
2. Mi hermana no **miente**. ________________
3. Su gato **duerme** todo el día. ________________
4. Los niños **juegan** en la playa. ________________
5. ¿No **encuentras** el traje de baño? ________________
6. **¿Entiendes** la lección? ________________
7. Uds. **cierran** la puerta. ________________

8. ¿Qué **prefiere** Ud.? ______________________

**G.** ¿Qué hacen estas personas?

1. Juan y Pedro ______________________ hasta cien. (contar)
2. Los estudiantes ______________________ en la cafetería. (almorzar)
3. Yo ______________________ a trabajar. (empezar)
4. Tú ______________________ a casa. (volver)
5. Mi abuelo ______________________ la siesta. (dormir)
6. María y yo ______________________ el libro. (encontrar)
7. Uds. ______________________ la paciencia. (perder)
8. Ellas ______________________ la tienda. (cerrar)

## En la playa de una isla tropical

Now let's read a story about an adventure at the beach. Look for the stem-changing verbs of another type:

Es un día de sol brillante. Estamos en una playa casi desierta de una isla tropical. Vemos las olas del mar, la arena blanca y las palmeras que se mueven con la brisa. Allá, a lo lejos, vemos a dos personas. **Siguen** las huellas de su perro caminando lentamente por la orilla del mar, y **sonríen** mientras hablan. ¿Qué dicen?

**la brisa** *breeze*
**a lo lejos** *in the distance*
**seguir (i)** *to follow*
**la huella** *track, footprint*
**lentamente** *slowly*
**la orilla** *shore*
**sonreír (í)** *to smile*

LA CHICA: Oh, Fernando. ¡Qué contenta estoy! Esta isla es un paraíso. El mundo no existe.

EL CHICO: Sí, tienes razón. Estamos lejos de los problemas del mundo. Pero, ¿quieres saber una cosa? Hace muchos años había piratas en esta isla.

**hace** *ago* **había** *there were*

LA CHICA: ¿De veras? ¡Qué romántico! Entonces, es seguro que hay tesoros sepultados en la arena — perlas, diamantes, rubíes, monedas de oro . . .

EL CHICO: Quizás. Pero, ¿quién sabe dónde están?

**¿de veras?** *really?*
**seguro** *certain*
**el tesoro** *treasure*
**sepultado** *buried*
**la moneda** *coin* **oro** *gold*
**quizás** *maybe, perhaps*

En eso la chica ve una cosa que brilla en la arena. Se inclina para ver mejor. Es una botella. La recoge. Hay un papel viejo adentro.

LA CHICA: (**ríe** alegremente) Mira, parece un mapa. ¿Crees que **sirve**?

**en eso** *just then*
**inclinarse** *to bend down*
**recoger** *to pick up*
**reír (í)** *to laugh*
**parecer** *to seem*
**servir (i)** *to serve, be useful*

EL CHICO: Sí, parece un mapa de un tesoro. Pero eso es imposible. ¡Es ridículo!

LA CHICA: No es imposible, Fernando. Allí hay una piedra grande debajo de una palmera, como muestra el mapa. ¿Qué piensas? ¿Buscamos el tesoro allí?

**la piedra** *stone*
**mostrar (ue)** *to show*

Los dos empiezan a cavar con las manos y con piedras grandes. Después de veinte minutos, Fernando grita, «¡Mira, Juanita! ¡Hay algo aquí!»

**cavar** *to dig*

¿Qué descubren los dos jóvenes en la arena?

## ACTIVIDAD

**H.** Conteste en frases completas:

1. ¿Cómo es la isla?

_______________

2. ¿Quiénes están en la playa?

_______________

3. ¿Qué hacen en la playa?

_______________

4. ¿Qué piensa la chica sobre la isla?

______________________________________________

5. ¿Cuál es la opinión del chico?

______________________________________________

6. Según la chica, ¿qué hay sepultado en la arena?

______________________________________________

7. ¿Qué encuentra la chica en la arena?

______________________________________________

8. ¿Qué hay dentro de la botella?

______________________________________________

9. ¿Qué hay debajo de la palmera?

______________________________________________

10. En su opinión, ¿qué descubren los dos jóvenes?

______________________________________________

**7** There were four verbs in the story, **sonreír**, **servir**, **seguir**, and **reír**, which belong to a third class of stem-changing verbs. What type of verbs are these?

__________ Right, they are all –**IR** verbs. Let's see how they change:

| | servir | sonreír |
|---|---|---|
| **yo** | **sirvo** | **sonrío** |
| **tú** | **sirves** | **sonríes** |
| **Ud., él, ella** | **sirve** | **sonríe** |
| **nosotros** | **servimos** | **sonreímos** |
| **Uds., ellos, ellas** | **sirven** | **sonríen** |

Now you know. Some **-IR** verbs change the **e** in the stem to **i** in all forms of the present tense except for **nosotros**. This change is indicated in our vocabulary as follows: **repetir (i), reír (í)**.

## ACTIVIDADES

**I.** You overhear several youngsters in a Spanish restaurant. Each orders something different. Complete their orders with the correct form of the verb **pedir (i)**:

1. Yo ______________ arroz con pollo.

2. Fernando ______________ sopa de ajo.

3. Roberto y Carlos ______________ una tortilla de patatas.

4. Doris y yo ______________ una ensalada mixta.

5. Tú ______________ gazpacho.

6. El mesero pregunta: «¿Qué ______________ Uds.?»

**J.** You are explaining a game in which each person repeats what someone else has said. Complete the statements with the correct forms of **repetir (i)**:

1. Carlos ______________ lo que dices tú.

2. Tú ______________ lo que dice Alicia.

3. Yo ______________ lo que dice Carlos.

4. Alicia ______________ lo que digo yo.

5. Nosotros ______________ lo que dice Manuel.

6. Uds. ______________ lo que decimos nosotros.

7. Manuel y Jorge ______________ lo que dice Carlos.

**K.** Let's see what these people are doing at the beach:

1. Un niño ______________ aprender a nadar. (querer)

2. La madre ______________ bajo la sombrilla. (dormir)

3. El padre ______________ el fuego para la barbacoa. (encender)

4. Yo ______________ una soda en el quiosko. (pedir)

5. Mi hermanito ______________ jugar en la arena. (preferir)

6. Tú ______________ la pelota de playa. (perder)

7. Mario y José ______________ un caracol muy bonito. (encontrar)

8. Yo no ______________ lo que grita mi madre. (entender)

9. Ella ________________ sus palabras. (repetir)

10. Yo ________________: «¡Qué bien que no ________________ en el verano!» (pensar, nevar)

11. El salvavidas ________________. (sonreír)

12. Dos perros ________________ a mi hermanito. (seguir)

**L.** You are in a hotel in San Juan and want to say or ask in Spanish:

1. that you don't understand Spanish very well.

________________________________________

2. how much the room costs.

________________________________________

3. where you sleep.

________________________________________

4. that your family wants to be there five days.

________________________________________

5. what time they serve breakfast.

________________________________________

6. where you can take the bus.

________________________________________

7. what time they close the dining room.

________________________________________

8. if it rains there a lot.

________________________________________

9. that you prefer to go to the beach now.

________________________________________

10. that you are coming back to the hotel for lunch.

________________________________________

## DIÁLOGO

José llama a Carmen por teléfono. ¿Qué dice Carmen?

## PREGUNTAS PERSONALES

1. ¿Qué haces en la playa?

______________________________________________

2. ¿Vives cerca de una playa? ¿De cuál?

______________________________________________

3. ¿Lees libros sobre piratas? ¿Por qué?

______________________________________________

4. ¿Crees que hay tesoros sepultados en el mar? ¿Por qué?

______________________________________________

5. ¿En cuántas islas del Caribe hablan español?

______________________________________________

## INFORMACIÓN PERSONAL

Draw a treasure map. Write five sentences giving the clues necessary to find the treasure:

EXAMPLE: **Hay una piedra grande debajo de una palmera.**

1. ______________________________________________
2. ______________________________________________
3. ______________________________________________
4. ______________________________________________
5. ______________________________________________

# CÁPSULA CULTURAL

## Una isla ideal

Where would you like to go on your vacation? Would you like to go to a beautiful Caribbean island with miles of white, sandy beaches, towering mountain ranges, a tropical rain forest with streams and waterfalls — the home of hundreds of varieties of animal and plant life —, an island of eternal spring time with an average temperature of 75 degrees?

Nice, you say, but a bit too quiet to your liking. You would much rather spend your time in a bustling, modern metropolis. You prefer big-city life — ultramodern hotels, skyscrapers, department stores, theaters, restaurants, and discotheques. Well, there's no reason why you can't have both.

There is an island in the Caribbean, called Borinquén by the native Indians before the arrival of Columbus in 1493, now called Puerto Rico, which offers all of the above. Puerto Rico is really the peak of a submerged mountain range. It possesses all the natural beauty of a tropical paradise. San Juan, the capital, is a modern city that keeps a reminder of colonial times in "el viejo San Juan," a replica of a Spanish colonial town of the sixteenth century. You would also enjoy visiting el Morro, a fortress built in 1595 to protect San Juan Harbor from pirate attacks. So, what are you waiting for?

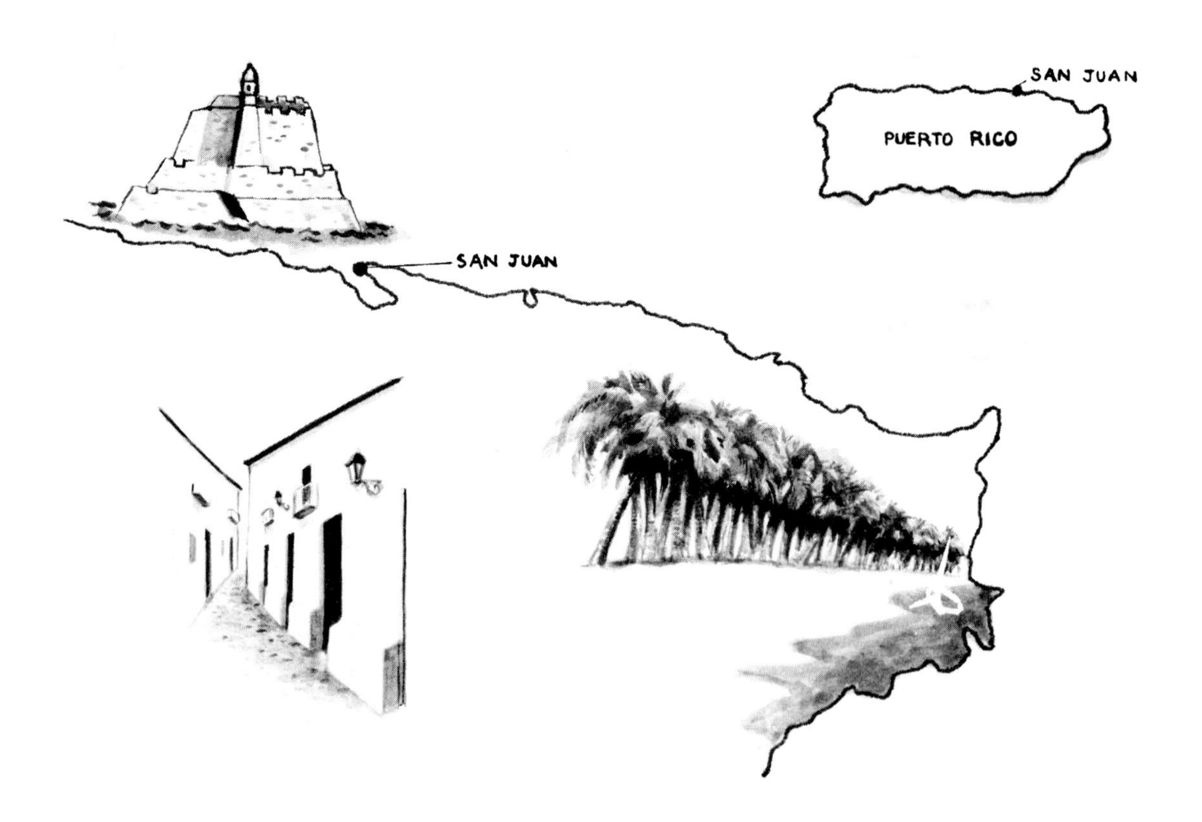

# 3 En la joyería

## Negative and Affirmative Expressions

### 1 Vocabulario

## ACTIVIDADES

**A.** Juan has a job in a jewelry store. The manager has told him to place labels on all the articles in the showcase for the big sale. Can you help him?

| | |
|---|---|
| **cadena de oro $100** | **brazalete de plata $150** |
| **anillo de diamantes $500** | **collar de esmeraldas $900** |
| **aretes de perlas $55** | **broche de rubíes $300** |

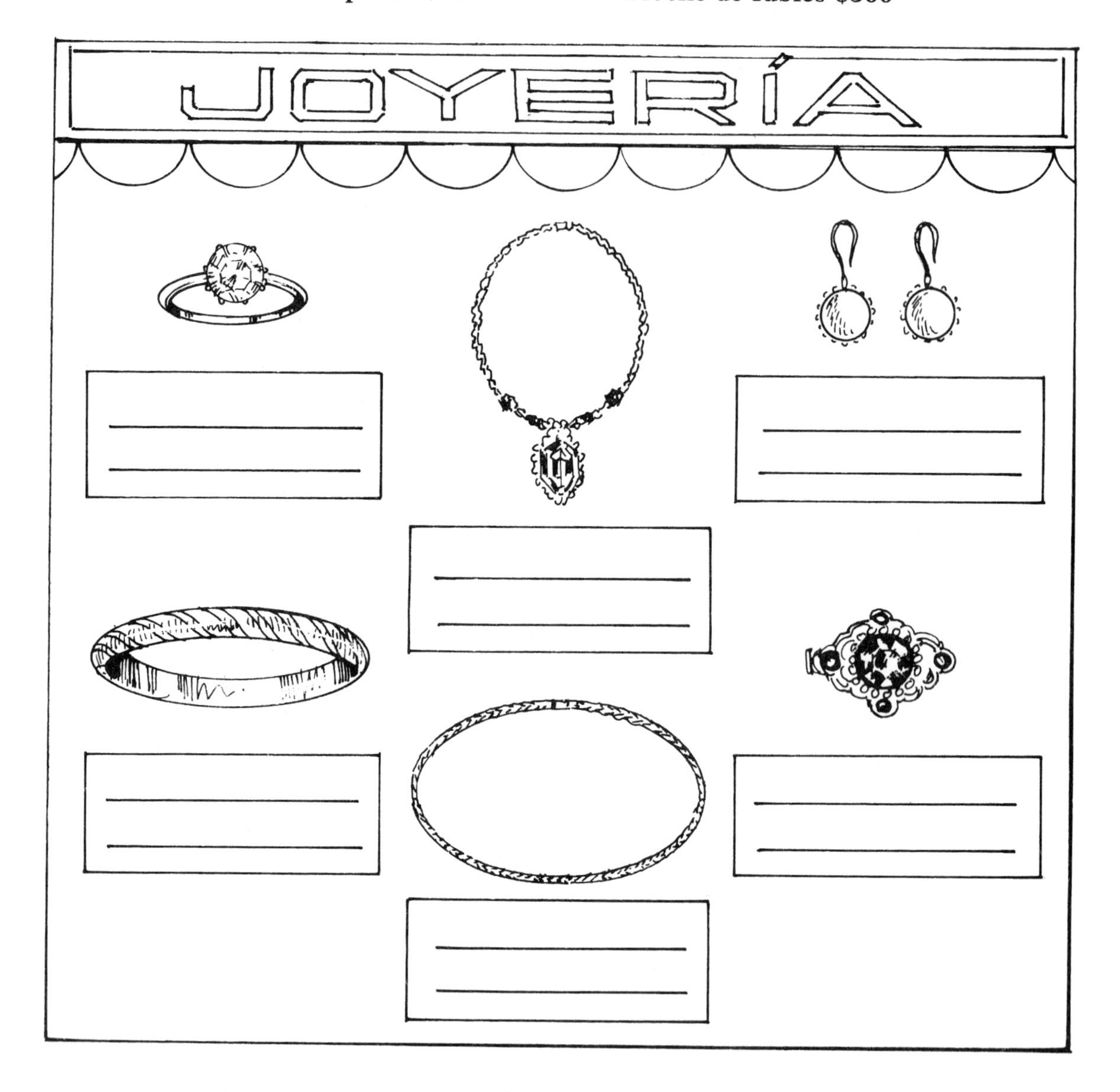


**B.** You are in the jewelry department of a department store buying holiday presents. What should you buy for these people on your list?

EXAMPLE: su padre: **Compro un reloj de pulsera para mi padre.**

1. su amigo Juan: ________________________________________

2. su amiga Carla: ______________________________

3. su madre: ______________________________

4. su hermana Clarita (16 años): ______________________________

5. su hermano Miguel (18 años): ______________________________

You already know the most common negative word in the Spanish language, **no.** To make any sentence negative, simply put ______ before the verb. There are, however, other important negative expressions in Spanish. Read the following story and pay careful attention to the new negatives and to their corresponding affirmatives.

## La magia

Un hombre está sentado en una silla delante de un grupo de gente, con la espalda hacia ellos. Tiene los ojos vendados. No puede ver **nada.** Su ayudante coge una cosa y dice: «Maestro, ahora tengo un objeto en la mano. ¿Qué es? ¿Cuál es la respuesta? Necesito la información. ¿Es un anillo de piedras preciosas, un brazalete o unos aretes?»

**la gente** *people*
**la espalda** *back*
**los ojos vendados** *blindfolded*
**coger** *to seize, take hold of*

El hombre piensa un momento y después contesta: «Veo **algo.** No es **ni** muy grande **ni** muy pequeño. **Tampoco** es pesado. Es, es . . . ¡un reloj!» «Estupendo, sensacional», grita el ayudante. «El maestro **nunca** comete un error. No se equivoca **jamás. Siempre** tiene razón. Un aplauso, por favor».

**ni. .ni** *neither . . nor*
**pesado** *heavy*
**nunca** *never*
**el error** *mistake*
**equivocarse** *to be wrong*
**jamás** *never*

Pero, ¿qué pasa aquí? ¿Es la magia de veras? ¿Es un mago el hombre? ¿Puede él ver cosas que **nadie** ve? O, ¿es un truco, una simple ilusión? Pues bien, si Ud. tiene buena memoria puede hacer lo mismo. Primero necesita una clave. Por ejemplo, en la clave del maestro cada letra del alfabeto tiene una palabra equivalente. El maestro sabe de memoria esta tabla de equivalentes.

**el mago** *magician*
**nadie** *nobody*
**el truco** *trick*
**la clave** *key* (to code)
**saber de memoria** *to know by heart*

¿Quiere **alguien** saber cómo descubre el maestro qué objetos coge su ayudante? Mire la primera palabra de cada frase que dice el ayudante:

| PALABRA | LETRA EQUIVALENTE |
|---|---|
| maestro | R |
| qué | E |
| cuál | L |
| necesito | O |
| es | J |

¿Comprende ahora cómo el mago hace su magia? Ahora Ud. **también** puede sorprender a sus amigos con su «poder mental».

**el poder** *power*

## ACTIVIDAD

**C.** Preguntas sobre el cuento:

1. ¿Dónde está sentado el mago?

 ___

2. ¿Por qué no puede ver nada?

 ___

3. ¿Qué dice primero el ayudante del mago?

 ___

4. ¿Qué tiene el ayudante en la mano?

 ___

5. ¿Qué es un truco?

 ___

6. ¿En qué consiste la clave del mago?

 ___

7. ¿Qué sabe de memoria el maestro?

 ___

8. ¿Qué palabra de cada frase es importante?

 ___

9. ¿Cuántas letras tiene la palabra reloj?

 ___

10. ¿Cuántas frases usa el ayudante del mago?

 ___

**3** Look for the words in bold type in the story and then insert the Spanish negatives and their corresponding affirmative expressions in the table:

| | | | |
|---|---|---|---|
| *nobody (no one)* | __________ | *somebody (someone)* | __________ |
| *nothing (not anything)* | __________ | *something* | __________ |
| *neither . . nor* | __________ | *or* | __________ |
| *never* | __________ | *always* | __________ |
| *never* | __________ | | |
| *neither* | __________ | *also, too* | __________ |

**4** Now read these sentences:

| | |
|---|---|
| ***No* puede ver *nada.*** | ***Nada* puede ver.** |
| ***No* comete *nunca* un error.** | ***Nunca* comete un error.** |
| ***No* es pesado *tampoco.*** | ***Tampoco* es pesado.** |
| **Cosas que *no* ve *nadie.*** | ***Cosas* que *nadie* ve.** |
| ***No* se equivoca *jamás.*** | ***Jamás* se equivoca.** |

Look at the right column. Where is the negative word placed?

____________________________________________________________

Right, directly before the verb. Now look at the left column. What word is placed directly before the verb? ______ Where is the negative word placed? ________________________ There are two ways of negating a sentence in Spanish:

**no** + verb + negative word
negative word + verb

## ACTIVIDADES

**D.** María likes to do what her older sister, Rosa, does. What does María say?

EXAMPLE: Yo no compro joyas. ¿Y tú?
**Yo tampoco compro joyas. / Yo no compro joyas tampoco.**

1. Yo no quiero el collar. ¿Y tú?

_______________

2. Yo no uso aretes. ¿Y tú?

_______________

3. Yo no encuentro el reloj. ¿Y tú?

_______________

4. Yo no sé hacer trucos. ¿Y tú?

_______________

5. Yo no puedo ir a la joyería. ¿Y tú?

_______________

**E.** Say that you don't ever do the following things:

EXAMPLE: comer chocolate
**Yo nunca (jamás) como chocolate.**
**Yo no como nunca (jamás) chocolate.**

1. trabajar los domingos

_______________

2. comprar joyas

_______________

3. tomar el sol

_______________

4. descubrir un tesoro

_______________

5. comer afuera

_______________

**F.** Fernando doesn't like certain foods. What does he tell his mother?

EXAMPLE: las frutas . . . las legumbres
**No me gustan ni las frutas ni las legumbres.**

1. el maíz . . . el arroz

_______________

2. la carne . . . el pescado

_______________

3. el pollo . . . el rosbif

______________________________

4. los tacos . . . las enchiladas

______________________________

5. las naranjas . . . las manzanas

______________________________

**5** When the object of a verb is a negative or an affirmative word referring to a person, the personal **a** is used:

**Veo *a* alguien.**
**No veo *a* nadie.**

## ACTIVIDADES

**G.** Miguel takes great pleasure in saying the opposite of what his twin brother Marcos says. Give Miguel's negative statements:

EXAMPLE: Yo escucho algo. ¿Y tú?
**Yo no escucho nada.**

1. Yo veo a alguien. ¿Y tú?

______________________________

2. Yo escribo algo. ¿Y tú?

______________________________

3. Yo busco a alguien. ¿Y tú?

______________________________

4. Yo tomo algo. ¿Y tú?

______________________________

5. Yo quiero a alguien. ¿Y tú?

______________________________

**H.** Your mother is asking you some questions. Answer them negatively:

1. ¿Haces algo ahora?

______________________________

2. ¿Conoces a alguien en México?

_______________________________________________

3. ¿Dices siempre la verdad?

_______________________________________________

4. ¿Qué prefieres hacer ahora, comer o mirar la televisión?

_______________________________________________

5. ¿Cuándo vas al cine con tus amigos?

_______________________________________________

6. ¿Llamas a alguien por teléfono?

_______________________________________________

6

There is one more negative word (**ninguno** *none, not any, no*) and one more affirmative word (**alguno** *any, some*) that need your special attention. Look at these examples:

| | |
|---|---|
| **¿Quieres hacer *alguna* pregunta?** | *Do you want to ask any question?* |
| **No, no quiero hacer *ninguna* pregunta.** | *No, I don't want to ask any question.* |
| ***Algún* día voy a visitar España.** | *Some day I'm going to visit Spain.* |
| **No quiero *ningún* consejo.** | *I don't want any advice.* |
| ***Algunos* días hace frío.** | *Some days it's cold.* |
| **No veo *ningunos* libros aquí.** | *I don't see any books here.* |
| **Quiero comprar *algunas* cosas.** | *I want to buy some things.* |
| **No creo en *ningunas* promesas.** | *I don't believe in any promises.* |

Did you observe that both **alguno** and **ninguno** agree in gender and number with nouns they accompany? What's more, they become **algún** and **ningún** before a masculine singular noun:

| | |
|---|---|
| **¿Tienes *algún* amigo español?** | *Do you have any Spanish friend?* |
| **No, no tengo *ningún* amigo español.** | *No, I don't have any Spanish friend.* |

## ACTIVIDADES

**I.** Your friend is offering you different things. Say that you don't want any:

EXAMPLE: ¿Quieres algún postre?
**No, gracias. No quiero ningún postre.**

1. ¿Quieres alguna torta?

_______________

2. ¿Quieres algunos discos?

_______________

3. ¿Quieres alguna fruta?

_______________

4. ¿Quieres algún libro?

_______________

5. ¿Quieres algún plato típico?

_______________

**J.** You are in a contrary mood today. Answer the following questions negatively:

1. Carlos no va a la fiesta. ¿Y tú?

_______________

2. ¿Sabes algo sobre el Paraguay?

_______________

3. ¿Cuándo va tu hermana al cine?

_______________

4. ¿Conocen tus padres a alguien en España?

_______________

5. ¿Qué libro vale mil dólares?

_______________

6. ¿Cuándo tienes exámenes?

_______________

7. ¿Está abierta alguna tienda hoy?

_______________

8. ¿Tienes algún trabajo para mañana?

_______________

9. ¿Qué quieres comer, un pastel o un sandwich?

_______________

10. ¿Ves algo interesante en esa joyería?

_______________

## DIÁLOGO

In this conversation, you have the role of Javier Jalapeño, an assistant to a great magician.

## PREGUNTAS PERSONALES

1. ¿Te gusta ver actos de magia? ¿Por qué (no)?

______________________________

2. ¿Qué significa la expresión «la mano es más rápida que el ojo»?

______________________________

3. ¿Conoces a algún mago?

______________________________

4. ¿Usas joyas? ¿Qué joyas usas?

______________________________

5. ¿Tienes un reloj de pulsera bonito? ¿Cómo es?

______________________________

## INFORMACIÓN PERSONAL

Complete the following sentences to tell us something about yourself:

1. Yo no ______________________________ a nadie.
2. No me gusta ni ______________ ni ______________.
3. Tampoco me gusta ______________________________.
4. Yo no ______________________________ nunca.
5. Los domingos ______________________________ nada.

## COMPOSICIÓN

You want to work as an assistant for a "mind reader" and have to give a small demonstration of your abilities. Think of an object in Spanish. Then make up a key and write the sentences that will help the magician to "read your mind."

______________________________

______________________________

______________________________

______________________________

# CÁPSULA CULTURAL

## Poderoso caballero es Don Dinero

We say "Money talks." The equivalent saying in Spanish in our title means "A powerful gentleman is Mr. Money." Anyway you look at it, money seems to be something we just can't do without.

In the United States, the basic monetary unit is the dollar (**el dólar**), which is also used in Puerto Rico (though Puerto Ricans call it **peso**). But, what about the other Spanish-speaking countries? What kind of money do you need if you want to go shopping in Spain, in Mexico, in Venezuela, or in Argentina? Well, the most common name for currency is **el peso** (though not all **pesos** have the same value); it is used in Mexico, Cuba, Colombia, Chile, the Dominican Republic, and Uruguay. Other countries have the following currencies:

**España — la peseta**
**Perú — el inti**
**Paraguay — el guaraní**
**Venezuela — el bolívar**
**Panamá — el balboa**
**Guatemala — el quetzal**
**Honduras — el lempira**
**Ecuador — el sucre**
**Nicaragua — el córdoba**
**Argentina — el austral**
**Bolivia — el boliviano**
**El Salvador** and **Costa Rica — el colón**

How many Mexican **pesos** can you buy with a dollar? How many **pesetas**? Check the foreign-exchange table in your local newspaper for the latest information.

# El fin de semana

## Formal and Familiar Commands

### Vocabulario

What can we do for fun on a weekend?

ir de compras

ir a una sala de conciertos

ver una película

patinar

jugar a los bolos

ir al teatro

nadar en la piscina

ver una exhibición en el museo

patinar en el hielo

montar a caballo

2 Do you enjoy any of the activities on page 41? How about inviting one or more of your friends to join you? It's very simple. Look at the examples:

| | |
|---|---|
| **¡*Vamos* a la fiesta!** | *Let's go to the party!* |
| **¡*Vamos a* jugar al monopolio!** | *Let's play monopoly!* |

**Vamos** is used to express *let's go.* **Vamos a** + infinitive is used to express *let's.*

## ACTIVIDADES

**A.** Tell your friend to do the following with you:

EXAMPLE: dance **Vamos a bailar.**

1. skate ______
2. see a horror movie ______
3. play soccer ______
4. dance ______
5. visit the museum ______
6. swim in the swimming pool ______

**B.** A friend of the family is flying in this weekend. Tell him/her to join you in five different activities:

EXAMPLE: **¡Vamos a escuchar un concierto de rock!**

1. ______
2. ______
3. ______
4. ______
5. ______

Did you notice the inverted exclamation mark (¡) before each sentence starting with **vamos?** In Spanish, sentences that have a normal exclamation mark at the end also have an inverted exclamation mark at the beginning.

## El hipnotismo

You now know how to tell somebody to do something along with you. How do you tell somebody to do something without including yourself? Let's read the following story about a hypnotist and find out:

Es sábado por la noche y la familia Colón da un paseo por la avenida, mientras decide cómo pasar la noche.

**dar un paseo** *to take a walk*
**pasar** *to spend (time)*

SR. COLÓN: Vamos al centro. Así podemos ir al cine y después tomar algo en uno de los cafés por ahí.
CHITO (un niño de 8 años): ¿Por qué no vamos a ver el partido de fútbol en el estadio? Dicen que va a ser estupendo.
MARILUZ (su hermana de 15 años): ¡Oh, no! Ese programa no me gusta. Yo prefiero ir a la fiesta en la plaza. Hay un concierto de rock con un grupo fabuloso.

**el centro** *downtown*
**por ahí** *over there*
**el partido** *game, match*

En ese momento pasan por delante del Teatro Real, famoso por sus programas de variedades.

CHITO: **¡Mira**, mamá! ¿Qué dice ese letrero?
MARILUZ: Tonto, ¿no sabes leer? Anuncian al hipnotista Mandrako, el Maravilloso.
CHITO: Pero, ¿qué es un hipnotista?
SR. COLÓN: Es un hombre que vive de la ignorancia de los demás.
SRA. COLÓN: Oh, Carlos. ¡No seas aguafiestas! El hipnotismo, hijo, es el arte de inducir un estado parecido al sueño en una persona, y así esa persona acepta órdenes del hipnotista.
SR. COLÓN: Sí, especialmente si la otra persona es un individuo de espíritu débil y de poca inteligencia.
MARILUZ: **¡Miren** Uds.! La función empieza a las siete y son las siete en punto. ¡Vamos a verla!
TODOS: Buena idea.

**el letrero** *sign*
**tonto** *silly*
**los demás** *the others, the rest*
**el aguafiestas** *spoilsport*
**parecido** *similar*
**débil** *weak*
**la función** *show*

La Sra. Colón compra las entradas y todos entran en el teatro oscuro y toman asiento. Mandrako, un hombre alto y flaco con barba y bigote y vestido todo de negro, está en el escenario. Ve al Sr. Colón y dice: «¡Señor! Sí, Ud. **Suba** por aquí, por favor».

**la entrada** *ticket*
**oscuro** *dark*
**tomar asiento** *to take a seat*
**la barba** *beard*
**el bigote** *mustache*
**el escenario** *stage*
**subir** *to go (come) up*

SR. COLÓN (a su familia): Son tonterías. Pero voy a participar sólo para demostrar que es una estupidez.

**tonterías** *nonsense*

MANDRAKO: **Tome** Ud. asiento, por favor. Ahora **mire** mi reloj. Ud. tiene sueño, mucho sueño. **Cierre** Ud. los ojos. Ahora, **abra** la boca y **ladre** como un perro. **Meta** un dedo en el oído y **salte** como un mono, **corra** como un gato. Muy bien. Ahora voy a contar hasta diez y puede abrir los ojos. No va a recordar nada.

**ladrar** *to bark*
**saltar** *to jump*
**recordar (ue)** *to remember*

Cuando el Sr. Colón vuelve a su asiento, dice:

«¿No les dije que el hipnotismo es una tontería? Un hombre inteligente como yo no es susceptible».

**no les dije** *didn't I tell you*

SRA. COLÓN: Por supuesto, mi amor. Pero, ¿por qué no sacas el dedo del oído?

**sacar** *to take out*

## ACTIVIDAD

**C.** Preguntas sobre el cuento:

1. ¿Qué hace la familia Colón?

______________________________

2. ¿Quién es Mandrako?

______________________________

3. ¿Qué es el hipnotismo?

______________________________

4. ¿Qué dice el Sr. Colón sobre el hipnotismo?

______________________________

5. ¿Cómo hipnotiza Mandrako al Sr. Colón?

______________________________

6. ¿Qué hace el Sr. Colón bajo la influencia de Mandrako?

______________________________

7. ¿Qué dice el Sr. Colón cuando vuelve a su asiento?

______________________________

8. ¿Qué dice la Sra. Colón?

______________________________

Mandrako gave a number of commands to Sr. Colón. In some he used the pronoun **Ud.** and in others he didn't. That's because the use of the pronoun is optional. Let's list some of Mandrako's commands:

| **-AR** verbs | **-ER** verbs | **-IR** verbs |
|---|---|---|
| ***Tome* Ud. asiento.** | ***Meta* un dedo en el oído.** | ***Suba* por aquí.** |
| ***Mire* mi reloj.** | ***Corra* como un gato.** | ***Abra* la boca.** |

Do you notice something strange about the endings? Right! In the formal command forms, **-AR** verbs end in **e**, **-ER** and **-IR** verbs end in **a**. So, it's very easy to give formal commands. Take the first person singular of the present tense (the **yo** form) and change the ending as follows:

| | | |
|---|---|---|
| **habl*ar*: (yo) habl~~o~~** | **Habl*e* (Ud.)** | *Speak.* |
| **com*er*: (yo) com~~o~~** | **Com*a* (Ud.)** | *Eat.* |
| **dorm*ir*: (yo) duerm~~o~~** | **Duerm*a* (Ud.)** | *Sleep.* |

If you want to tell more than one person to do something, simply add the letter **n** to the singular command:

| SINGULAR | PLURAL |
|---|---|
| ***Cierre* (Ud.) la ventana.** | ***Cierren* (Uds.) la ventana.** |
| **No *sirva* (Ud.) el café ahora.** | **No *sirvan* (Uds.) el café ahora.** |
| ***Repita* (Ud.) la lección.** | ***Repitan* (Uds.) la lección.** |

## ACTIVIDADES

**D.** You are doing certain things and you want to tell somebody else to do the same things:

EXAMPLE: Miro el programa de televisión.
**Mire (Ud.) el programa de televisión también.**

**1.** Leo el periódico.

______________________________

**2.** Compro una camisa roja.

______________________________

**3.** Tomo el autobús ahora.

______________________________

**4.** Visito la exhibición en el museo.

______________________________

5. Bebo café en la cafetería.

______________________________

6. Estudio la lección para mañana.

______________________________

7. Monto a caballo.

______________________________

8. Duermo la siesta.

______________________________

9. Como afuera los sábados.

______________________________

10. Nado en la piscina por la tarde.

______________________________

**E.** Now tell your classmates to do the following:

1. cerrar la puerta

______________________________

2. no mentir

______________________________

3. entrar en la clase

______________________________

4. abrir el libro de español

______________________________

5. no dormir en clase

______________________________

6. repetir las palabras del profesor

______________________________

7. aprender un poema de memoria

______________________________

**6** Some verbs in Spanish have an irregular **yo** form. These verbs also follow the same rule to form the formal command:

| | | | |
|---|---|---|---|
| **decir:** (*to say*) | **yo digo** | **Dig*a* Ud.** | **Dig*an* Uds.** |
| **hacer:** (*to do*) | **yo hago** | **Hag*a* Ud.** | **Hag*an* Uds.** |

| | | | |
|---|---|---|---|
| **oír:** (*to hear*) | **yo oig~~o~~** | **Oig*a* Ud.** | **Oig*an* Uds.** |
| **poner:** (*to put*) | **yo pong~~o~~** | **Pong*a* Ud.** | **Pong*an* Uds.** |
| **salir:** (*to go out*) | **yo salg~~o~~** | **Salg*a* Ud.** | **Salg*an* Uds.** |
| **tener:** (*to have*) | **yo teng~~o~~** | **Teng*a* Ud.** | **Teng*an* Uds.** |
| **traer:** (*to bring*) | **yo traig~~o~~** | **Traig*a* Ud.** | **Traig*an* Uds.** |
| **venir:** (*to come*) | **yo veng~~o~~** | **Veng*a* Ud.** | **Veng*an* Uds.** |

**7** There are three important verbs that do not follow the rule for formal commands: **dar, ir,** and **ser.** You will have to memorize these forms:

| | |
|---|---|
| ***Dé* Ud. el libro a Juan.** | *Give the book to John.* |
| ***Vaya* Ud. a casa.** | *Go home.* |
| **No *sea* tonto.** | *Don't be foolish.* |

## ACTIVIDADES

**F.** Complete the following commands with the correct form of the verb in parentheses:

**1.** (dar) ________________ Ud. la información al policía.

**2.** (oír) ________________ Uds. lo que dice su padre.

**3.** (poner) ________________ Ud. el libro sobre la mesa.

**4.** (salir) No ________________ Uds. a patinar ahora.

**5.** (tener) ________________ Ud. mucho cuidado.

**6.** (venir) ________________ Uds. mañana por la mañana.

**7.** (ser) ________________ Ud. bueno con su hermanita.

**8.** (decir) ________________ Ud. la verdad.

**9.** (ir) No ________________ Uds. de compras al centro.

**10.** (hacer) ________________ Ud. el trabajo bien.

**G.** Tell your teacher the following in Spanish:

**1.** Give an example!

________________________________________

2. Bring a Spanish film!

______________________________

3. Don't leave now!

______________________________

4. Say something!

______________________________

5. Go to the cafeteria now!

______________________________

8 You now know how to give formal commands. But what happens if you want to tell a friend or somebody you address as **tú** to do something? It's even simpler: You just take the third person singular of the present tense and give the command:

| | | |
|---|---|---|
| **Él *lee* el libro.** | **¡*Lee* el libro!** | *Read the book!* |
| **Ella *compra* los discos.** | **¡*Compra* los discos!** | *Buy the records!* |
| **Él *abre* la ventana.** | **¡*Abre* la ventana!** | *Open the window!* |

NOTE: Exclamation marks with commands are optional, depending on how strongly you wish to express them.

## ACTIVIDAD

**H.** Tell one of your friends to do the following:

1. visitar el museo

______________________________

2. escribir en español

______________________________

3. comprar entradas para el cine

______________________________

4. jugar a los bolos

______________________________

5. patinar en el parque

______________________________

6. almorzar a las doce

______________________________

7. hablar por teléfono

______________________________

8. comer la manzana

______________________________

9. ayudar a los amigos

______________________________

10. volver a casa temprano

______________________________

**9** If you want to tell a friend not to do something, just add an **s** to the formal command form:

| | |
|---|---|
| **¡*Salga* Ud.!** | **¡No *salgas* tú!** |
| **¡*Abra* Ud. la ventana!** | **¡No *abras* tú la ventana!** |
| **¡*Mire* Ud. ese programa!** | **¡No *mires* tú ese programa!** |

## ACTIVIDAD

**I.** Express the following commands in the familiar form in Spanish:

1. Write all the words. Don't write only the first word.

______________________________

2. Eat all your lunch. Don't eat only the dessert.

______________________________

3. Speak with your father. Don't speak with your mother.

______________________________

4. Study the whole lesson. Don't study only the vocabulary.

______________________________

5. Listen to the teacher. Don't listen to your friend.

______________________________

6. Call on Monday. Don't call on Tuesday.

______________________________

**10** Many verbs have irregular familiar command forms. Here are some of the most common:

| | | | |
|---|---|---|---|
| **decir:** | ***di*** | **salir:** | ***sal*** |
| **hacer:** | ***haz*** | **ser:** | ***sé*** |
| **ir:** | ***ve*** | **tener:** | ***ten*** |
| **poner:** | ***pon*** | **venir:** | ***ven*** |

The negative forms of these commands are regular:

**No *digas* tú.**
**No *hagas* tú.**
**No *vayas* tú.**
**No *pongas* tú.**
**No *salgas* tú.**
**No *seas* tú.**
**No *tengas* tú.**
**No *vengas* tú.**

## ACTIVIDADES

**J.** Complete the following commands to your friend with the correct form of the verb in parentheses:

**1.** (poner) ¡No ________________ la mesa allí!

**2.** (ir) ¡No ________________ a la tienda ahora!

**3.** (comprar) ¡________________ los libros hoy!

**4.** (comer) ¡________________ temprano para salir después!

**5.** (hacer) ¡________________ las tareas esta noche!

**6.** (decir) ¡________________ siempre la verdad!

**7.** (venir) ¡________________ temprano! ¡No ________________ tarde!

**8.** (salir) ¡________________ del cuarto!

**9.** (vender) ¡________________ tu carro!

**10.** (ir) ¡________________ a ver la película!

**K.** Your mother tells you to do certain things and not do others. Express her commands in the familiar form in Spanish:

**1.** Go to school. Don't go to the movies.

________________________________________

2. Do your homework. Don't look at television now.

3. Be good. Don't tell lies.

4. Be careful. Don't run.

5. Close the door, go to your room, and put your coat there.

6. Read a good book. Don't listen to records.

## PREGUNTAS PERSONALES

1. Generalmente, ¿qué haces el sábado por la noche?

2. En el invierno, ¿vas a patinar en el hielo?

3. ¿Qué tipo de películas te gusta ver?

4. ¿Vas al teatro? ¿Te gustan las comedias o los dramas?

5. ¿Sabes montar a caballo?

6. ¿Asistes a conciertos de música clásica?

7. ¿Te gusta jugar a los bolos? ¿Hay una bolera (*bowling alley*) cerca de tu casa?

8. ¿Qué deportes practicas?

## DIÁLOGO

You are talking with a friend and she is asking your advice about several things. Tell her what to do:

## INFORMACIÓN PERSONAL

You have been selected to play the part of "El Gran Fandango," the world's greatest hypnotist. Using some of the commands you have just learned, tell a subject what you wish him/her to do:

1. ______________________________

2. ______________________________

3. ______________________________

4. ______________________________

5. ______________________________

6. ______________________________

# CÁPSULA CULTURAL

## Vamos a comer

It's six o'clock on a Friday evening. You are in Madrid and you are hungry. You want to have dinner. But no restaurant seems to be open! The cafés and bars, though, are full of people. What's going on?

Well, dinner time in Spain doesn't start until late, in fact it's not unusual to have dinner around 9 or 10 p.m. So, in the meantime, you sit in a café. Spaniards go there not only to have coffee or a glass of wine or a snack but also to meet friends, chat, celebrate a good day, finish a business deal, write letters, read a book, study, or simply sit and look at the world going by.

Lunch, too, is eaten much later in Spain than in the U.S. And it's not something to be gulped down in a rush. It's a full meal (soup, meat, rice, vegetables, dessert, coffee), savored and appreciated, which sometimes doesn't end until 3 p.m.

If you go to a place where people are eating, you wish them **¡Buen provecho!**, that is, roughly, "Enjoy your meal!" They respond **Igualmente** (*Same to you*). Food is very important, so much so that there are many sayings attesting to it. For example, to earn one's living is **ganarse el pan** (*to earn one's bread*) or **ganarse las habichuelas** (*to earn one's beans*); and something that is "as good as gold" is **bueno como el pan**.

# 5 Cartas al periódico

## Position of Adjectives; Shortened Forms; Adverbs

### 1 Vocabulario

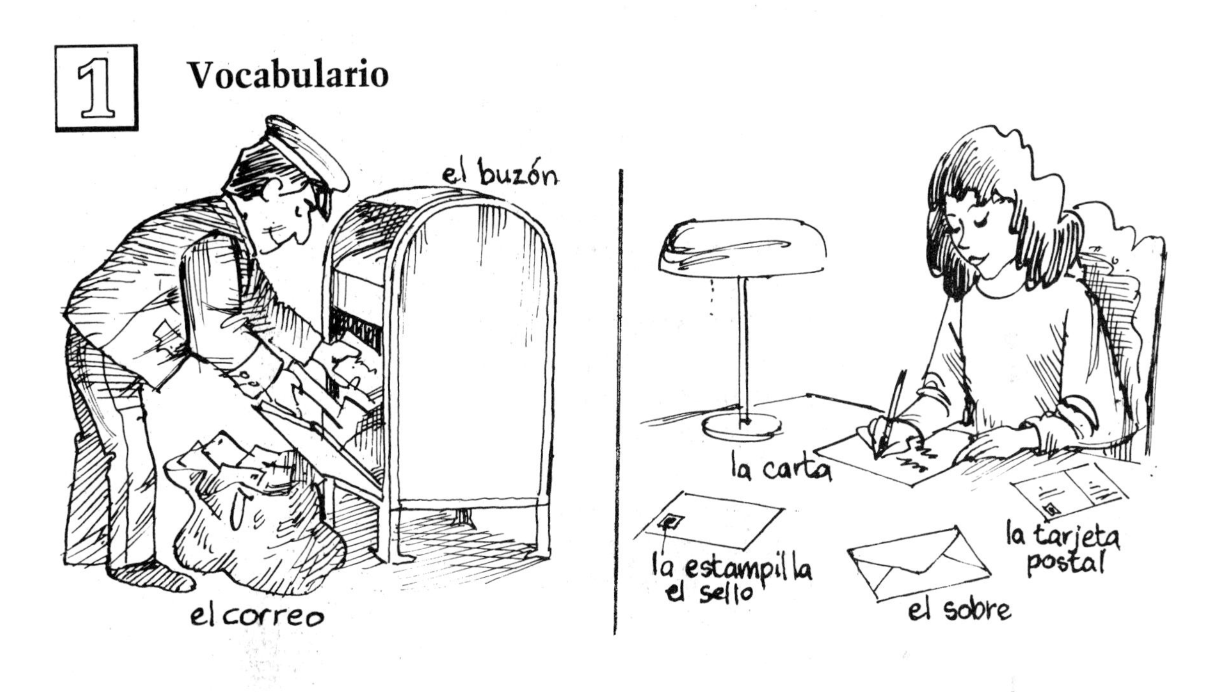

## ACTIVIDADES

**A.** List five activities required for writing and mailing a letter:

EXAMPLE: **Compro una estampilla.**

1. ____________________

2. ____________________

3. ____________________

4. ____________________

5. ____________________

**B.** Here are a couple of pages of a daily newspaper. Can you label the various sections in Spanish?

When we speak about someone or something, we use adjectives to describe that person or thing. You already know that adjectives in Spanish agree in gender (masculine or feminine) and number (singular or plural) with the noun they describe. Do you remember how to make an adjective feminine?

| | |
|---|---|
| **Él es *simpático*.** | **Ella es** ________________. |
| **Él es *inteligente*.** | **Ella es** ________________. |
| **Él es *joven*.** | **Ella es** ________________. |

Adjectives ending in **o** change the **o** to ______ in the feminine form. Other adjectives remain unchanged. Remember, however, that there is an exception: Adjectives of nationality ending in a consonant add an **a** for the feminine form:

| | |
|---|---|
| **Carlos es *español*.** | **María es *española*.** |
| **Jean es *francés*.** | **Monique es *francesa*.** |

3

How do we describe more than one person or thing?

| | |
|---|---|
| **Él es *pequeño*.** | **Ellos son** ________________. |
| **Ella es *pequeña*.** | **Ellas son** ________________. |
| **Él/Ella es *fuerte*.** | **Ellos/Ellas son** ________________. |
| **Él/Ella es *popular*.** | **Ellos/Ellas son** ________________. |

The rules are very simple: If the singular adjective ends in a vowel, we add **s.** If it ends in a consonant, we add **es.**

You also know that descriptive adjectives usually follow the noun:

| | |
|---|---|
| **Compro un *sobre azul*.** | *I buy a blue envelope.* |
| **Leo un *periódico argentino*.** | *I read an Argentinian newspaper.* |

## ACTIVIDAD

**C.** One of your classmates describes some people or objects to you. You want to know about other people or things:

EXAMPLE: Your classmate: Miguel es mexicano. (Isabel)
You: **¿Es Isabel mexicana también?**

1. Your classmate: La nueva profesora es española. (el director)

   You: ______________________________
2. Your classmate: El español es fácil. (las matemáticas)

   You: ______________________________
3. Your classmate: El carro de Eduardo es amarillo. (su casa)

   You: ______________________________
4. Your classmate: Mi perro es grande y gordo. (tus gatos)

   You: ______________________________
5. Your classmate: El padre de Raúl es alto y rubio. (la madre)

   You: ______________________________
6. Your classmate: Mis hermanas son feas. (tus hermanos)

   You: ______________________________

**4** Do you remember **alguno** and **ninguno?** They stand before the noun and drop the final **o** before a masculine singular noun:

| | |
|---|---|
| **¿Conoces a *algún* periodista?** | *Do you know any newspaperman?* |
| **No, no conozco a *ningún* periodista.** | *No, I don't know any newspaperman.* |

There is a special group of adjectives that may stand before or after the noun. Look at the following examples:

| | | |
|---|---|---|
| **Luis es un chico *bueno*.** | **Luis es un *buen* chico.** | *Louis is a good boy.* |
| **José es un alumno *malo*.** | **José es un *mal* alumno.** | *Joe is a bad student.* |
| **Leo el capítulo *primero*.** | **Leo el *primer* capítulo.** | *I read the first chapter.* |
| **Vivo en el piso *tercero*.** | **Vivo en el *tercer* piso.** | *I live on the third floor.* |

The sentences in both Spanish columns mean the same thing. What happened to the adjectives in the right column? ______________________ Right, they dropped the final **o.** The adjective was shortened. What is the gender of the nouns described by those adjectives?________________. Are they singular or plural? ________________.

Now look at these sentences:

| | |
|---|---|
| **El español es mi *tercera* clase.** | *Spanish is my third class.* |
| **Ellas son *malas* alumnas.** | *They are bad students.* |
| **Los *primeros* capítulos son largos.** | *The first chapters are long.* |
| **Luis y Carlos son *buenos* chicos.** | *Louis and Charles are good boys.* |

Were the adjectives shortened in the above sentences? ______ Here's the easy rule: **bueno, malo, primero,** and **tercero** are shortened only before a masculine singular noun.

## ACTIVIDADES

**D.** Complete the following sentences with the correct form of the adjective:

1. Siempre saco ______________ notas en álgebra. (malo)
2. ¿Tienes ______________ problema? (alguno)
3. Cuando hace ______________ tiempo, leo un ______________ libro. (malo, bueno)
4. Es la ______________ vez que repito lo mismo. (tercero)
5. Me gustan los dos ______________ días de clase. (primero)
6. Al ______________ día ya pienso en las vacaciones. (tercero)
7. La ______________ página de la lección es fácil. (primero)
8. ______________ día voy a hablar bien el español. (alguno)
9. Hoy no tengo ______________ examen. (ninguno)
10. Quiero comer un ______________ desayuno. (bueno)

**E.** Francisco is always saying the opposite of his twin brother Fernando:

EXAMPLE: Carlos es un buen amigo.
**No, Carlos es un mal amigo.**

1. María es una mala estudiante.

______________________________________________

2. Hoy hace buen tiempo.

______________________________________________

3. El hijo de la Sra. Pérez es un mal chico.

_______________

4. Ella saca buenas notas en español.

_______________

5. Leer es un mal hábito.

_______________

**6** The adjective **grande** can also stand before or after the noun. But look what happens:

| | |
|---|---|
| **Buenos Aires es una ciudad *grande*.** | *Buenos Aires is a large city.* |
| **Buenos Aires es también una *gran* ciudad.** | *Buenos Aires is also a great city.* |
| **Mi tío es un hombre *grande*.** | *My uncle is a large man.* |
| **Mi tío es un *gran* escritor.** | *My uncle is a great writer.* |
| **Nueva York tiene edificios *grandes*.** | *New York has large buildings.* |
| **Nueva York tiene *grandes* edificios.** | *New York has great buildings.* |

Is the meaning of **grande** the same in each pair of examples? ______ How do you express *great* before a singular noun (masculine or feminine)? ________ Before a plural noun (masculine or feminine)? ______________ Where is the adjective **grande(s)** meaning *large, big*? ______________.

## ACTIVIDAD

**F.** Do you know five great people? List them, indicating why they are (or were) great:

EXAMPLE: **Simón Bolívar: un gran general**

1. _______________
2. _______________
3. _______________
4. _______________
5. _______________

## Problemas de amor

Let's read now about a special section of a newspaper—**el consultorio sentimental** (*advice to the lovelorn*):

Todos los días millones de personas por todo el mundo compran periódicos. ¿Qué leen estas personas? ¿las noticias? ¿los anuncios? ¿los artículos? Claro que sí. Pero también leen una sección importante para ellos: «El consultorio sentimental».

¿Te sientes triste y solo? ¿Tienes problemas personales que no puedes resolver? Tal vez necesitas la ayuda profesional de Doña Lupita. Todos los días miles de personas escriben cartas a su «Consultorio Sentimental» del periódico para pedir consejo. ¿Estás de acuerdo con los consejos que da la gran Lupita?

**sentir (ie)** *to feel*
**resolver (ue)** *to solve*
**tal vez** *perhaps*
**el consejo** *advice*
**estar de acuerdo** *to agree*

Querida Lupita:

Tengo trece años y estoy enamorada seriamente por primera vez. Él tiene catorce años y está en mi tercera clase del día. Es amable, inteligente, simpático y alegre. Baila divinamente y participa activamente en muchos deportes. Yo soy seria, estudiosa, cuidadosa y sincera. Tengo un gran sentido del humor y muchas personas dicen que soy atractiva. Mi problema es que quiero salir con él, pero soy tímida y no puedo ni siquiera iniciar una conversación con él. ¿Qué debo hacer? Ayúdeme, por favor.

Desesperada

**enamorado** *in love*
**cuidadoso** *careful*
**tímido** *shy*
**ni siquiera** *not even*
**deber** *should*

Querida Desesperada:

¡Eres una gran chica! Debes tener confianza en ti misma. No eres ni mentirosa ni cruel. Los chicos prefieren una chica como tú, bonita, seria y simpática. Tal vez pareces arrogante porque no hablas mucho. Tienes que darle una oportunidad al chico de conocerte como eres realmente. ¿Por qué no lo llamas por teléfono? ¿O le escribes una nota? Buena suerte.

Lupita

**confianza en ti misma** *self-confidence*
**mentiroso** *liar*

## ACTIVIDAD

**G.** Preguntas sobre el cuento:

**1.** ¿Quiénes escriben cartas a Doña Lupita?

______________________________

**2.** ¿Cómo se llama la sección del periódico para personas con problemas personales?

______________________________

**3.** ¿Quién es Desesperada?

______________________________

**4.** ¿Cuál es el problema de Desesperada?

______________________________

**5.** ¿Cómo es Desesperada?

______________________________

**6.** ¿Cómo es el chico que ella describe?

______________________________

**7.** ¿Qué consejos da Doña Lupita?

______________________________

**8.** ¿Estás de acuerdo con sus consejos? ¿Por qué (no)?

______________________________

______________________________

**8** There are some new words in the story ending in **-mente.** Do you recall them? **activamente, divinamente, seriamente,** and so on. These are called adverbs — expressions that describe another adverb, an adjective, or a verb. How are they formed? Very simply, **muy fácilmente:** Just add the ending **-mente** to the feminine singular form of the adjective. (**-mente** is usually equivalent to English *-ly*.) Let's look at some examples:

| FEMININE FORM OF ADJECTIVE | ADVERB |
|---|---|
| **rápida** | **rápida*mente*** |
| **seria** | **seria*mente*** |
| **fácil** | **fácil*mente*** |

Can you continue giving the adverbs formed from the following adjectives?

| | | |
|---|---|---|
| **atento** | *attentive; polite* | ______________ |
| **ciego** | *blind* | ______________ |
| **loco** | *crazy* | ______________ |
| **popular** | *popular* | ______________ |
| **útil** | *useful* | ______________ |
| **hábil** | *skillful* | ______________ |

## ACTIVIDADES

**H.** Julia was chosen for the lead role in the school play. Tell why:

EXAMPLE: Ella es hábil. Ella actúa **hábilmente.**

1. Ella es seria. Ella actúa ______________________________.
2. Ella es natural. Ella actúa ______________________________.
3. Ella es inteligente. Ella actúa ______________________________.
4. Ella es magnífica. Ella actúa ______________________________.
5. Ella es dulce. Ella actúa ______________________________.

**I.** You are asked to describe how some of your friends do certain things:

EXAMPLE: Víctor participa **activamente** en los deportes.

1. Rosa habla ______________ el francés. (perfectly)
2. Fernando estudia ______________ las matemáticas. (seriously)
3. Carlos siempre entra ______________ en la clase. (quickly)
4. Tomás habla ______________. (intelligently)
5. Miguel come ______________. (carefully)
6. Simón aprende ______________ el español. (easily)
7. Juanita es ______________ inteligente. (really)
8. Susana siempre actúa ______________. (crazily).

**9** There are other common adverbs that are not formed from adjectives. Here is a list of the most important ones:

**ahora** *now*
**bastante** *enough*
**bien** *well*
**casi** *almost*
**cerca** *near, nearby*
**demasiado** *too (much)*
**despacio** *slowly*
**después** *later, afterwards*
**hoy** *today*
**lejos** *far, far away*
**mal** *badly, poorly*
**mañana** *tomorrow*
**más** *more*
**menos** *less*
**mucho** *a lot, much*
**muy** *very*
**poco** *little*
**pronto** *soon*
**siempre** *always*
**tarde** *late*
**temprano** *early*
**ya** *already*

## ACTIVIDADES

**J.** Margarita always says the opposite of what her mother says. What does Margarita say?

EXAMPLE: Tu padre baila bien.
**No, mi padre baila mal.**

1. Tu hermanito come poco.

______________________________

2. Tú vas a llegar tarde a la escuela.

______________________________

3. Tu hermana debe trabajar menos.

______________________________

4. Tus abuelos viven cerca del teatro Colón.

______________________________

5. Tú debes salir ahora.

______________________________

**K.** Tell your teacher when you are going to do the following things:

1. Voy a hacer la tarea de español ______________. (tomorrow)
2. Voy a ir al cine ______________. (today)
3. Voy a escribir una carta ______________. (afterwards)
4. Voy a salir de la clase ______________. (soon)
5. Voy a leer el periódico ______________. (now)

**Bien** and **bueno; mal** and **malo**

Remember that **bien** and **mal** are adverbs. They describe actions and don't change their form. **Bueno** and **malo** are adjectives. They describe nouns and agree with them in gender and number:

| | |
|---|---|
| **María es *buena*.** | **Pablo es *malo*.** |
| **Jorge es *bueno*.** | **Rosa es *mala*.** |
| **María y Jorge son *buenos*.** | **Pablo y Rosa son *malos*.** |

But:

| | |
|---|---|
| **María escribe *bien*.** | **Pablo escribe *mal*.** |
| **María y Jorge escriben *bien*.** | **Pablo y Rosa escriben *mal*.** |

## ACTIVIDADES

**L.** Complete with the correct word, **bien** or **bueno** (**buen, buena, buenos, buenas**):

1. La película es ________________.
2. Roberto es un ________________ amigo.
3. Yo estoy ________________, gracias.
4. Tú cantas y bailas muy ________________.
5. Leo una ________________ novela.
6. ¿Tienes ________________ noticias de tu familia?
7. Hoy hace ________________ tiempo.
8. El bebé duerme ________________.

**M.** Now repeat Actividad L, using **mal** or **malo** (**mal, mala, malos, malas**):

1. La película es ____________.
2. Roberto es un ____________ amigo.
3. Yo estoy ____________.
4. Tú cantas y bailas muy ____________.
5. Leo una ____________ novela.

6. ¿Tienes ____________ noticias de tu familia?

7. Hoy hace ____________ tiempo.

## PREGUNTAS PERSONALES

1. ¿Qué periódico lees?

______________________________________________

2. ¿Qué sección del periódico prefieres?

______________________________________________

3. ¿Te gusta escribir cartas? ¿Escribes muchas?

______________________________________________

4. ¿Tienes alguna colección de estampillas?

______________________________________________

5. ¿Cuál es tu novela favorita?

______________________________________________

6. ¿Reciben mucho correo en tu casa?

______________________________________________

7. ¿Publica tu escuela algún periódico? ¿Es bueno?

______________________________________________

8. ¿Crees que es posible recibir consejos profesionales del «Consultorio sentimental» de un periódico? ¿Por qué (no)?

______________________________________________

## INFORMACIÓN PERSONAL

Tell how you do these things:

1. Yo aprendo español ______________________________________________.

2. Yo hablo ______________________________________________.

3. Yo como ______________________________________________.

4. Yo contesto ______________________________________________ en clase.

5. Yo camino ______________________________________________.

## DIÁLOGO

La consejera de la escuela habla con Marta sobre un problema personal. **¿Qué dice Marta?**

## COMPOSICIÓN

You are writing to the "Consultorio Sentimental" of a newspaper. Tell them your name and age, describe yourself, and ask advice to solve a real or imaginary problem:

_____ de __________ de 19____

Querido(a) ______________:

______________________________________________

______________________________________________

______________________________________________

______________________________________________

______________________________________________

______________________________________________

Un cordial saludo de

# CÁPSULA CULTURAL

## México lindo

What makes Mexico different from every other country in Latin America? Answer: Mexico is the only Spanish-speaking country that shares a border with the United States. In fact, Mexico is the only Spanish-speaking country that is part of the North American continent. These facts alone would be sufficient to insure that Mexico is of vital importance and concern to the United States.

But there are many more factors. Mexico has a population of more than 80 million people, the largest of all the Spanish-speaking countries in the world. Its capital, (**la Ciudad de) México,** is the most populous Spanish-speaking city in the world and one of the fastest-growing. In territory, Mexico is the fifth largest country in the Western Hemisphere, surpassed only by the United States, Canada, Brazil, and Argentina.

What kind of a country is Mexico? It is a land of enormous contrasts. In its cities, it is not unusual to see Indian people dressed in their traditional costumes walking past modern skyscrapers. Mexico City, the capital, is located in a semitropical zone yet enjoys a moderate climate of eternal spring owing to its location at an altitude almost 7,500 feet above sea level.

Today, Mexico is a country in transition, passing from an agricultural economy to an industrial one, producing everything from chemicals and textiles to automobiles. It also has some of the largest oil reserves in the world. Because of its picturesque beauty and proximity to our country, more than two million American tourists visit Mexico every year.

When are you going?

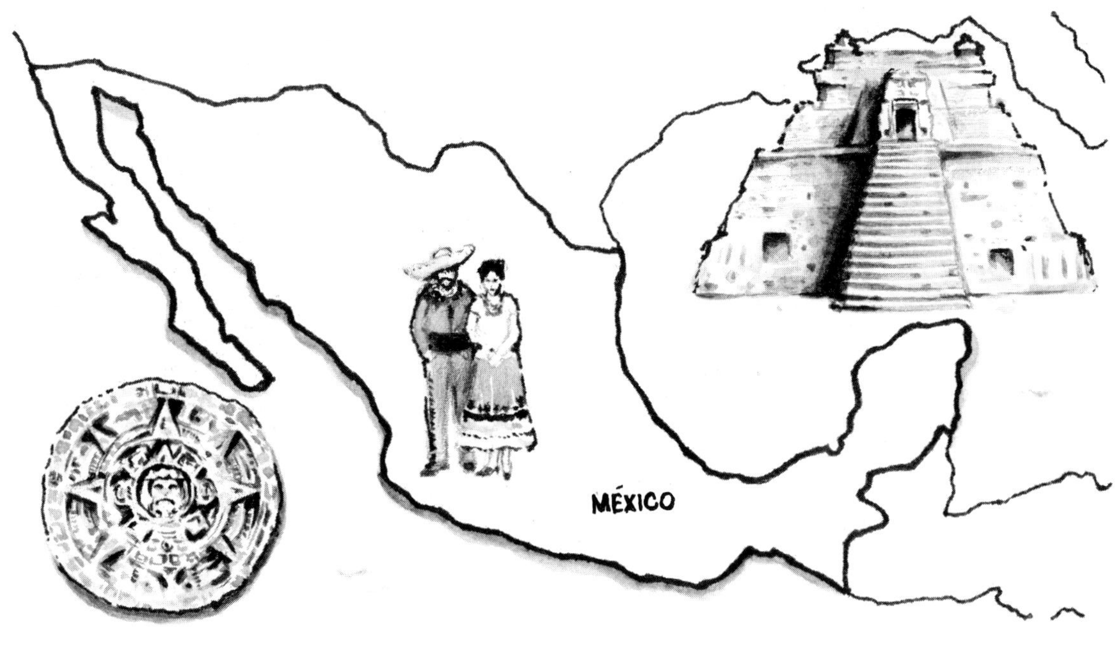

# *Repaso I (Lecciones 1–5)*

## Lección 1

**a.** Question words in Spanish:

**¿por qué?** *why?*
**¿cómo?** *how?*
**¿qué?** *what? which?*
**¿cuál(es)?** *what? which one(s)?*
**¿quién(es)?** *who?*
**¿a quién(es)?** *whom?*
**¿de quién(es)?** *whose?*
**¿dónde?** *where?* **¿adónde?** *where (to)?*
**¿cuándo?** *when?*
**¿cuánto (-a, -os, -as)?** *how much (many)?*

**b. Conocer** and **saber** mean *to know.* **Conocer** is used in the sense of *to be acquainted, to be familiar with;* **saber** means *to know facts, to have information about* something:

**Conozco ese libro.** *I know (I am familiar with) that book.*
**Sé que ella viene mañana.** *I know that she's coming tomorrow.*

**Saber** followed by an infinitive means *to know how to:*

**Él sabe hablar español.** *He knows how to speak Spanish.*

## Lección 2

Some Spanish verbs have stem changes in all forms of the present tense, except for **nosotros.** There are three types of changes:

(1) **-AR, -ER,** and **-IR** verbs that change **e** to **ie:**

**pensar:** **p*ie*nso, p*ie*nsas, p*ie*nsa, pensamos, p*ie*nsan**
**perder:** **p*ie*rdo, p*ie*rdes, p*ie*rde, perdemos, p*ie*rden**
**mentir:** **m*ie*nto, m*ie*ntes, m*ie*nte, mentimos, m*ie*nten**

(2) **-AR, -ER,** and **-IR** verbs that change **o** to **ue:**

**almorzar:** **alm*ue*rzo, alm*ue*rzas, alm*ue*rza, almorzamos, alm*ue*rzan**
**volver:** **v*ue*lvo, v*ue*lves, v*ue*lve, volvemos, v*ue*lven**
**dormir:** **d*ue*rmo, d*ue*rmes, d*ue*rme, dormimos, d*ue*rmen.**

**Jugar** changes the **u** to **ue: j*ue*go, j*ue*gas, j*ue*ga, jugamos, j*ue*gan**

(3) **-IR** verbs that change **e** to **i:**

**repetir:** **rep*i*to, rep*i*tes, rep*i*te, repetimos, rep*i*ten**

## Lección 3

**a.** Spanish negatives and their corresponding affirmative expressions:

| NEGATIVE | AFFIRMATIVE |
|---|---|
| **nadie** *no one, nobody* | **alguien** *someone, somebody* |
| **nada** *nothing, not anything* | **algo** *something* |
| **ni . . ni** *neither . . nor* | **o** *or* |
| **nunca** *never*<br>**jamás** *never* | **siempre** *always* |
| **tampoco** *neither* | **también** *also, too* |
| **ninguno (-a, -os, -as)** *no, none* | **alguno (-a, -os, -as)** *any, some* |

**b.** There are two ways of negating a sentence in Spanish:

| | | |
|---|---|---|
| **no** + verb + negative word: | **No quiero nada.** | *I don't want anything.* |
| negative word + verb: | **Nada quiero.** | |

**c.** When the object of a verb is a negative or an affirmative word referring to a person, the personal **a** is used:

**Llamo a alguien.**
**No llamo a nadie. / A nadie llamo.**

## Lección 4

**a. Vamos a** + infinitive is used in Spanish to express *let us*:

***Vamos a jugar* al tenis.** *Let's play tennis.*

**Vamos** is used to express *let's go*:

***Vamos* a la fiesta.** *Let's go to the party.*

**b.** Singular formal commands are formed by changing the ending **-o** of the first person singular of the present tense to **-e** for **-AR** verbs and to **-a** for **-ER** and **-IR** verbs. Plural formal commands are formed by adding **-n** to the singular command:

| INFINITIVE | FIRST PERSON PRESENT TENSE | FORMAL COMMANDS Singular | Plural |
|---|---|---|---|
| **hablar** | **habl~~o~~** | **Habl*e* (Ud.)** | **Habl*en* (Uds.)** |
| **comer** | **com~~o~~** | **Com*a* (Ud.)** | **Com*an* (Uds.)** |
| **dormir** | **duerm~~o~~** | **Duerm*a* (Ud.)** | **Duerm*an* (Uds.)** |

| | | |
|---|---|---|
| **dar:** | **Dé (Ud.)** | **Den (Uds.)** |
| **ir:** | **Vaya (Ud.)** | **Vayan (Uds.)** |
| **ser:** | **Sea (Ud.)** | **Sean (Uds.)** |

c. Familiar commands are identical with the third person singular of the present tense:

| INFINITIVE | THIRD PERSON SINGULAR | FAMILIAR COMMAND |
|---|---|---|
| **hablar** | **habla** | **Habla (tú).** |
| **comer** | **come** | **Come (tú).** |
| **dormir** | **duerme** | **Duerme (tú).** |

d. Negative familiar commands add **s** to the singular formal command:

| FORMAL COMMAND | NEGATIVE FAMILIAR COMMAND |
|---|---|
| **Salga (Ud.).** | **No salga*s* (tú).** |

e. Many verbs have irregular familiar command forms:

| | | | | | | | |
|---|---|---|---|---|---|---|---|
| **decir:** | **di** | **ir:** | **ve** | **salir:** | **sal** | **tener:** | **ten** |
| **hacer:** | **haz** | **poner:** | **pon** | **ser:** | **sé** | **venir:** | **ven** |

## Lección 5

a. Adjectives agree in gender and number with the nouns they describe. Adjectives that end in **o** change the **o** to **a** in the feminine form. Other adjectives remain unchanged, except for adjectives of nationality, which have feminine forms in **-a: el alumno español, la alumna español*a*.**

To form the plural of adjectives, add **s** to an adjective ending in a vowel and **es** to an adjective ending in a consonant.

Descriptive adjectives in Spanish usually follow the noun.

b. The adjectives **alguno** and **ninguno** stand before the noun and drop the final **o** before a masculine singular noun:

**¿Tienes *algún* periódico?**
**No, no tengo *ningún* periódico.**

c. **Bueno, malo, primero**, and **tercero** may stand before or after the noun. They are shortened before a masculine singular noun:

**Voy a un *buen* hotel. / Voy a un hotel *bueno*.**
**Es un *mal* consejo. / Es un consejo *malo*.**
**Lean el *primer* capítulo. / Lean el capítulo *primero*.**
**Vivo en el *tercer* piso. / Vivo en el piso *tercero*.**

d. **Grande** means *large* when it stands after the noun. It means *great* when it stands before the noun. **Grande** becomes **gran** before a singular noun:

| | |
|---|---|
| **Madrid es una *gran* ciudad.** | *Madrid is a great city.* |
| **Mi abuelo es un hombre *grande*.** | *My grandfather is a large man.* |

e. Adverbs describe another adverb, an adjective, or a verb. Adverbs are usually formed by adding **-mente** to the singular feminine form of the adjective:

**rápida** **rápida*mente***

Some common adverbs are not formed from adjectives.

f. The adverbs **bien** and **mal** do not change form. The adjectives **bueno** and **malo** agree in gender and number with the noun they describe:

**Ella habla *bien* (*mal*). / Ellas hablan *bien* (*mal*).**
**Ella es *buena* (*mala*). / Ellas son *buenas* (*malas*).**

## ACTIVIDADES

**A.** Here are ten pictures of people doing things. Complete the description below each picture by using the correct form of one of these verbs:

| | | | | |
|---|---|---|---|---|
| almorzar | costar | jugar | preferir | servir |
| comenzar | dormir | pensar | querer | sonreír |

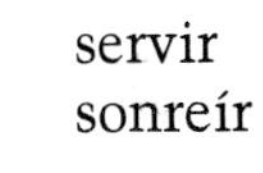

**1.** El bebé ________________ la siesta.

**2.** Los alumnos ________________ en la cafetería.

**3.** La Sra. Gómez ________________ empanadas.

**4.** Anita y Juanita ________________.

**5.** La mamá pregunta: «¿Qué traje de baño ________________?»

**6.** Jorge ________________ en Rosita.

7. ¿Cuánto ________________ esta cadena?

9. Carlitos ________________ las gafas de sol.

8. Los muchachos ____________.

10. La película ________________ pronto.

**B.** **¿Quién es Mandrako el mago?** Read the following sentences and then decide which one of the five men they describe. Put an X in the correct circle:

No lleva nunca sombrero.
No lleva corbata tampoco.
Sonríe siempre.
Usa un arete en una oreja.
También lleva una cadena de oro.
Jamás lleva traje.
No tiene mucho pelo pero tiene barba.
Lleva gafas muy grandes.

**C.** How many of these words do you remember? Fill in the Spanish words, then read down the boxed column of letters. What do Miguel and Rosa see at the beach?

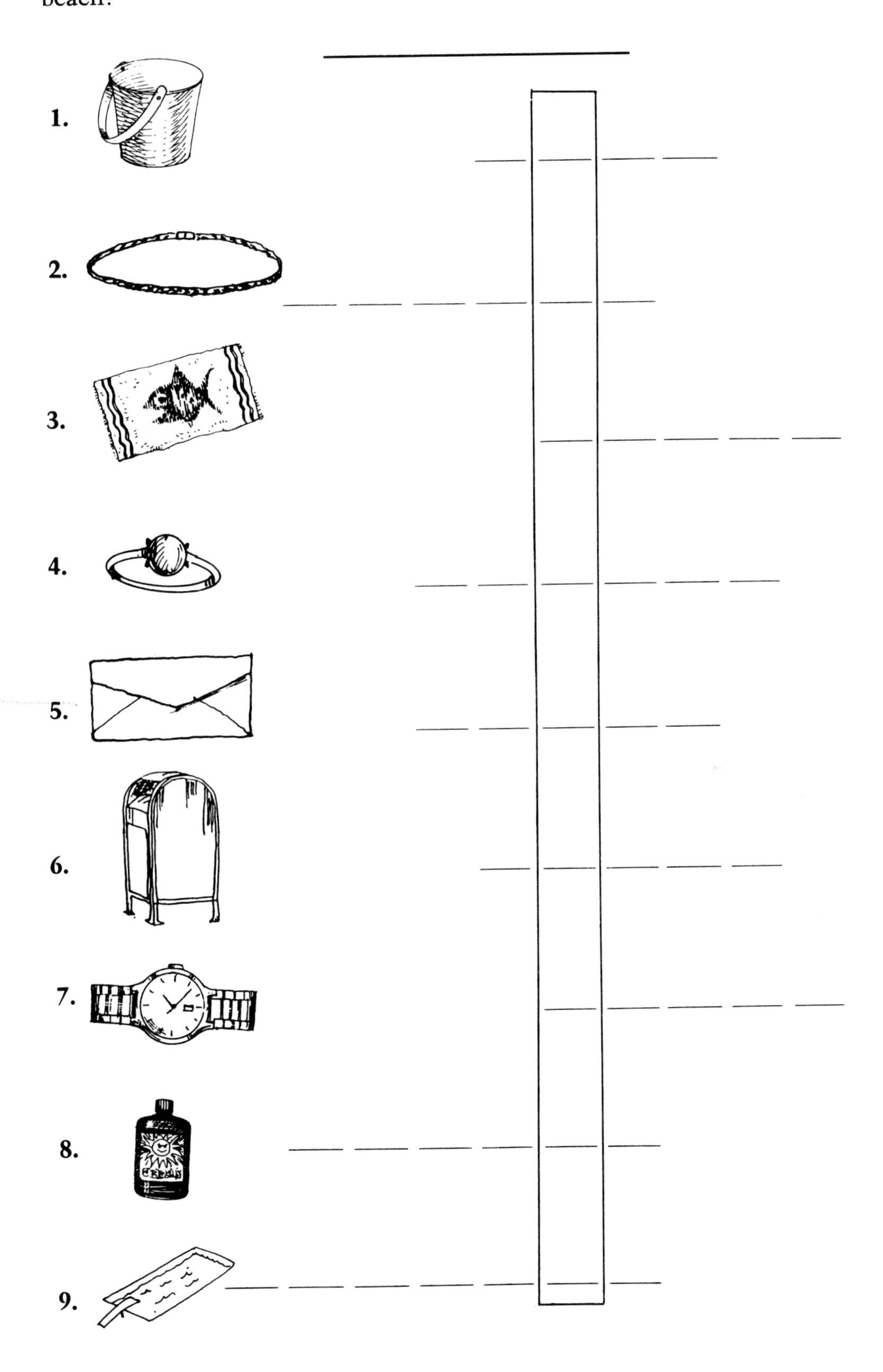

**D.** Hidden in the puzzle below are

8 adjectives 16 adverbs

__________ __________ __________

__________ __________ __________

__________ __________ __________

__________ __________ __________

__________ __________ __________

__________ __________ __________

__________ __________ __________

__________ __________ __________

Find the hidden words, circle them in the puzzle, and then write them in the space above. The words may read from left to right, right to left, up or down, or diagonally:

| | | | | | | | | | |
|---|---|---|---|---|---|---|---|---|---|
| C | A | S | I | E | M | P | R | E | E |
| H | F | S | O | N | E | M | R | T | L |
| U | O | C | Á | Ñ | B | U | E | N | A |
| O | I | Y | U | M | I | C | E | I | M |
| G | R | A | N | D | E | H | D | N | S |
| E | E | S | U | O | N | O | R | G | O |
| I | S | L | C | E | R | C | A | U | J |
| C | C | O | D | I | M | Í | T | N | E |
| E | P | R | O | N | T | O | C | O | L |
| H | Á | B | I | L | M | E | N | T | E |

**E.** Here are eight pictures. Write an appropriate command form under each of these pictures, using the following verbs:

| | | | | |
|---|---|---|---|---|
| cerrar | ir | poner | venir | traer |
| comprar | mirar | salir | volver | |

1. ¡No ____________________ la televisión ahora!

2. Manuela, ¡____________________ Ud. a la pizarra!

3. ¡____________________ Ud. el televisor allí!

4. ¡No ____________________ el vestido rojo, ____________________ el azul!

5. ¡____________________ a jugar afuera!

6. ¡____________________ a la tienda y ____________________ pan!

7. ¡No ____________________ a casa tarde!

8. ¡____________________ Ud. la ventana, por favor!

**F.** Unscramble the words. Then unscramble the letters in the circles to find out the message you received by mail after responding to an ad in a newspaper:

| | |
|---|---|
| **EROCOR** | ◯ ☐ ☐ ☐ ☐ ◯ |
| **ATACR** | ☐ ◯ ☐ ◯ ☐ |
| **DIERÓCIPO** | ☐ ☐ ☐ ◯ ☐ ☐ ◯ ☐ ☐ |
| **NUACISON** | ☐ ◯ ☐ ☐ ☐ ☐ ☐ ◯ |

**Recibimos buenas** ____________________.

**G.** Let's do something special this weekend. What? To find the answer, identify the pictures, then write the letters in the blanks below:

**¡Vamos a** __ __ __ __ __ __ __ __ __ __ __
7 12 13 10 4 9 6 11 3 5 8

__ __ __ __ __
1 2 14 16 15

## H. Crucigrama

HORIZONTALES

1. Sabe hacer trucos.
3. Una forma de dinero.
5. Imperativo (*command*) de **ser.**
7. Lee noticias en el ____.
8. Imperativo de **reír.**
9. Persona que mira la televisión.
14. Contrario de **siempre.**
15. Se usa en la oreja.
16. Los ____ clasificados.
20. ¿Tienes problemas? ¿Necesitas ____?
21. Sirve para meter arena en un cubo.
22. Necesitas ____ para escribir.
23. En verano hay mucho ____.
24. Imperativo de **contar.**
25. Imperativo de **venir.**
27. El turista manda una ____ postal.
28. ¡____ como un perro!
29. No hay luz. La casa está ____.
30. Presente de **nevar.**

VERTICALES

1. Contrario de **bien.**
2. Contrario de **alguien.**
3. Hombre casado.
4. Contrario de **nunca.**
6. Marido y mujer.
8. ¿Qué hora es? Mire el ____.
10. Imperativo de **ir.**
11. El artículo de fondo.
12. Está sepultado.
13. Hay mucha en la playa.
17. No puede ver. Es ____.
18. Piedras preciosas.
19. Escribes un ____ para el periódico
20. Lugar donde ves películas.
21. Dinero español.
22. Imperativo de **perder.**
23. ¡____ como un mono!
25. Barco de ____.
26. Contrario de **algo.**
27. Imperativo de **tener.**

**I.** Picture Story. Can you read this story? Whenever you come to a picture, read it as if it were a Spanish word:

# Segunda Parte

# 6 *Por la mañana / Por la noche*

## Reflexive Verbs

### 1 Vocabulario

The new words that follow are all verbs. They belong to a special family of verbs called REFLEXIVE VERBS. See if you can guess their meanings:

## ACTIVIDAD

**A.** Match the descriptions with the pictures:

| | |
|---|---|
| **Él se peina.** | **Nosotras nos acostamos.** |
| **Ellas se visten.** | **Uds. se cepillan los dientes.** |
| **Tú te despiertas.** | **Carlos se levanta.** |
| **Yo me lavo.** | **Mi papá se afeita.** |

1. ______________________

2. ______________________

3. ______________________

4. ______________________

5. ______________________

6. ______________________

7. ______________________

8. ______________________

A verb is reflexive when the subject does something to itself. To use a verb "reflexively," we add a special pronoun, called a reflexive pronoun, to indicate that the subject and object of the verb refer to the same person or thing. It's really not very difficult once you get the hang of it. You probably noticed, however, that some English verbs do not seem to be reflexive while their Spanish equivalents are.

For example, *to get up* is **levantarse.** The verb **levantar** by itself, without the reflexive pronoun, means simple *to raise* or *to lift*:

| | |
|---|---|
| **Él *levanta* la mesa.** | *He lifts the table.* |
| But: | |
| **Él *se levanta.*** | *He gets up* (literally, *he lifts himself*) |

Let's look at some more reflexive verbs in Spanish that are not reflexive in English. Just remember that the reflexive pronoun in Spanish REFLECTS the action expressed by the verb on the subject:

| | |
|---|---|
| **La abuela *divierte* a los niños.** | *The grandmother amuses the children.* |
| **La abuela *se divierte.*** | *The grandmother has fun (amuses herself).* |
| **El papá *acuesta* al bebé.** | *The father puts the baby to bed.* |
| **El papá *se acuesta.*** | *The father goes to bed (puts himself to bed).* |
| ***Llamo* a Luis.** | *I call Louis.* |
| ***Me llamo* Luis.** | *My name is Louis (I call myself Louis).* |

## ACTIVIDAD

**B.** In each group, underline the sentence with a reflexive verb:

1. Se lava con agua fría.
   Lava el carro con agua fría.
2. La muchacha mira la televisión.
   La muchacha se mira en el espejo.
3. Mi madre viste a mi hermana.
   Mi madre se viste.
4. Ud. se despierta temprano.
   Ud. despierta a su mamá temprano.
5. José pone el abrigo en la silla.
   José se pone el abrigo.

## 3 El ciclismo

Let's read a story about a very popular sport — bicycle racing. How many reflexive verbs can you identify?

En España y en muchos países hispanoamericanos, el ciclismo es más que un deporte — es una pasión. En Colombia, por ejemplo, cada año más de sesenta ciclistas participan en una carrera, la Vuelta a Colombia, que dura varios días. El ganador es un héroe nacional y recibe mucho dinero y regalos.

**la carrera** *race*
**la vuelta** *circuit*
**durar** *to last*
**el ganador** *winner*

Escuchemos una entrevista con un joven que se llama Víctor Veloz, un ciclista muy popular:

EL PERIODISTA: Buenos días, Víctor. Queremos saber cómo vive un campeón. ¿Puedes describir un día típico de tu vida?

VÍCTOR: Bueno. Por lo general, me despierto muy temprano, a las cinco de la mañana. Me gusta entrenar cuando no hace mucho calor.

**entrenar** *to train*

EL PERIODISTA: Sí, claro. ¿Qué haces de especial para comenzar el día?

VÍCTOR: Después de levantarme, me lavo la cara y las manos, me afeito y me cepillo los dientes.

EL PERIODISTA: Sí, sí, comprendo. Eso hacemos todos. Pero, ¿qué haces para llevarle ventaja a todos los demás ciclistas, para hacerte campeón?

VÍCTOR: Tomo un desayuno ligero. Me visto, me pongo los zapatos, me peino y salgo a entrenar dos o tres horas. Luego vuelvo a casa, me baño y almuerzo. Después del almuerzo, que es bastante grande, me acuesto a descansar un poco.

**llevar ventaja a** *to have the advantage over*
**hacerse** *to become*
**ligero** *light*
**ponerse** *to put on*
**descansar** *to rest*

EL PERIODISTA: Y después, ¿qué haces por la tarde?

VÍCTOR: Más o menos lo mismo. Hago ejercicios y monto en bicicleta dos o tres horas más. Me siento a comer a las siete y media y me acuesto antes de las diez. Necesito mucho descanso y no tengo tiempo para divertirme.

**sentarse (ie)** *to sit down*
**divertirse** *to have fun*

EL PERIODISTA: Muy interesante. Veo que no haces nada excepcional. Todos los jóvenes tienen la misma oportunidad de hacerse campeones. No tienes ninguna ventaja sobre los demás. A propósito, tienes una bicicleta bonita. ¿Cuánto vale?

VÍCTOR: Diez mil dólares.

**valer** *to be worth, to cost*

## ACTIVIDADES

**C.** Conteste en frases completas:

1. ¿Qué es el ciclismo para muchos hispanoamericanos?

   ______________________________________________

2. ¿Qué recibe generalmente el ganador?

   ______________________________________________

3. ¿Qué quiere saber el periodista sobre Víctor Veloz?

   ______________________________________________

4. ¿Por qué se levanta Víctor tan temprano?

   ______________________________________________

5. ¿Qué hace Víctor después de levantarse?

   ______________________________________________

6. ¿Qué clase de desayuno toma Víctor?

   ______________________________________________

7. ¿Se acuesta Víctor después de almuerzo? ¿Por qué?

   ______________________________________________

8. Según el periodista, ¿qué oportunidades tienen todos los jóvenes?

   ______________________________________________

9. ¿Qué hace Víctor de especial?

   ______________________________________________

10. ¿Qué necesita Ud. para hacerse campeón en un deporte?

    ______________________________________________

**D.** **Sí o no.** Víctor Veloz is talking about himself. If a statement is incorrect, change it to make it correct:

1. Me despierto a las siete de la mañana.

   ______________________________________________

2. Me lavo antes de levantarme.

   ______________________________________________

3. Me visto antes del desayuno.

   ______________________________________________

4. Me siento a descansar después del almuerzo.

______________________________

5. Me baño cuando me levanto por la mañana.

______________________________

6. Me afeito después del desayuno.

______________________________

7. Me acuesto a medianoche.

______________________________

8. Necesito poco descanso.

______________________________

**E.** What do you do in the morning?

EXAMPLE: 

**Me despierto.**

1. ______________________________

3. ______________________________

2. ______________________________

4. ______________________________

5. ______________________________

6. ______________________________

**F.** What do you do in the evening?

1. ______________________________

4. ______________________________

2. ______________________________

5. ______________________________

3. ______________________________

6. ______________________________

**4** Now you can answer the following questions: In the sentence **Yo me lavo,** whom am I washing? ____________ Is the action being performed on the subject or on someone else? ________________ Do the subject (**yo**) and the reflexive pronoun (**me**) refer to the same person or to two different people?

______________________________

What do we mean by a reflexive verb? ____________________________

______________________________________________________________

What is the position of the reflexive pronoun with respect to the subject?

____________________ With respect to the verb? ____________________

Different subjects require different reflexive pronouns:

**Yo *me* lavo**
**Tú *te* lavas**
**Ud. *se* lava**
**Él *se* lava**
**Ella *se* lava**

**Nosotros *nos* lavamos**
**Uds. *se* lavan**
**Ellos / Ellas *se* lavan**

## ACTIVIDADES

**G.** What is Gerardo's routine? Look at the picture and say what Gerardo does at the time indicated:

EXAMPLE:

**Gerardo se despierta a las seis y media de la mañana.**

**1.** ______________________________________________________________

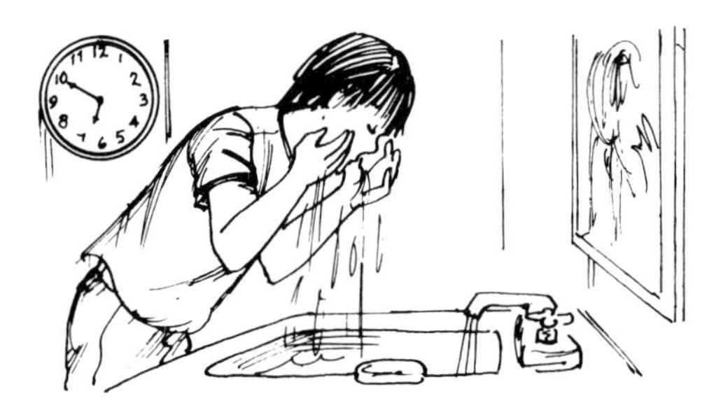

2. ______________________________________________

3. ______________________________________________

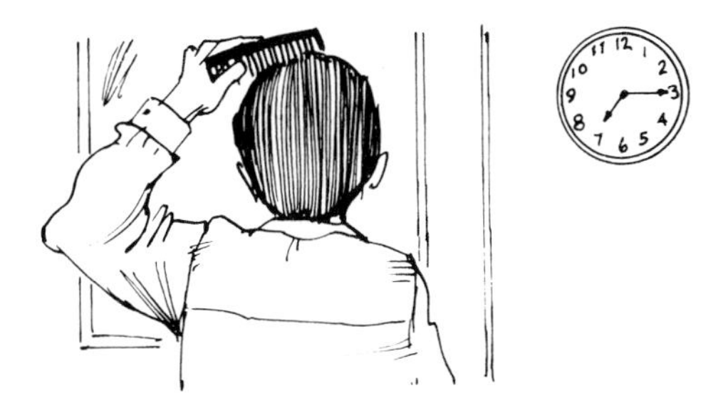

4. ______________________________________________

5. ______________________________________________

**H.** Complete each sentence with the correct reflexive pronoun:

**1.** Yo ____________ despierto a las seis.

**2.** Ellos siempre ____________ levantan tarde.

3. ¿A qué hora ____________ acuestan Uds.?

4. Nosotros ____________ vestimos antes de salir.

5. ¿Cuándo ____________ baña Ud.?

6. Tú ____________ lavas las manos antes de comer.

7. Marta ____________ peina tres veces al día.

8. Nosotras ____________ cepillamos el pelo todas las noches.

**I.** What are all these people doing? Complete the sentences with the correct form of the verb in parentheses:

1. (acostarse) Yo ______ ____________________ temprano.
2. (bañarse) Ella ______ ____________________ con agua fría.
3. (sentarse) Tú ______ ____________________ cuando estás cansado.
4. (peinarse) Rosa ______ ____________________ antes de ir a la fiesta.
5. (dormirse) Los niños ______ ____________________ después de mirar la televisión.
6. (ponerse) Ud. ______ ____________________ el suéter que compró.
7. (despertarse) Nosotros ______ ____________________ tarde los domingos.
8. (vestirse) Uds. ______ ____________________ rápido.
9. (quitarse) Yo ______ ____________________ los zapatos cuando llego a casa.
10. (afeitarse) Mis hermanos ______ ____________________ dos veces al día.

**6** In Spanish reflexive constructions, we do not use the possessive adjective with parts of the body or wearing apparel, since the reflexive pronoun obviously refers to the subject. The definite article is used instead:

| | |
|---|---|
| **Tú te lavas *el* pelo.** | *You wash your hair.* |
| **Él se pone *los* zapatos.** | *He puts on his shoes.* |
| **Yo me cepillo *los* dientes.** | *I brush my teeth.* |
| **Ud. se quita *el* abrigo.** | *Your take off your coat.* |

## ACTIVIDAD

**J.** Your mother wants to know what takes you so long in the morning. You tell her that

1. you wash your face.

______________________________

2. you brush your teeth.

______________________________

3. you brush your hair.

______________________________

4. you take off your pajamas.

______________________________

5. you put on your shoes and your socks.

______________________________

**7** In all the sentences up to this point, the reflexive pronoun came directly before the conjugated verb: **Yo me lavo con agua fría.** In a negative sentence, the reflexive pronoun is not separated from the verb. The word **no** stands before the reflexive pronoun:

| | |
|---|---|
| **Yo *no me lavo* con agua y jabón.** | *I don't wash myself with water and soap.* |
| **Tú *no te acuestas* a las seis.** | *You don't go to bed at six o'clock.* |

## ACTIVIDAD

**K.** Say that one of the persons listed doesn't do an activity at a certain time:

| | | |
|---|---|---|
| Carlos | acostarse | las siete de la mañana |
| Yo | despertarse | las once de la noche |
| Mis padres | peinarse | las doce de la noche |
| Tú | desvestirse | las seis de la mañana |
| Mi hermano y yo | dormirse | medianoche |
| Uds. | levantarse | las cuatro de la tarde |
| Ud. | sentarse | las dos de la tarde |
| Mi madre | cepillarse los dientes | mediodía |

EXAMPLE: **Tú no te peinas a medianoche.**

1. ______________________________

2. ______________________________

3. ______________________________

4. ______________________________

5. ______________________________

6. ______________________________

**8** How are reflexive verbs used to give commands? Look at this short game of **Simón dice** and then answer the questions that follow:

| | | |
|---|---|---|
| **Simón dice a sus amigos:** | **¡*Levántense* Uds.!**<br>**¡*Lávense* Uds.!**<br>**¡*Vístanse* Uds.!** | **¡No *se levanten* Uds.!**<br>**¡No *se laven* Uds.!**<br>**¡No *se vistan* Uds.!** |
| **Simón dice a Josefina:** | **¡*Levántate*!**<br>**¡*Lávate*!**<br>**¡*Vístete*!** | **¡No *te levantes*!**<br>**¡No *te laves*!**<br>**¡No *te vistas*!** |
| **Simón dice al Sr. López:** | **¡*Levántese* Ud.!**<br>**¡*Lávese* Ud.!**<br>**¡*Vístase* Ud.!** | **¡No *se levante* Ud.!**<br>**¡No *se lave* Ud.!**<br>**¡No *se vista* Ud.!** |

Where is the reflexive pronoun in relationship to the verb? In the affirmative (*yes*) command, the reflexive pronoun is __________ the verb and attached to it. Note also that all the affirmative commands of reflexive verbs have an accent mark to retain the original stress. In a negative (*no*) command, the reflexive pronoun is __________ the verb; **no** is placed __________ the reflexive pronoun.

## ACTIVIDADES

**L.** Tell a friend to do the following:

**1.** wake up ______________________________

**2.** take a bath ______________________________

3. brush his/her teeth

_______________

4. have fun

_______________

5. go to bed

_______________

6. comb his/her hair

_______________

**M.** Make the commands in Actividad L negative:

1. _______________
2. _______________
3. _______________
4. _______________
5. _______________
6. _______________

**N.** Tell the students in the class to do the following:

1. wake up early

_______________

2. take off their coat(s)

_______________

3. wash their hands

_______________

4. sit down now

_______________

5. have fun

_______________

6. comb their hair

_______________

**O.** Make the commands in Actividad N negative:

1. _______________
2. _______________
3. _______________
4. _______________
5. _______________
6. _______________

**P.** Tell your teacher to do or not do the following:

1. not take off her/his hat

_______________

2. put on her/his coat

_______________

3. get up from the chair

_______________

4. not wash his/her face

_______________

5. not sit down

_______________

6. have fun

_______________

**9** What happens when the reflexive verb is used as an infinitive? Look at the following examples:

| | |
|---|---|
| **Voy a *bañarme* ahora.** | *I'm going to take a bath now.* |
| **El bebé no quiere *acostarse*.** | *The baby doesn't want to go to bed.* |
| **No debes *dormirte* en clase.** | *You shouldn't fall asleep in class.* |

Where is the reflexive pronoun placed? ______________________________

Right, it is placed after the verb and attached to it.

## ACTIVIDADES

**Q.** Complete the following sentences, using the correct Spanish form of the verb in parentheses:

1. (to wash) Él no quiere ________________ las manos con jabón.
2. (to sit down) Felipe y yo queremos ________________ allí.
3. (to go to bed) ¡________________ Ud. ahora mismo!
4. (to fall asleep) El niño no puede ________________.
5. (to have fun) Nosotros vamos a ________________ en las vacaciones.
6. (to take a bath) No tengo tiempo de ________________ ahora.
7. (to get up) El ciclista debe ________________ temprano.
8. (to brush) ¡________________ (tú) el pelo bien!
9. (to sit down) ¡________________ Ud. aquí, por favor!
10. (to put on) Cuando hace frío tengo que ________________ un suéter.

**R.** You are writing a letter to a pen pal in Mexico. Tell him the following in Spanish:

1. You always have fun on weekends.

   ______________________________________________

2. You go to bed early on Sundays.

   ______________________________________________

3. Every morning your mother says to you "Get up now!"

   ______________________________________________

4. Your sister never wants to wake up to go to school.

_______________

5. Your little brother is learning to put on his shoes.

_______________

6. At school the teacher is always saying, "Sit down quietly!"

_______________

7. You want to live in a country where it's not cold and you don't have to put on a coat and a hat.

_______________

## PREGUNTAS PERSONALES

1. ¿Te diviertes en las vacaciones?

_______________

2. ¿Sabes montar en bicicleta?

_______________

3. ¿A qué hora te despiertas los domingos?

_______________

4. ¿Cuántas veces al día te cepillas los dientes?

_______________

5. ¿Ves alguna vez carreras de bicicletas?

_______________

## INFORMACIÓN PERSONAL

List five things you do in the morning before leaving for school:

1. _______________
2. _______________
3. _______________
4. _______________
5. _______________

## DIÁLOGO

Ud. es un(a) ciclista famoso(a). Un periodista quiere escribir un artículo para un periódico y le hace varias preguntas:

# CÁPSULA CULTURAL

## ¿A qué hora?

A simple, elementary question? Not always. What if your plane left Barajas Airport in Madrid at 18,30? When should you be there? If your guide scheduled a trip to the Prado Museum that leaves your hotel at 15,00, would that be before or after lunch?

Although Spaniards use the twelve-hour system (1:00 to 12:00) most of the time, trains, buses, and airline schedules, theater and sporting events, among others, use a 24-hour system to avoid A.M. or P.M. Thus, a hotel restaurant might have this schedule posted on its window:

| HORARIO | |
|---|---|
| **Desayuno** | **de 7,30 a 10,30** |
| **Almuerzo** | **de 13,00 a 15,00** |
| **Cena** | **de 20,00 a 23,00** |

To express the time in the 24-hour system, you just add 12 to any hour after noon.

Now then, can you tell at what time lunch and dinner are served at the hotel and when your plane leaves the airport? And when does the tour to the museum start?

# 7 *Una novela policíaca*

Preterite Tense

**Vocabulario**

## ACTIVIDADES

**A.** **¿Qué pasa?** Write five sentences in Spanish to describe what's going on in the picture:

**1.** ______________________________

**2.** ______________________________

**3.** ______________________________

**4.** ______________________________

**5.** ______________________________

**B.** You are writing a detective story. List the names of six different characters and their roles:

EXAMPLE: **Carmen López, una testigo**

1. ______________ 4. ______________

2. ______________ 5. ______________

3. ______________ 6. ______________

**2** Up to now we have talked about things happening **ahora** (*now*), **hoy** (*today*), and even **mañana** (*tomorrow*). How do you express actions or events that took place **anoche** (*last night*), **ayer** (*yesterday*), **la semana pasada** (*last week*), or **el año pasado** (*last year*)? Of course, you need to use verbs in a past tense. One such past tense in Spanish is the preterite.

## 3 Las joyas robadas

Here's a story about a theft and a smart detective. Pay special attention to the verbs in bold type. They are in the preterite tense:

**Paró** de llover a las dos de la tarde. El inspector Delgado **abrió** la ventana de su despacho y **miró** hacia la calle. De repente, **sonó** el teléfono. La señora Laura Moreno, muy excitada, **preguntó** si un detective podía ir a su casa inmediatamente. El inspector **salió** de su despacho y **llegó** veinte minutos más tarde a la casa de la señora Moreno. **Tocó** a la puerta.

**parar** *to stop*
**el despacho** *office*
**de repente** *suddenly*
**sonar** *to sound, to ring*
**más tarde** *later*
**tocar** *to knock*

Laura **abrió** de inmediato y **dijo**: «Pase, pase, Sr. Delgado. ¡**Ocurrió** algo terrible! **Salí** temprano esta mañana para visitar a mi amiga Fernanda y cuando **regresé** hace una hora, **encontré** la puerta de la casa abierta. **Entré** y **vi** la sombra de un hombre en el estudio de mi marido. En ese momento el hombre me **vio** y **saltó** por la ventana. **Corrió** por el jardín y yo **corrí** detrás de él, pero él **entró** rápidamente en un carro estacionado al frente de la casa y **se escapó**. En el estudio **encontré** abierta la caja fuerte y **descubrí** que el ladrón **se llevó** mis joyas. Valen una fortuna, casi un millón de dólares. Afortunadamente están aseguradas».

**la sombra** *shadow*
**estacionado** *parked*
**escaparse** *to get away*
**la caja fuerte** *safe*
**llevarse** *to take away*
**asegurado** *insured*

INSPECTOR DELGADO: ¿**Reconoció** Ud. al hombre?
LAURA: No estoy completamente segura porque no le **vi** la cara, pero pienso que el ladrón puede ser Juan, un empleado que **despedimos** la semana pasada. Él sabe dónde guardo mis joyas. Además, **encontré** esta gorra en el jardín. Es de Juan.

**reconocer** *to recognize*
**seguro** *sure*
**despedir** *to dismiss*
**guardar** *to keep*
**la gorra** *cap*

El inspector **escuchó** todo con mucha atención, **examinó** el estudio, los muebles en desorden, y **salió** al jardín. **Vio** las huellas de unos zapatos de hombre en la tierra blanda y mojada.

**el desorden** *disorder*
**blando** *soft*
**mojado** *wet*

LAURA: Sr. Delgado, ¿quiere más información sobre Juan? Puedo darle toda la ayuda necesaria para atrapar al ladrón.
INSPECTOR DELGADO: ¡Señora, quiero saber la verdad y no las mentiras que **contó** Ud.!

**atrapar** *to catch*

¿Cómo sabe el inspector que la historia de Laura es falsa?

¿Qué creen Uds. que **pasó** realmente? ¿Quién **robó** las joyas?

**robar** *to steal*

* * *

Solución: Según Laura, ella **corrió** por el jardín detrás del ladrón. Pero en el jardín el inspector **encontró** solamente las huellas de un hombre.

## ACTIVIDAD

**C.** Conteste con frases completas:

1. ¿Quién llamó al inspector Delgado?

______________________________

2. ¿A qué hora llegó el inspector a casa de la Sra. Moreno?

______________________________

3. ¿Qué vio Laura en el estudio de su marido?

______________________________

4. ¿Cómo reaccionó el hombre cuando vio a Laura?

______________________________

5. Según Laura, ¿cómo se escapó el ladrón?

_______________

6. ¿Qué encontró Laura en el jardín?

_______________

7. ¿Qué examinó el inspector?

_______________

8. ¿Qué vio el inspector en el jardín?

_______________

9. ¿Contó Laura la verdad?

_______________

10. ¿Quién cree Ud. que robó las joyas?

_______________

To form the preterite tense of regular verbs, simply remove the **-ar, -er,** or **-ir** ending of the verb and substitute another ending:

| | rob *ar* | corr *er* | descubr *ir* |
|---|---|---|---|
| **yo** | **rob** *é* | **corr** *í* | **descubr** *í* |
| **tú** | **rob** *aste* | **corr** *iste* | **descubr** *iste* |
| **Ud., él, ella** | **rob** *ó* | **corr** *ió* | **descubr** *ió* |
| **nosotros** | **rob** *amos* | **corr** *imos* | **descubr** *imos* |
| **Uds., ellos, ellas** | **rob** *aron* | **corr** *ieron* | **descubr** *ieron* |

5

There is only one **-AR** verb (**dar**) that takes the **-er** endings in the preterite tense instead of the regular **-ar** endings:

| | | | |
|---|---|---|---|
| **yo** | *di* | **nosotros** | *dimos* |
| **tú** | *diste* | | |
| **Ud., él, ella** | *dio* | **Uds., ellos, ellas** | *dieron* |

## ACTIVIDADES

**D.** You were a witness to a bank robbery and are testifying in court. Complete the sentences with the correct form of the verb in parentheses:

1. (entrar) Yo _______________ en el banco a las once de la mañana.

2. (entrar, cerrar) Dos hombres ____________ detrás de mí y ____________ la puerta.

3. (comenzar) Una señora y yo ____________ a gritar.

4. (escuchar, llamar) El director del banco ____________ los gritos y ____________ a la policía.

5. (llegar) La policía ____________ pronto.

6. (robar) Los ladrones no ____________ nada.

7. (dar) El director del banco ____________ las gracias a la policía.

**E.** On Monday morning, your teacher wants to know what the students did on Sunday. Complete the sentences with the correct form of the verb in parentheses:

1. (dormir) Yo ____________ hasta las diez.
2. (comer) Manuel ____________ en casa de sus abuelos.
3. (ver) Jorge y Raúl ____________ una película de horror.
4. (salir) Tú ____________ de compras con tus padres.
5. (recibir) Mis hermanos y yo ____________ amigos en el aeropuerto.
6. (dar) Uds. ____________ un paseo por el parque.
7. (correr) Rosario ____________ tres millas.
8. (escribir) Pablo y María ____________ cartas.

**F.** You have just returned from a weekend at a friend's house and your little brother wants to know what you did. Answer his questions:

1. ¿Saliste a comer en un restaurante?

____________________________________________

2. ¿Qué comiste?

____________________________________________

3. ¿Viste alguna película buena?

______________________________________________

4. ¿Compraste el regalo para mamá?

______________________________________________

5. ¿A qué hora te despertaste el domingo?

______________________________________________

6. ¿Nadaste en la piscina?

______________________________________________

7. ¿Diste un paseo por el centro de la ciudad?

______________________________________________

8. ¿Te divertiste mucho?

______________________________________________

9. ¿Te gustaron los padres de tu amigo?

______________________________________________

10. ¿Invitaste a tu amigo a venir a nuestra casa?

______________________________________________

## 6

**-AR** and **-ER** verbs with stem changes in the present tense have regular forms in the preterite. **-IR** verbs with stem changes in the present tense (**e** to **ie, o** to **ue,** and **e** to **i**) change **e** to **i** and **o** to **u** in the third person singular and plural of the preterite. Let's look at some examples:

| | PRESENT TENSE | PRETERITE |
|---|---|---|
| **encontrar (ue)** | **yo enc*ue*ntro** | **encontré, encontraste, encontró . . .** |
| **pensar (ie)** | **yo p*ie*nso** | **pensé, pensaste, pensó . . .** |
| **perder (ie)** | **yo p*ie*rdo** | **perdí, perdiste, perdió . . .** |
| **volver (ue)** | **yo v*ue*lvo** | **volví, volviste, volvió . . .** |

But:

| | | |
|---|---|---|
| **mentir (ie)** | yo **m*ie*nto** | **mentí, mentiste, *mintió*, mentimos, *mintieron*** |
| **dormir (ue)** | yo **d*ue*rmo** | **dormí, dormiste, *durmió*, dormimos, *durmieron*** |
| **pedir (i)** | yo **p*i*do** | **pedí, pediste, *pidió*, pedimos, *pidieron*** |
| **servir (i)** | yo **s*i*rvo** | **serví, serviste, *sirvió*, servimos, *sirvieron*** |

## ACTIVIDAD

**G.** You went with some friends to a restaurant last night. Say what each of you ordered:

1. Yo ________________ un bistec con papas fritas.
2. Manuel ________________ el pollo frito.
3. Rosa ________________ una ensalada de camarones.
4. Tú ________________ la sopa del día.
5. Los hermanos Gómez ________________ hamburguesas.
6. María ________________ sopa y una hamburguesa.

**7** There are many verbs in Spanish with irregular preterite forms. Some have the same endings but change their stem completely. Read the following dialog and see how many verbs in this category you can recognize. Most of these verbs have an irregular **yo** form and/or stem changes in the present tense:

Did you recognize the verbs in the dialog? Try to determine the infinitives of these irregular preterite stems:

| | | | |
|---|---|---|---|
| **estuv-** | ________________ | **quis-** | ________________ |
| **hic-** | ________________ | **tuv-** | ________________ |
| **pud-** | ________________ | **vin-** | ________________ |
| **pus-** | ________________ | | |

Now let's take some of the sentences in the dialog to figure out the common endings of these verbs:

| | | |
|---|---|---|
| **yo** | **tuv** | ***e*** |
| **tú** | **hic** | ***iste*** |
| **María (Ud./él)** | **vin** | ***o*** |
| **nosotras** | **pus** | ***imos*** |
| **Uds. (ellos/ellas)** | **pud** | ***ieron*** |

Can you complete the table below?

| | **estar** | **hacer** | **poder** | **poner** | **querer** | **tener** | **venir** |
|---|---|---|---|---|---|---|---|
| **yo** | **estuve** | **hice** | **pud—** | **pus—** | **quis—** | **tuv—** | **vin—** |
| **tú** | **estuviste** | **hiciste** | ____ | | | | |
| **Ud.** | **estuvo** | **hizo** | ____ | | | | |
| **él/ella** | **estuvo** | **hizo** | ____ | | | | |
| **nosotros** | **estuvimos** | **hicimos** | ____ | | | | |
| **Uds.** | **estuvieron** | **hicieron** | ____ | | | | |
| **ellos/ellas** | **estuvieron** | **hicieron** | ____ | | | | |

Note that the stem of the verb **hacer** undergoes a small change (**c** to **z**) in the third person singular to keep the **c** sound.

## ACTIVIDADES

**H.** Complete each sentence with the correct form of the verb in parentheses:

**1.** (querer) El sábado pasado yo no ________________ ir a la fiesta.

2. (venir) Mis abuelos ________________ a visitarnos ayer.

3. (ponerse) Esta mañana Ud. ______ ________________ los jeans nuevos.

4. (estar) ¿Dónde ________________ tú el verano pasado?

5. (poder) Nosotros no ________________ terminar las tareas anoche.

6. (tener) El verano pasado ellas ________________ que trabajar.

7. (hacer) ¿Qué ________________ Uds. el fin de semana pasado?

8. (estar) ¿Quién ________________ ausente el lunes pasado?

9. (poner) ¿Dónde ________________ tú los periódicos que compré?

**I.** The following things are happening today. How would you say they happened yesterday?

1. Yo no puedo ver esa película.

________________________________________

2. Ellos hacen todo el trabajo.

________________________________________

3. Mi mamá pone la comida en la mesa.

________________________________________

4. Los ladrones pueden escaparse.

________________________________________

5. Nosotros tenemos que ir a la escuela.

________________________________________

6. Tú no quieres comer afuera.

________________________________________

7. María hace un viaje a México.

________________________________________

8. Yo no tengo tiempo.

________________________________________

9. ¿Dónde ponen Uds. los periódicos?

________________________________________

10. Ud. viene por la mañana.

________________________________________

**8** There are two verbs that share the same irregular forms in the preterite, **ser** and **ir**. Only the context makes clear what the meaning is:

| | **ser** | **ir** |
|---|---|---|
| **yo** | *fui* | *fui* |
| **tú** | *fuiste* | *fuiste* |
| **Ud., él, ella** | *fue* | *fue* |
| **nosotros** | *fuimos* | *fuimos* |
| **Uds., ellos, ellas** | *fueron* | *fueron* |

**Mi hermana *fue* testigo del robo.** — *My sister was a witness to the robbery.*

**Ella *fue* a declarar a la estación de policía.** — *She went to testify at the police station.*

## ACTIVIDADES

**J.** After the summer vacation, you and your friends tell each other where you went:

1. ¿Adónde __________ tú, Javier?
2. Yo __________ a un campamento de verano.
3. Y Uds., Margarita y Rosario, ¿adónde __________?
4. Nosotras __________ al Perú.
5. ¿Adónde __________ Roberto?
6. Roberto y sus padres __________ a California.

**K.** You are on a school trip to Madrid and are keeping a diary. Complete the following entries with the correct form of the verb in parentheses:

Ayer nuestro grupo __________ (hacer) muchas cosas. Por la mañana nosotros __________ (ir) al Museo del Prado y __________ (ver) varias exhibiciones. Jorge y Darío no __________ (querer) ir con nosotros y ellos __________ (ir) de compras. Por la tarde yo __________ (salir) a dar un paseo con María por el Parque del Retiro. Ella ________ (ponerse) zapatos nuevos y no ________ (poder) caminar mucho. Nosotros ________ (tener) que tomar un taxi para regresar al hotel. Por la noche un amigo español ________ (venir) al hotel y nosotros dos ________ (salir) a comer afuera. En el restaurante mi amigo ________ (pedir) una comida típica española. El mesero ________ (servir) muy despacio. Nosotros ________ (estar) en el restaurante hasta muy tarde y yo ________ (acostarse) después de medianoche.

**9** Verbs ending in a vowel + **-er** or **-ir** share some common irregularities in the preterite. Let's look at two of them:

| | **creer** (*to believe*) | **oír** (*to hear*) |
|---|---|---|
| **yo** | **cre*í*** | **o*í*** |
| **tú** | **cre*í*ste** | **o*í*ste** |
| **Ud., él, ella** | **cre*y*ó** | **o*y*ó** |
| **nosotros** | **cre*í*mos** | **o*í*mos** |
| **Uds., ellos, ellas** | **cre*y*eron** | **o*y*eron** |

Note that the **i** has an accent mark in the **yo, tú,** and **nosotros** forms. In the other two forms, the **i** changes to **y**. Can you complete the table below?

| | **leer** (*to read*) | **caerse** (*to fall down*) |
|---|---|---|
| **yo** | **leí** | **me caí** |
| **tú** | ________ | ________ |
| **Ud., él, ella** | ________ | ________ |
| **nosotros** | ________ | ________ |
| **Uds., ellos, ellas** | ________ | ________ |

## ACTIVIDAD

**L.** You have heard rumors about a trip to Mexico during the holiday break. Complete the sentences with the correct preterite tense form of the verb **oír:**

1. Yo ____________ que la escuela planea un viaje a México.
2. ¿____________ tú lo mismo?
3. Yo no, pero Juan ____________ eso también.
4. Y Julia y Mercedes ____________ que no va a costar mucho.
5. ¿Qué ____________ Uds.?
6. Nosotros ____________ que el viaje va a ser en diciembre.

**10** Remember the endings shared by some irregular verbs? **-e, -iste, -o, -imos, -ieron.** There are two verbs (**decir** [*to say*] and **traer** [*to bring*]) with similar irregular stems that have the same endings except for the third person plural (**-eron** instead of **-ieron**):

| | **decir** | **traer** |
|---|---|---|
| **yo** | **dij** ***e*** | **traj** ***e*** |
| **tú** | **dij** ***iste*** | **traj** ***iste*** |
| **Ud., él, ella** | **dij** ***o*** | **traj** ***o*** |
| **nosotros** | **dij** ***imos*** | **traj** ***imos*** |
| **Uds., ellos, ellas** | **dij** ***eron*** | **traj** ***eron*** |

## ACTIVIDADES

**M.** Somebody organized a surprise party for you and you want to know who brought the different foods. Complete the sentences with the correct preterite form of **traer:**

1. ¿Qué ____________ tú, Daniel?
2. Yo ____________ los sandwiches.
3. Y Ud., Srta. López, ¿qué ____________?
4. Margarita y yo ____________ las sodas.
5. Rosa ____________ la torta.
6. José y su hermano ____________ los globos (*balloons*).

**N.** Answer the following questions in complete Spanish sentences:

1. ¿Leyó Ud. el periódico ayer?

___

2. ¿Quién fue el primer presidente de los Estados Unidos?

___

3. ¿Dónde estuvo Ud. el domingo pasado?

___

4. ¿Qué tiempo hizo el fin de semana pasado?

___

5. ¿Quién vino tarde a la clase hoy?

___

6. ¿Quién oyó las noticias en su casa anoche?

___

7. ¿Para qué clase tuvo Ud. que hacer tareas anoche?

___

8. ¿Qué dijo la profesora hoy en la clase?

___

## PREGUNTAS PERSONALES

1. ¿Adónde fuiste el sábado pasado por la noche?

___

2. ¿Qué hiciste anoche?

___

3. ¿A qué hora saliste de casa esta mañana?

___

4. ¿A qué hora te acostaste anoche?

___

5. ¿Trabajaste la semana pasada?

___

## DIÁLOGO

You were found at night near the scene of a crime, and next day a policeman wants to question you. Here are your answers. What are the questions?

## INFORMACIÓN PERSONAL

Make a list of five things you did yesterday:

1. ______________________________
2. ______________________________
3. ______________________________
4. ______________________________
5. ______________________________

## COMPOSICIÓN

You witnessed a robbery. Fill out the following police report:

INFORME DEL TESTIGO

| ______________ | ______________ | ______________ |
|---|---|---|
| Apellido | Nombre | Edad |

| ______________________ | ______________ |
|---|---|
| Dirección | Teléfono |

1. ¿Qué vio Ud.?

   ______________________________

   (Say that you saw a robbery)

2. ¿Dónde tuvo lugar el incidente?

   ______________________________

   (Say that it was in a store downtown)

3. ¿Qué hicieron los ladrones?

   ______________________________

   (Say that they entered the store and took the money.)

4. ¿Pudo ver la cara de los ladrones?

   ______________________________

   (Say that you couldn't see their faces well.)

5. ¿Adónde fueron los ladrones después?

   ______________________________

   (Say that they left quickly and ran away.)

# CÁPSULA CULTURAL

## **¡Auxilio, policía!** (Help, police!)

When you are in trouble in a strange land, where do you go for assistance? To a police officer, naturally. But, which kind? In Spain, for example, there are three different kinds of police.

The **Policía Nacional** is found in the cities. Men of the **Policía Nacional** wear brown uniforms, are armed, and can be seen guarding official buildings. Another countrywide group is the **Guardia Civil.** Its members patrol in cars or on motorbikes and are usually found in the rural areas. They wear green uniforms and a distinctive three-cornered hat called **el tricornio** or **sombrero de tres picos.** A third group is the **Policía Municipal** or **los Urbanos.** These officers work for the various city governments and are basically traffic policemen, although they do get involved in other matters concerning the public order. They usually wear blue uniforms in the winter and white ones in the summer.

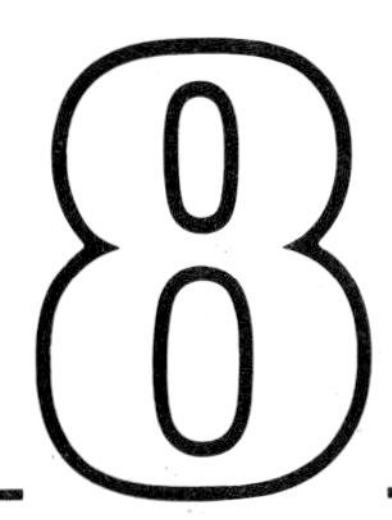

# Las vacaciones

## Imperfect Tense

### Vocabulario

## ACTIVIDADES

**A.** Here's a picture of a wonderful resort place. Can you describe some of the things people are doing?

**B.** Sometimes you need the right equipment to be able to enjoy an activity. Can you name the activities in which you would use these pieces of equipment?

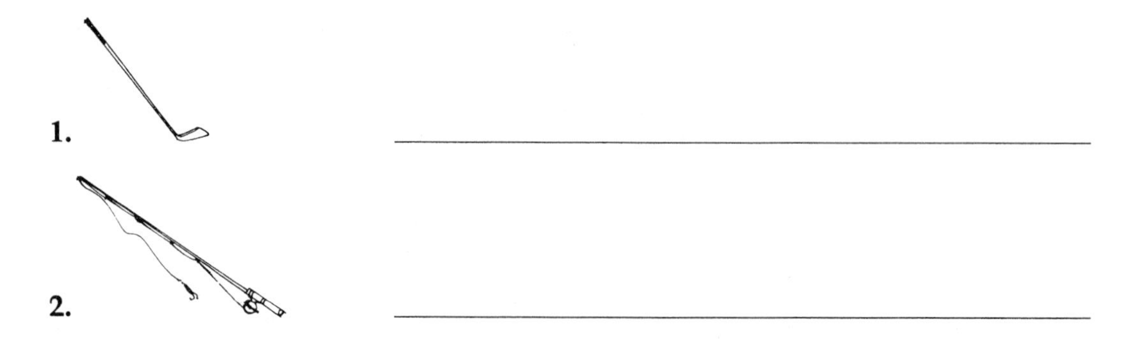

1.

2.

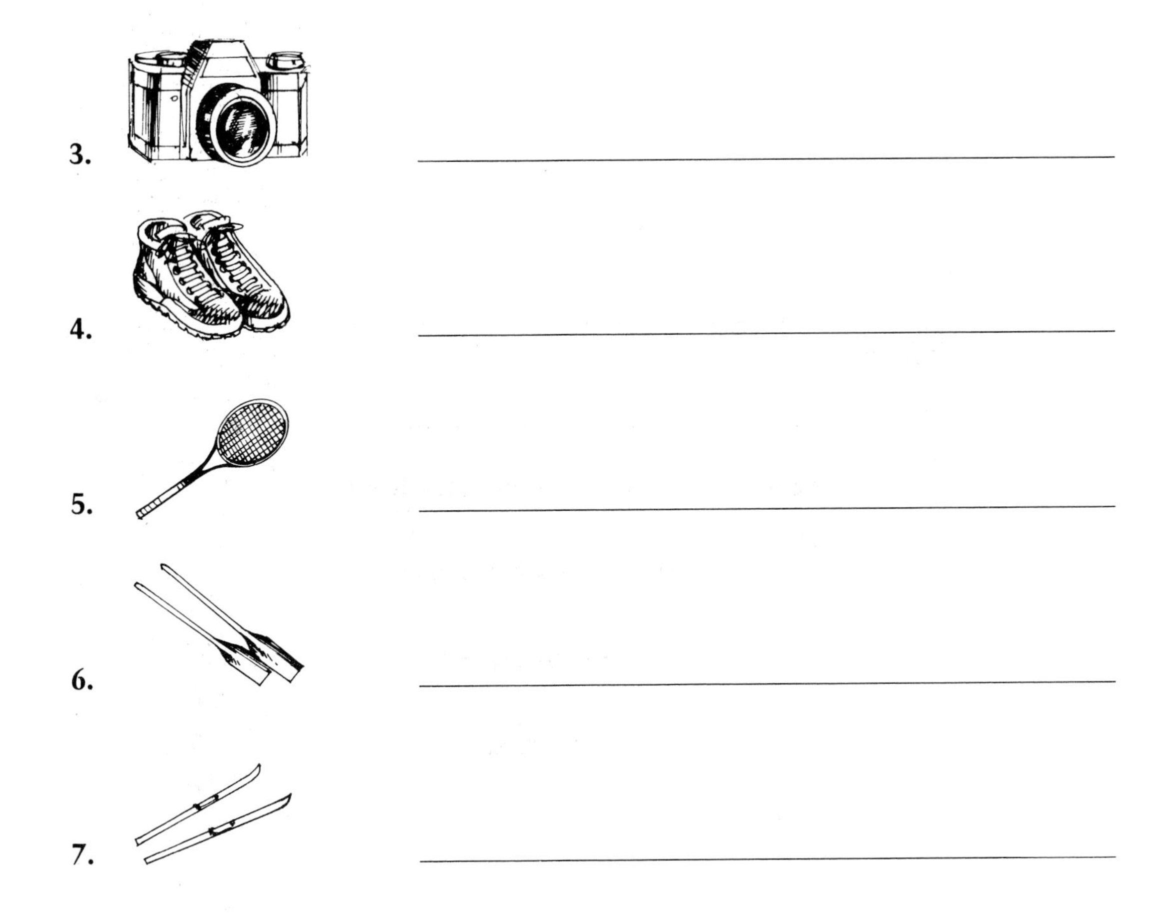

3. ____________________

4. ____________________

5. ____________________

6. ____________________

7. ____________________

## Doctor, tengo muchos problemas

Let's read a one-act play about a man with a lot of problems. Pay attention to the verbs in bold type. These verbs are in the imperfect, another past tense in Spanish:

ESCENA: El consultorio del famoso psiquiatra Salvador Sesohueco. La enfermera está en el despacho de al lado. El paciente está recostado en el sofá mientras el doctor toma nota de lo que dice en su libreta.

**el consultorio** *doctor's office*
**estar recostado** *to be lying down*
**la libreta** *notebook*

DOCTOR: Dígame, Sr. Comequeso, ¿desde cuándo tiene esos sentimientos de inseguridad?
PACIENTE: Toda mi vida, doctor.
DOCTOR: ¿De veras? Muy interesante. Pero, ¿cómo **se llevaba** con sus amiguitos cuando **era** niño?
PACIENTE: Casi no **tenía** amigos. No **veía** a nadie. **Me quedaba** en casa todos los días con mi mamá.
DOCTOR: Pero cuando Ud. ya **era** un joven de diez y seis o diez y siete años, ¿con quién **salía** Ud.?

**desde** *since*
**el sentimiento** *feeling*
**llevarse** *to get along*
**quedarse** *to stay*

PACIENTE: Con mi mamá.
DOCTOR: Ajá. ¿Cuántos años tiene Ud. ahora?
PACIENTE: Tengo treinta y cinco años.
DOCTOR: ¿Está casado?
PACIENTE: Sí, señor.
DOCTOR: ¿Adónde **iba** Ud. de vacaciones cuando **estaba** soltero?
PACIENTE: Mi mamá y yo **íbamos** al campo a descansar. Ahora voy con mi mujer a casa de mi suegra.
DOCTOR: Pero, ¿no tiene Ud. deseos de divertirse, de jugar al golf o al tenis, de hacer un crucero?
PACIENTE: Sí, doctor, pero mi mujer no me da permiso.
DOCTOR: Señor Comequeso, no necesito oír más. Ya veo cuál es su problema. Ud. no tiene ninguna confianza en sí mismo. Ud. **dependía** antes de su mamá y ahora depende de su mujer. Voy a idear un programa para convertirlo en un hombre libre e independiente como yo. Hago lo que quiero.
PACIENTE: Gracias, señor doctor. Yo **quería** ser independiente cuando **era** joven y ahora quiero ser como Ud.. Yo lo admiro mucho.
LA ENFERMERA entra y dice: Hay una llamada para Ud., doctor. Es su esposa.
DOCTOR (en el teléfono): Hola, Silvia. ¿Cómo estás, mi vida? No, claro que no estoy ocupado para ti. ¿Cómo? ¿Quieres llevar a tu mamá esta noche con nosotros? Claro que sí, no hay problema. Tú sabes que yo estoy de acuerdo con todo lo que tú decides.

**estar casado** *to be married*
**soltero** *single*
**la suegra** *mother-in-law*
**el permiso** *permission*
**idear** *to devise*
**convertir en** *to turn into*
**libre** *free*
**la llamada** *call*

## ACTIVIDAD

**C.** Conteste en frases completas:

**1.** ¿Dónde está el Sr. Comequeso?

______________________________

**2.** ¿Qué hace el doctor mientras el paciente habla?

______________________________

3. ¿Cuántos amigos tenía el paciente cuando era niño?

______________________________

4. ¿Con quién salía cuando tenía 17 años?

______________________________

5. ¿Adónde iba el paciente a pasar las vacaciones con su mamá?

______________________________

6. ¿Por qué no hace un crucero el Sr. Comequeso?

______________________________

7. Según el psiquiatra, ¿cuál es el problema del paciente?

______________________________

8. ¿Qué va a hacer el psiquiatra?

______________________________

9. ¿Quién llama por teléfono?

______________________________

10. En su opinión, ¿qué tipo de hombre es el doctor?

______________________________

**3** In Spanish, we use two past tenses to express actions in the past. You have already learned one of them, the preterite. Now let's learn the other one, the imperfect. Later on, we'll see the differences in use between the two. Look at the following examples:

| | |
|---|---|
| **Yo *jugaba* al tenis todos los días.** | *I used to play tennis every day.* |
| **Tú *descansabas* en el campo.** | *You used to rest in the country.* |
| **Ud. *remaba* en el lago.** | *You used to row in the lake.* |
| **Ella *nadaba* en la piscina.** | *She used to swim in the swimming pool.* |
| **Nosotros *montábamos* a caballo.** | *We used to go horseback riding.* |
| **Uds. *sacaban* muchas fotos.** | *You used to take a lot of pictures.* |
| **Ellos *pescaban* en el río.** | *They used to fish in the river.* |

All the above verbs are **-AR** verbs. What endings were added to the stem to form the imperfect?

| | |
|---|---|
| **yo** | ***-aba*** |
| **tú** | ***-abas*** |
| **Ud., él, ella** | ***-aba*** |
| **nosotros** | ***-ábamos*** |
| **Uds., ellos, ellas** | ***-aban*** |

## ACTIVIDAD

**D.** You are reminiscing with a friend about your childhood. Complete the sentences with the correct form of the imperfect of the verb in parentheses:

1. (jugar) Yo ________________ todos los días en el parque.
2. (trabajar) Mi madre ________________ por las mañanas.
3. (visitar) Mi hermanito y yo ________________ a los abuelos los domingos.
4. (pasar) Mis padres ________________ las vacaciones en la playa.
5. (comprar) Tus abuelos nos ________________ muchos dulces.
6. (despertarse) Yo _____ ________________ muy temprano.
7. (mirar) Por las tardes tú y yo ________________ la televisión.
8. (hablar) Mi hermana ________________ por teléfono todo el tiempo.
9. (tomar) Tú ________________ el almuerzo en mi casa.
10. (nevar) En el invierno ________________ mucho.

**4** Now let's look at these examples:

**Yo *comía* en la cafetería.**
**Tú *corrías* rápido.**
**Ud. *quería* ser dentista.**
**Él *hacía* bien las tareas.**
**Nosotros *teníamos* mucho dinero.**
**Uds. *leían* en español.**
**Ellas *sabían* la lección.**

**Yo *salía* temprano.**
**Tú nunca *mentías*.**
**Ud. *dormía* mucho.**
**Ella *vivía* en Nueva York.**
**Nosotras *decíamos* siempre la verdad.**
**Uds. se *reían* mucho.**
**Ellos *servían* la comida.**

All verbs in the left column are **-ER** verbs. All verbs in the right column are **-IR** verbs. Are the endings different? ______ Can you give the endings to form the imperfect of **-ER** and **-IR** verbs?

| | | | |
|---|---|---|---|
| **yo** | __________ | **nosotros** | __________ |
| **tú** | __________ | | |
| **Ud., él, ella** | __________ | **Uds., ellos, ellas** | __________ |

## ACTIVIDADES

**E.** Here's a description of what's going on in the classroom now. Say that the same thing used to happen last year by changing the sentences to the correct form of the imperfect:

EXAMPLE: La maestra dice buenos días.
**El año pasado la maestra también decía buenos días.**

1. Un alumno abre las ventanas.

______________________________

2. Yo quiero hablar en español.

______________________________

3. Los alumnos saben contestar bien.

______________________________

4. Nosotros tenemos muchas tareas.

______________________________

5. Tú lees y escribes en español.

______________________________

6. El director viene a nuestra clase.

______________________________

7. Uds. se duermen en clase.

______________________________

8. Yo entiendo la lección.

______________________________

9. Ud. cree todo lo que dice la maestra.

______________________________

10. Los alumnos conocen a todos los profesores.

______________________________

**F.** Using the following verbs, write five things you used to do two years ago:

| | | | |
|---|---|---|---|
| dormir | vivir | leer | hacer |
| trabajar | pasar | escribir | nadar |

EXAMPLE: **Hace dos años yo vivía en otra ciudad.**

1. ______________________________

2. ______________________________

3. ______________________________

4. ______________________________

5. ______________________________

**5** There are only three verbs with irregular forms in the imperfect tense. One of them (**ver**) keeps the **e** of the **-er** ending in all forms:

| | |
|---|---|
| **yo ve*ía*** | **nosotros ve*íamos*** |
| **tú ve*ías*** | |
| **Ud., él, ella ve*ía*** | **Uds., ellos, ellas ve*ían*** |

**Ser** and **ir** are completely irregular. Memorize their forms:

| | **ser** | **ir** |
|---|---|---|
| **yo** | ***era*** | ***iba*** |
| **tú** | ***eras*** | ***ibas*** |
| **Ud., él, ella** | ***era*** | ***iba*** |
| **nosotros** | ***éramos*** | ***íbamos*** |
| **Uds., ellos, ellas** | ***eran*** | ***iban*** |

## ACTIVIDADES

**G.** You are talking with some friends about the past. Complete the sentences with the correct form of the imperfect of **ser**:

1. Tú ______________ bueno en matemáticas.
2. Javier ______________ mi mejor amigo.
3. Yo ______________ capitán del equipo de fútbol.
4. La maestra ______________ muy justa.
5. Tú y yo ______________ los campeones de tenis.
6. María y Rosa ______________ las muchachas más bonitas de la clase.
7. Uds. ______________ malos estudiantes.

**H.** Where did these people go when you were little?

EXAMPLE: mi hermana ______
**Cuando yo era niño, mi hermana iba a la universidad.**

1. mis padres ______________________________
2. yo ______________________________
3. mi abuelo ______________________________
4. Ud. ______________________________
5. tú ______________________________
6. Uds. ______________________________

**I.** You want to ask your mother questions about her life when she was a child. You have her answers. What were your questions?

Mami, cuando eras niña,

1. ______________________________
Yo vivía en una ciudad muy grande.

2. ______________________________
En las vacaciones mis padres y yo íbamos a las montañas.

3. ______________________________
Sí, yo tenía muchos amigos.

4. ______________________________
Yo veía a mis abuelos todos los domingos.

5. ______________________________
Yo iba a la escuela en bicicleta.

6. ______________________________
Los fines de semana salía al parque y jugaba allí.

## PREGUNTAS PERSONALES

1. ¿Sabías nadar cuando eras niño(a)?

______________________________

2. ¿Dónde vivías hace cinco años?

______________________________

3. ¿A qué escuela ibas entonces?

_______________

4. ¿Eras buen(a) alumno(a)?

_______________

5. ¿Quién era tu mejor amigo(a)?

_______________

## INFORMACIÓN PERSONAL

You are a psychiatrist who just opened a new office. Your first client is lying on the couch. Think of five questions you want to ask about his or her childhood. Use five of the following verbs:

| | | | |
|---|---|---|---|
| vivir | ir | jugar | ser |
| hacer | tener | saber | querer |

1. _______________
2. _______________
3. _______________
4. _______________
5. _______________

## COMPOSICIÓN

The school nurse is trying to set up a summer program and needs some information from the students about how they spent their vacations as children. Tell

1. where you used to go.
2. how you traveled there.
3. what the weather was like.
4. what you usually did there.
5. why you liked or disliked the vacation.

_______________

_______________

_______________

_______________

_______________

## DIÁLOGO

Because of the problems he's been having lately, Mr. Bocachica is undergoing psychoanalysis. What does he tell the psychiatrist?

# CÁPSULA CULTURAL

## Las estaciones

Do you want to go to the beach in December or in February and enjoy a hot sun? No problem. Since much of South America is below the Equator, the seasons there are the opposite of those here. July, August, and September are winter months. January, February, and March are summer months.

You can spend the cold winter months in internationally famous resorts like Mar del Plata in Argentina, Viña del Mar in Chile, or Punta del Este in Uruguay. You say you don't want to travel so far south? Well, how about going to Colombia? The country is right on the Equator, and temperatures don't change much during the year. In fact, they depend on how high you are above sea level. You can swim at a beach in Cartagena or Santa Marta in the morning and then climb a mountain in the Andes and see some snow.

Do you want to go skiing next July? See you in Chile!

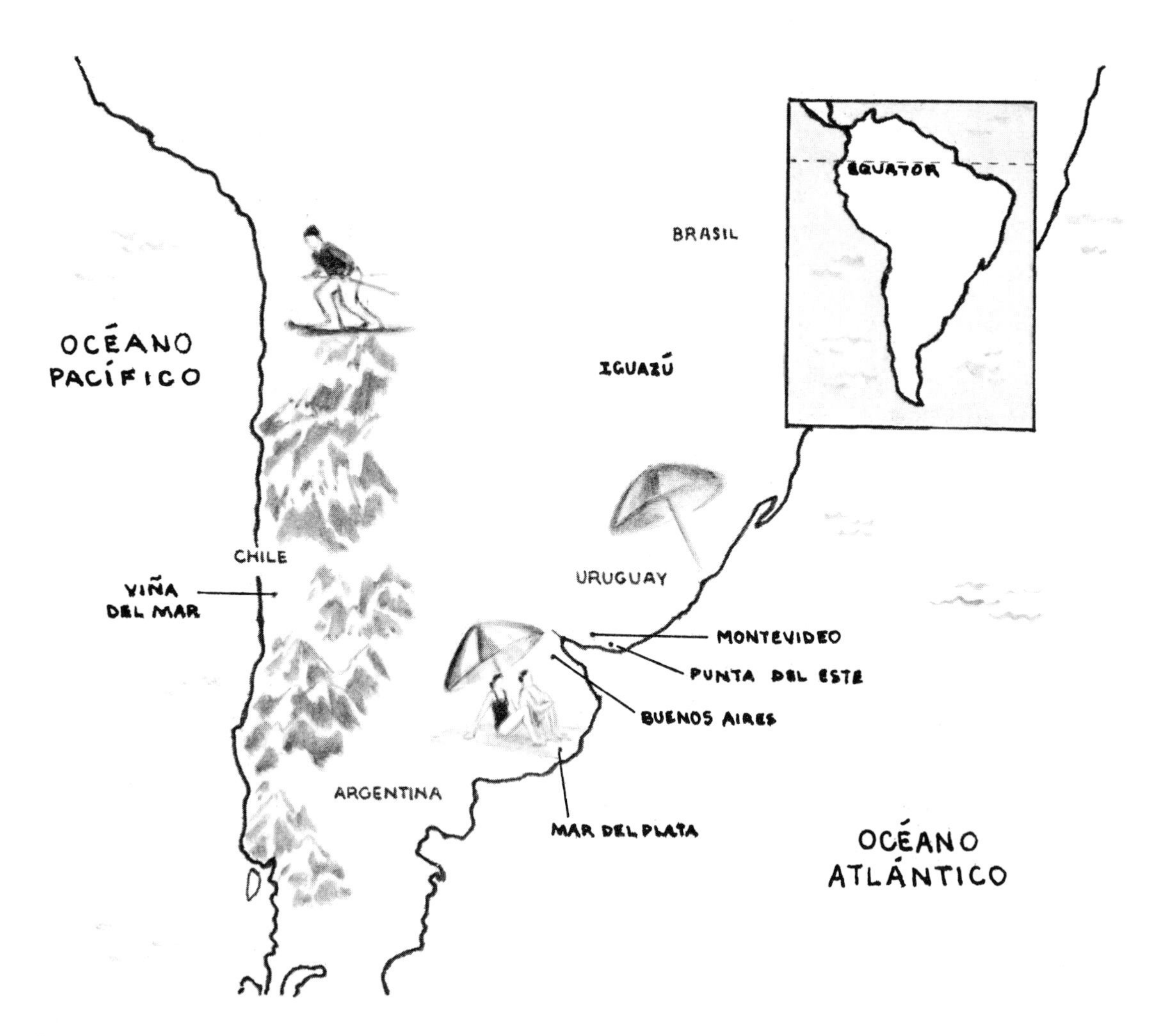

# 9 ¿Cuándo?

## Imperfect and Preterite Tenses Compared

### 1 Vocabulario

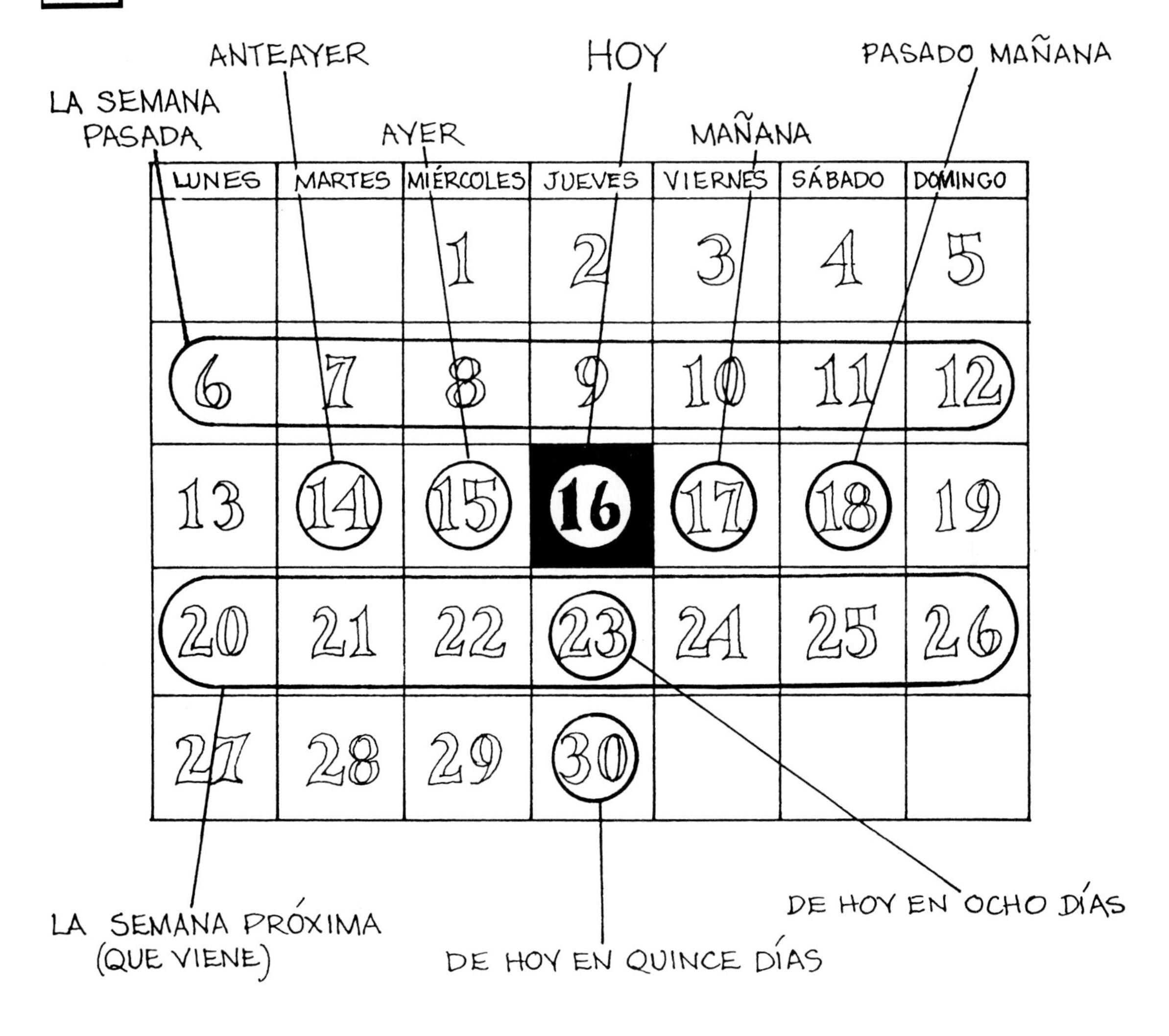


**un minuto = 60 segundos**
**una hora = 60 minutos**
**un día = 24 horas**
**una semana = 7 días**
**un mes = 30/31 días (4 semanas)**
**un año = 12 meses**
**un siglo = 100 años**
**la eternidad**

## ACTIVIDADES

**A.** Si hoy es el primero de enero. ¿Cuándo fue o va a ser

1. el 31 de diciembre? ______________________
2. el 30 de diciembre? ______________________
3. el 2 de enero? ______________________
4. el 3 de enero? ______________________
5. el 8 de enero? ______________________
6. el 15 de enero? ______________________

**B.** Match the expressions in the left column with their definitions in the right column. Write the matching letter in the space provided:

1. 60 minutos ______
2. 60 segundos ______
3. 12 meses ______
4. en dos semanas ______
5. el día antes de ayer ______
6. el día después de hoy ______
7. cien años ______
8. en una semana ______
9. el día después de mañana ______
10. el tiempo infinito ______

**a.** un minuto
**b.** de hoy en ocho
**c.** de hoy en quince
**d.** una hora
**e.** pasado mañana
**f.** ayer
**g.** la eternidad
**h.** anteayer
**i.** mañana
**j.** un siglo
**k.** un año

## La adivina

Since we are learning about time expressions and the past, let's read a story about a fortune teller (**una adivina**):

ROSANA: Josefina, ¿quieres venir conmigo a consultar a la vieja gitana, doña Matilda? Todas nuestras

**la gitana** *Gypsy*

amigas dicen que ella puede ver el pasado y adivinar el futuro.

**adivinar** *to foretell, guess*

JOSEFINA: ¡Me sorprendes! Tú eres una persona inteligente y racional. Y sin embargo crees en esas cosas. Yo no voy a botar mi dinero así. Pero, si insistes, como eres mi mejor amiga, te acompaño.

**sin embargo** *nonetheless*
**botar** *to throw away*
**acompañar** *to go with*

ROSANA: De acuerdo. Vamos pasado mañana, viernes, por la tarde.

**de acuerdo** *agreed*

Llega el viernes y las dos amigas están sentadas alrededor de una mesa. En el centro de la mesa hay una bola de cristal. La gitana habla.

MATILDA: Voy a comenzar con el pasado de la Srta. Rosana. Cuando Ud. era niña, Ud. contaba con los dedos de las manos y de los pies. Solamente hace poco aprendió Ud. a sumar y a restar.

**sumar** *to add*
**restar** *to subtract*

ROSANA: Al contrario. De niña yo era muy buena en matemáticas. Gané mi primer premio en matemáticas cuando tenía diez años.

**ganar** *to win*

MATILDA: Cuando Ud. tenía 16 años estaba tan celosa de una de sus amigas, que siempre contaba mentiras sobre ella.

**celoso** *jealous*

ROSANA: ¡Jamás!

MATILDA: Finalmente, en su clase de español, Ud. escribía notas anónimas a los muchachos guapos.

**guapo** *handsome*

ROSANA: Todo esto es ridículo. No quiero escuchar más. Vamos, Josefina. Tú tenías razón. ¡Qué estúpida soy!

MATILDA: Un momento. Veo algo interesante en la bola de cristal sobre su amiga.

JOSEFINA: ¿Oh? ¡Diga qué ve Ud.!

MATILDA: Veo a una muchacha tímida que se chupaba los dedos aún a los diez años.

**chuparse el dedo** *to suck one's finger*

JOSEFINA: Cierto.

MATILDA: No le gustaban los huevos fritos y una vez que su mamá los preparó para el desayuno, Ud. los echó por la ventana.

**echar** *to throw*

JOSEFINA: Sí, sí, me acuerdo. Siga, siga. Es increíble, Ud. lo sabe todo.

**acordarse (ue)** *to remember*

MATILDA: Eso es todo por hoy. Si quieren, la semana que viene les digo la buenaventura.

**decir la buenaventura** *to tell someone's fortune*

Las dos jóvenes salen a la calle.

JOSEFINA: No comprendo cómo ella sabía todas esas cosas de mi pasado. De veras, ¡es una maravilla!
ROSANA: ¡Qué va! Tu hermana la visitó la semana pasada y tú sabes la boca grande que ella tiene.

**¡qué va!** *nonsense*

## ACTIVIDAD

**C.** Conteste en frases completas:

1. ¿Quién es y cómo se llama la adivina?

_______________________________________________

2. Según Rosana, ¿qué puede hacer la adivina?

_______________________________________________

3. ¿Cree Josefina en esas cosas?

_______________________________________________

4. ¿Qué tiene la adivina en el centro de la mesa?

_______________________________________________

5. ¿Conocía la adivina el pasado de Rosana?

_______________________________________________

6. ¿Conocía la adivina el pasado de Josefina?

_______________________________________________

7. ¿Qué piensa Rosana de la adivina?

_______________________________________________

8. ¿Qué piensa Josefina de la adivina?

_______________________________________________

9. Según Rosana, ¿por qué sabe la adivina cosas del pasado de Josefina?

_______________________________________________

10. ¿Cree Ud. en los adivinos? ¿Por qué (no)?

_______________________________________________

You have now learned the two most important past tenses in Spanish. Let's look at them side by side:

| IMPERFECT TENSE | PRETERITE TENSE |
|---|---|
| **Generalmente** ***llegaba*** tarde, | pero **un domingo** ***llegó*** temprano. |
| **Siempre** ***iba*** a la escuela en carro, | pero **un día** ***tuve*** que ir en bus. |
| **Todos los sábados** ***venía*** mi tío | pero **el sábado pasado** no ***vino.*** |

What time expressions are used in the clauses on the left?

______________________________________________

What do they tell us about the actions described?

______________________________________________

Right, in Spanish we use the imperfect to express what used to happen or happened over and over again — that is, repeated or habitual actions in the past. That's why the imperfect is often used with expressions like **por lo general** (*in general*), **a menudo** (*often*), **siempre** (*always*), **todos los días** (every day).

What time expressions are used in the clauses on the right?

______________________________________________

**Un día, un domingo,** or **el sábado pasado** imply that the action happened at a specific time. In Spanish, we use the preterite to express specific events that are not habitual, that started and ended within a specific time frame. That's why the preterite is often used with expressions that determine a specific time, like **anoche** (*last night*), **ayer** (yesterday), **esta mañana** (*this morning*), **el lunes pasado** (*last Monday*), and others.

## ACTIVIDADES

**D.** The preterite and imperfect forms of the verb are given in each of the following sentences. Underline the correct choice:

1. (Iban, Fueron) al cine a menudo.
2. ¿Quién (hizo, hacía) las tareas anoche?
3. (Paró, Paraba) de llover a las doce.
4. Ella (salía, salió) de casa temprano esta mañana.
5. ¿Dónde (tomabas, tomaste) siempre el autobús?
6. ¿Dónde (tomabas, tomaste) el autobús ayer?
7. Por lo general, yo (corría, corrí) en el parque.
8. Los domingos Juan (visitaba, visitó) a sus abuelos.
9. Todos los viernes (llegábamos, llegamos) temprano a casa.
10. El viernes pasado (llegábamos, llegamos) tarde.

**E.** You are at a party where everyone is talking about the past. Using the cues provided, make statements about the way it was. Be careful, some verbs have to be used in the preterite and some in the imperfect:

1. Yo / ir todos los sábados al cine.

_______________________________________________

2. Nosotros / estar una semana en Nueva York.

_______________________________________________

3. Yo / salir a dar un paseo todas las noches.

_______________________________________________

4. Juan / leer dos novelas el verano pasado.

_______________________________________________

5. Nosotros / nadar a menudo en la piscina.

_______________________________________________

6. Mis padres / viajar a Europa hace un año.

_______________________________________________

7. Uds. / ir a la playa todos los veranos.

_______________________________________________

8. Tu hermana / trabajar por lo general hasta tarde.

_______________________________________________

9. Mi tío / venir de España hace cinco años.

_______________________________________________

10. Tú / llegar siempre tarde a la escuela.

_______________________________________________

**4** There is still more to learn about the past. Look carefully at these sentences:

| | |
|---|---|
| **Yo *dormía* cuando *sonó* el teléfono.** | *I was sleeping when the telephone rang.* |
| **Ud. *estaba* en casa cuando *llamé*.** | *You were at home when I called.* |
| **Rosa *escribía* una carta cuando *llegó* su amiga.** | *Rose was writing a letter when her friend arrived.* |
| ***Hacía* sol cuando *salimos*.** | *The sun was shining when we left.* |

How many actions are described in each sentence? ____________ How many verb tenses are used in each sentence? ____________ Which tenses are they?

__________ and __________. Which word combines the two clauses describing the two actions? __________.

Let's summarize: The IMPERFECT describes an ongoing or continuous past action lasting an unspecified amount of time. In English, we usually say *was* (*were*) + . . . *ing*. The PRETERITE expresses a specific past action that happened at one point while the other action was in progress. Imagine two cameras — an instant and a video camera. Which one would represent the imperfect? __________ the preterite? __________.

## ACTIVIDADES

**F.** Complete the sentence with the correct form of the preterite or the imperfect of the verb in parentheses:

1. (llegar) Eran las cuatro de la tarde cuando tú __________ a casa.
2. (jugar) El sábado pasado Juan __________ al fútbol con sus hermanos.
3. (levantarse) Yo siempre ______ __________ temprano.
4. (leer, llamar) Mi padre __________ cuando mi madre __________.
5. (ir) El año pasado ellas __________ a Colombia.
6. (ver, llevar) Cuando yo __________ a Luis, él __________ un traje muy elegante.
7. (hacer) Por lo general, ellos __________ las tareas juntos.
8. (recibir) Tú siempre __________ muchas cartas.
9. (lavarse, tocar) Yo ______ __________ cuando alguien __________ a la puerta.
10. (nacer, vivir) Cuando mi hermano __________, nosotros __________ en Miami.

**G.** Your neighbor's window was broken in a ball game, and she complained to your father. Answer his questions:

1. ¿Dónde estabas esta tarde cuando yo entré en casa?

_______________________________________________

2. ¿Con quién jugabas cuando te llamé?

_______________________________________________

3. ¿A qué jugaban Uds.?

_______________________________________________

4. ¿Qué hiciste al ver que la pelota caía en otra casa?

_______________________________________________

5. ¿Qué hacía la vecina (*neighbor*) cuando la pelota cayó en su casa?

_______________________________________________

6. ¿Dónde estaba tu madre cuando Uds. terminaron de jugar?

_______________________________________________

7. ¿Qué le dijiste a tu mamá sobre la ventana?

_______________________________________________

**5** Read this short description of a holiday:

> **Era** el diez de junio y **eran** las siete de la mañana. El sol ya **brillaba** y **hacía** un tiempo precioso. **Estábamos** en un hotel al lado de la playa y por la ventana yo **veía** el mar. En la playa **había** un hombre. **Era** alto y **llevaba** un traje de baño rojo. Yo **quería** bajar a nadar, pero **tenía** que esperar a mis padres. Yo **tenía** solamente ocho años.

Which tense did the narrator use? _______________ Right, he used the imperfect to describe circumstances and conditions in the past. The circumstances and conditions may refer to time, dates, weather, attitudes, states of mind, physical descriptions, age, or locations. All circumstances described in the imperfect happen over an unspecified amount of time.

What happens if the narrator wants to tell about an action that occurred at a specific point in time? Let's pick up the story from the last sentence.

> Yo **tenía** solamente ocho años. Mis padres **dormían** y como yo no **quería** esperar más, **decidí** despertarlos. **Abrí** su puerta y **grité** «¡Buenos días!»

Which tense is used to describe the narrator's actions? _______________

## ACTIVIDADES

**H.** You have to write a short paragraph describing your first years. Underline the correct form of the verb in parentheses:

Cuando yo (era, fui) niño, mi familia (vivió, vivía) en Chicago, en un apartamento pequeño. Mi padre (trabajaba, trabajó) de mecánico en un garaje. Él siempre (llegó, llegaba) temprano a casa y él y yo (salimos, salíamos) a jugar pelota al parque. En invierno mi madre (preparaba, preparó) chcolate caliente y (se sentó, se sentaba) a contarme cuentos. Yo (iba, fui) a una escuela cerca de casa.

**I.** Imagine that you spent last summer in Mexico. Tell your friends in Spanish about a special excursion you took one day. Be careful! You have to decide when to use the imperfect and when to use the preterite:

1. It was August and I was in Mexico City.

 ______________________________

2. I was in a hotel downtown.

 ______________________________

3. One day I woke up early because I was going on a trip.

 ______________________________

4. I wanted to be ready on time.

 ______________________________

5. I opened the window and saw that the sun was shining.

 ______________________________

6. We were going in an old bus and I dressed comfortably.

 ______________________________

7. The bus driver was a young man and he spoke English well.

 ______________________________

8. During the trip, he told many stories about the Indians.

 ______________________________

9. We were going to see the pyramids.

 ______________________________

10. The pyramids were very beautiful and I had a lot of fun.

 ______________________________

**J.** You are telling what you saw this morning on your way to school. Complete the paragraph with the correct form of the preterite or the imperfect of the verb in parentheses:

Esta mañana ________________ (llover) cuando yo ________________ (salir) de casa. Yo ________________ (venir) rápidamente cuando yo ________________ (oír) a un señor que ________________ (gritar) en la calle. ________________ (ser) un hombre que ________________ (correr) detrás de un perro muy grande. Al parecer (*apparently*) el hombre ________________ (encontrar) a un amigo en la calle y el perro ________________ (escaparse) cuando los dos amigos ________________ (hablar).

**6** Remember the verbs **saber** and **conocer?** They have special meanings in the preterite tense, different from their meanings in the imperfect. Let's first conjugate both in the preterite. **Conocer** is regular, but **saber** is irregular:

| | **conocer** | **saber** |
|---|---|---|
| **yo** | **conocí** | ***supe*** |
| **tú** | **conociste** | ***supiste*** |
| **Ud., él, ella** | **conoció** | ***supo*** |
| **nosotros** | **conocimos** | ***supimos*** |
| **Uds., ellos, ellas** | **conocieron** | ***supieron*** |

Now look at these examples:

**¿*Conocías* a Juan?**
*Did you know John?*
**Sí, lo *conocí* hace dos meses.**
*Yes, I met him two months ago.*

***¿Sabías que tenemos un examen hoy?***
*Did you know that we have a test today?*
**Sí, pero *supe* muy tarde y no tuve tiempo de estudiar.**
*Yes, but I found out too late and I didn't have time to study.*

## ACTIVIDADES

**K.** Express the following conversation in Spanish:

1. Do you know Mary?

_______________________________________________

2. Yes, I met Mary at a party yesterday.

_______________________________________________

3. Do you know where she lives?

_______________________________________________

4. Yes, I found out that she lives near my house.

_______________________________________________

5. Did you also meet her sister Rose?

_______________________________________________

6. Yes, I met Rose. Did you know that they are Cuban?

_______________________________________________

**L.** You are a fortune teller, but your client doesn't understand English. Tell him/her the following in Spanish:

1. You used to play football when you were 14 years old.

_______________________________________________

2. When you were little, you lived in a large city.

_______________________________________________

3. Last summer you went to the beach.

_______________________________________________

4. You used to get up early and swim a lot.

_______________________________________________

5. You would write postcards to all your friends.

_______________________________________________

6. The last week of your vacation you didn't write any postcards.

_______________________________________________

7. You used to like horror films.

_______________________________________________

8. One day your sister screamed when you were watching a horror film.

_______________________________________________

9. Your mother said that you couldn't see any more horror films.

_______________________________________________

## DIÁLOGO

You went to a fortune teller. To find out if she's any good, you asked her to tell you some things about your past. React to what she says:

## PREGUNTAS PERSONALES

1. ¿Qué tiempo hacía hoy por la mañana cuando te despertaste?

_______________

2. ¿Llamó alguien anoche cuando Uds. cenaban?

_______________

3. ¿Dónde estaba tu madre ayer cuando llegaste de la escuela?

_______________

4. ¿Cuántos años tenía tu padre cuando tú naciste?

_______________

5. Hace dos años, ¿quién era tu mejor amigo(a)?

_______________

## INFORMACIÓN PERSONAL

You have been asked to "tell about yourself." Describe some interesting or important facts or events from your past. (You don't really have to tell the truth. No one is going to check. So, go ahead, be outrageous!)

_______________

_______________

_______________

_______________

# CÁPSULA CULTURAL

## El misterioso mundo del pasado

We have been talking about the past. There is a past we know because of written documents, but there are still many mysteries to be unraveled, some of them in Latin America.

In **Rapa Nui** (Easter Island), a Chilean island in the Pacific, there are more than 600 gigantic stone statues (ranging from 10 to 37 feet) and ruins of giant stone walls about which not very much is known. Who were the people who built these statues? Why did they do it? What do they represent?

In 1911, the "lost city of the Incas," **Machu-Picchu,** was discovered by an American archaeologist near Cuzco in Peru. It is the most extraordinary ruin in the Americas because it was found almost intact. Little is known, however, about who lived there and when. Was it a military fortress? A sacred city? Why didn't the Spaniards find out about it when they conquered the Incan empire? Did people still live there?

In Colombia, in a region of cold, foggy mountains, there is a parklike place called San Agustín, where more than a thousand stone sculptures can be seen. Some have human forms and some represent all kinds of animals — tigers, owls, lizards, monkeys, birds, frogs, and others. San Agustín is thought to have been a sacred place, but its artisans had already disappeared when the Spaniards arrived in the sixteenth century. Who were these people? What do these gigantic statues, some of which date from the first century, represent?

You can visit all these places and many more in Latin America and marvel at the craftsmanship of the unknown peoples who built them.

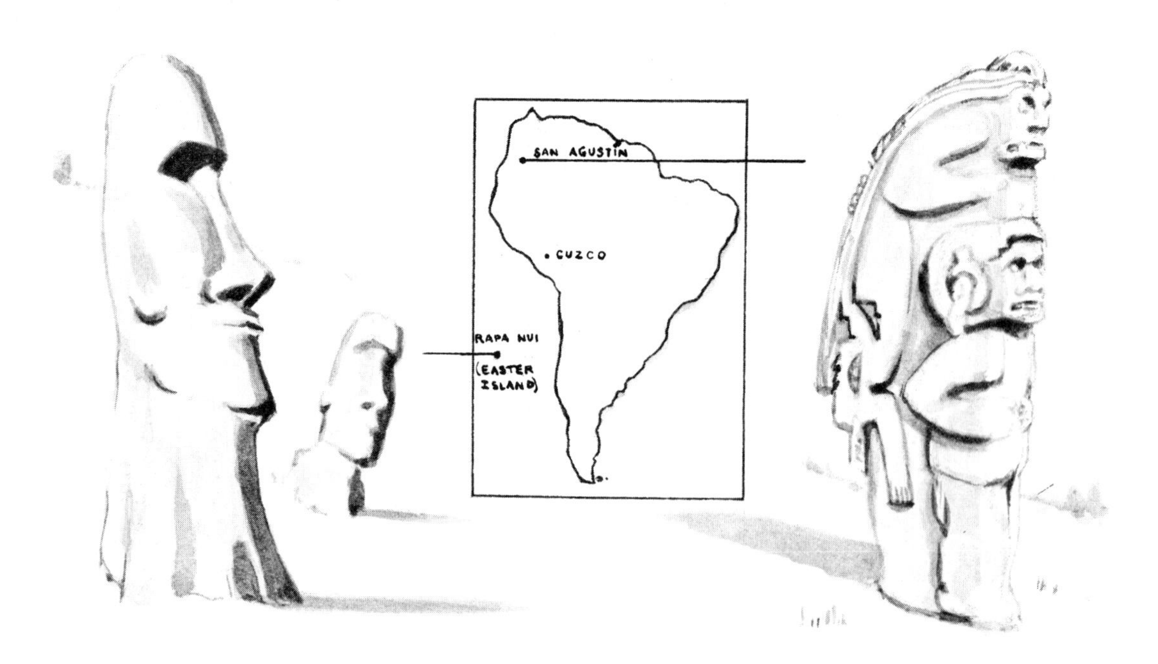

# 10 Los deportes

## Demonstrative Adjectives and Pronouns

### Vocabulario

## ACTIVIDADES

**A.** Mr. Gonzalez needs sports equipment for his gym classes. Can you help him choose some items?

Para jugar al béisbol necesita ______________________________.

Para jugar al básquetbol necesita ______________________________.

Para esquiar necesita ______________________________.

Para jugar al fútbol americano necesita ______________________________.

Para la natación necesita ______________________________.

Para el tenis necessita ______________________________.

Para el volibol necesita ______________________________.

Para el boxeo necesita ______________________________.

**B.** What sports activities are these people engaged in?

1. ______________________ 2. ______________________

3. ______________________________ 5. ______________________________

4. ______________________________ 6. ______________________________

## El karate

Let's read about another popular sport, **el karate:**

Con un simple golpe de pie o de mano, una persona puede romper una tabla de madera o hacer pedazos un ladrillo. ¿Imposible? No. Es muy posible si Ud. sabe ese antiguo arte oriental llamado karate. La palabra karate significa «mano vacía» en japonés. Eso quiere decir que no se usan armas. Para combatir se utilizan solamente ciertas partes del cuerpo como las manos, los pies, los codos y las rodillas.

**el golpe** *blow*
**romper** *to break*
**la tabla** *board*
**hacer pedazos** *to smash*
**el ladrillo** *brick*
**vacío** *empty*
**querer decir** *to mean*
**el codo** *elbow*
**la rodilla** *knee*

Se sabe que hace más de dos mil años unos monjes budistas en la India usaban una forma de este combate para defenderse de los animales salvajes. El karate se desarrolló gradualmente a través de los siglos, principalmente en Japón y luego en Corea, como método de defensa propia. Hoy día, además de ser un arte marcial, es un deporte de competición que se practica en todos los países del mundo.

**se sabe** *it is known*
**el monje** *monk*
**salvaje** *wild*
**desarrollarse** *to develop*
**a través** *through*
**defensa propia** *self-defense*

Los estudiantes avanzan desde el grado de principiantes hasta el de expertos. Cada grado tiene un cinturón de un color diferente. Los principiantes, por ejemplo, llevan cinturón blanco y los expertos, negro. Muchas de las asociaciones de karate tienen

**el grado** *stage*
**la asociación** *society*

reglas estrictas de comportamiento para evitar la violencia. Sus miembros juran:

1. dedicar sus esfuerzos al desarrollo intelectual y físico.
2. ser corteses y recordar siempre la virtud de la modestia.
3. respetar a los demás, superiores e inferiores, amigos o enemigos.
4. evitar todo incidente innecesario y utilizar el karate sólo en emergencias.
5. ser buenos ciudadanos.

**el comportamiento** *behavior*
**evitar** *to avoid*
**jurar** *to swear*
**el esfuerzo** *effort*
**recordar (ue)** *to remember*
**el ciudadano** *citizen*

El estudiante que quiere tener éxito tiene que pasar muchos años de práctica. Por ejemplo, tiene que demostrar su fuerza rompiendo dos o tres ladrillos con un solo golpe de pie. ¿Todavía está Ud. interesado en aprender? Buena suerte. Pero, ¡tenga cuidado con los dolores de pies!

**la fuerza** *strength*

## ACTIVIDAD

**C.** Conteste en frases completas:

**1.** Una persona que sabe karate, ¿qué puede hacer con un golpe?

______________________________

**2.** ¿Qué quiere decir la palabra karate en japonés?

______________________________

**3.** ¿Qué partes del cuerpo se usan en el karate?

______________________________

**4.** ¿Quién utilizó originalmente un método parecido?

______________________________

**5.** ¿Qué es el karate hoy día?

______________________________

**6.** ¿Cómo se indican los diferentes grados?

______________________________

**7.** ¿Por qué muchas de las asociaciones de karate tienen reglas estrictas?

______________________________

**8.** ¿Está Ud. de acuerdo con esas reglas? ¿Por qué (no)?

______________________________

**3** The demonstratives *this, these, that,* and *those* are used in English to point out specific persons or things. In Spanish, there are many more demonstratives. Let's take a look:

How many possibilities are there in Spanish to point out things? __________

**Este** (*this*) refers to a person or thing that is *here* (**aquí**), next to you. **Ese** (*that*) refers to a person or thing that is *there* (**ahí**), either close to you or next to the person you are talking to. **Aquel** (*that*) refers to a person or thing that is *over there* (**allí**), far from you and the person you are talking to. **Este, ese,** and **aquel** are demonstrative adjectives agreeing in number and gender with the noun they accompany.

**4** Let's look at the forms of **este:**

**est*e*** hombre **est*a*** mujer **est*os*** hombres **est*as*** mujeres

Can you complete the following?

____________ traje ____________ guantes

____________ camisa ____________ medias

**5** The forms of **ese** have the same endings:

**es*e*** árbol **es*a*** casa **es*os*** árboles **es*as*** casas

Easy? Now you do some:

____________ caballo ____________ gatos

____________ vaca ____________ gallinas

6 Finally, forms of **aquel** also have the same endings, but an extra **l** is placed before them:

**aquel** chico **aquel*la*** chica **aquel*los*** chicos **aquel*las*** chicas

Do the following:

__________ disco __________ cuadros

__________ ventana __________ puertas

Note that in Spanish the demonstrative adjective has to be repeated before each noun:

**Quiero comprar *esos* periódicos y *esas* revistas.**
*I want to buy those newspapers and (those) magazines.*

## ACTIVIDADES

**D.** You are in a sports store and want to find out how much certain things cost:

EXAMPLE: esquíes
**¿Cuánto cuestan estos esquíes?**

**1.** guante de béisbol

________________________________________

**2.** bate

________________________________________

**3.** balones de fútbol

________________________________________

**4.** raqueta de tenis

________________________________________

**5.** cestas

________________________________________

**6.** cascos

________________________________________

**7.** pelota

________________________________________

**8.** bicicletas

________________________________________

**E.** You take your mother to the store to show her what you would like for your birthday:

EXAMPLE: camisa
**Me gusta esa camisa.**

1. abrigo

_______________

2. sortija de rubíes

_______________

3. gafas de sol

_______________

4. zapatos

_______________

5. reloj de pulsera

_______________

6. lociones

_______________

7. trajes de baño

_______________

8. cadena de oro

_______________

**F.** You are watching a parade with your friend and are calling each other's attention to things you see:

EXAMPLE: caballo
**¡Mira aquel caballo!**

1. traje largo

_______________

2. músicos

_______________

3. muchacha bonita

_______________

4. banderas

_______________

5. banda

______________________________________________

6. policías

______________________________________________

7. coche

______________________________________________

8. flores

______________________________________________

**G.** You are going shopping at the supermarket. Say what you are going to buy:

EXAMPLE: pan / aquí
**Voy a comprar *este* pan.**

torta / ahí
**Voy a comprar *esa* torta.**

frutas / allí
**Voy a comprar *aquellas* frutas.**

1. helado / aquí

______________________________________________

2. sodas / allí

______________________________________________

3. pollo / ahí

______________________________________________

4. carne / aquí

______________________________________________

5. manzanas / ahí

______________________________________________

6. huevos / allí

______________________________________________

7. crema / ahí

______________________________________________

8. legumbres / aquí

______________________________________________

9. jugo / allí

______________________________________________

**7** Now look at the following sentences:

**Me gusta esta camisa pero no *aquélla*.** — *I like this shirt but not that one.*
**¿Qué película vas a ver, *ésta* o *ésa*?** — *Which film are you going to see, this one or that one?*
**Quiero comprar ese libro, no *éste*.** — *I want to buy that book, not this one.*
**¿Quieres escuchar estos discos o *ésos*?** — *Do you want to listen to these records or those ones?*

When **aquel, este,** and **ese** are used by themselves (without nouns), they are called demonstrative pronouns. The form of the demonstrative pronoun depends on the gender and number of the noun it represents. Demonstrative pronouns have the same forms as demonstrative adjectives, except that the pronouns have an accent mark on the stressed syllable:

**éste**
**ésta** } *this one*

**éstos**
**éstas** } *these*

**ése**
**ésa** } *that one*

**ésos**
**ésas** } *those*

**aquél**
**aquélla** } *that one*

**aquéllos**
**aquéllas** } *those*

## ACTIVIDADES

**H.** Marcos went to summer camp and found signs telling him what to do everywhere. Circle the demonstrative pronoun that completes the sentence correctly:

1. Ponga su ropa en esta silla, no en
   (a) éste (b) ésos (c) aquélla
2. Entre por esa puerta, no por
   (a) aquél (b) ésta (c) éste
3. Duerma en aquel cuarto, no en
   (a) ése (b) ésos (c) aquélla
4. Abra estas ventanas, no
   (a) aquéllos (b) éstos (c) ésas
5. Use esos zapatos, no
   (a) éstas (b) aquéllos (c) ése
6. Báñese en este baño, no en
   (a) ésa (b) aquéllas (c) ése
7. Siga esas reglas, no
   (a) ésos (b) éstas (a) aquél
8. Corra por aquel patio, no por
   (a) ésa (b) éste (c) éstas

**I.** Complete the following sentences in Spanish:

1. Quiero ____________ sombrero, no ____________. (this / that one)
2. Necesito ____________ libros, no ____________. (those / those over there)
3. Prefiero ____________ flores rojas. (these)
4. ____________ lección no es difícil, pero ____________ sí lo es. (that / this one)
5. ¿Ve Ud. ____________ avión en la distancia? (that)
6. ____________ cuadro es muy famoso, pero me gusta más ____________. (this / that one)
7. Abre ____________ ventana y cierra ____________. (this / that one over there)
8. ____________ papeles son importantes. (those over there)
9. ____________ soldados son españoles; ____________ son franceses. (those/ these)
10. ____________ niño es mi hermano; ____________ es su amigo. (that/ that one over there)

## PREGUNTAS PERSONALES

1. ¿Practicas algún deporte? ¿Cuál(es)?

____________________________________________

2. ¿Qué equipos de deporte hay en tu escuela?

____________________________________________

3. ¿Sabes algún arte marcial? ¿Cuál(es)?

____________________________________________

4. ¿Vas a los partidos de fútbol americano de tu escuela?

____________________________________________

5. ¿Cuál es tu equipo de fútbol americano preferido en las ligas profesionales?

____________________________________________

## DIÁLOGO

Rafael wants to join a team at school. He's talking with the head of the Physical Education Department:

## INFORMACIÓN PERSONAL

You want to convince the coach of your favorite sport that you would be a good addition to the team. Complete the following sentences:

**1.** A mí me gusta mucho ______________________________.

**2.** Ese deporte es ______________________________.

**3.** Yo creo que soy ______________________________.

**4.** El año pasado ______________________________.

**5.** Quiero ______________________________.

## COMPOSICIÓN

You have a new friend from Chile who doesn't know how to play baseball. Tell him how many players are on a team, how the game is played, the rules of the game, and which is your favorite professional team. You will find the following words useful:

**tirar** *to throw*
**batear** *to bat*
**el árbitro** *umpire*
**el bateador** *batter*
**el jugador** *player*
**el jonrón** *homerun*
**el lanzador** *pitcher*
**el aficionado** *fan*
**el receptor** *catcher*

______________________________________________________________

______________________________________________________________

______________________________________________________________

______________________________________________________________

______________________________________________________________

______________________________________________________________

# CÁPSULA CULTURAL

## Los deportes en el mundo hispano

Everybody knows that soccer is a passion in Spain and Latin America. Most large cities and many small ones have their own teams, and national games are very important. In almost every empty lot in every town, you can see boys of all ages playing soccer and dreaming of being the next international star.

What is less known is that other sports, like baseball, have also been popular in certain Hispanic countries. In the Caribbean, in Cuba, the Dominican Republic, Puerto Rico, Mexico, Nicaragua, and Venezuela, baseball is as important or even more important than soccer. There are many baseball players of Hispanic origin in the United States.

Cycling is very important in Spain, Colombia, Mexico, Cuba, Chile, and Costa Rica. Each country has its **Vuelta,** a race that lasts a couple of weeks. The winner is a national hero.

There is also a lesser known, very ancient sport, **jai-alai,** which has its origins in the Basque region of Spain. It's rather dangerous and probably the fastest game in the world. It's played with a hard ball and a basketlike container called **cesta** on a court (**cancha**) with high walls. It resembles handball, except for the **cesta.** This sport is popular in Spain, Cuba, Mexico, and Venezuela, as well as in Florida and Connecticut.

Which of these sports do you like best? Why?

# *Repaso II (Lecciones 6–10)*

## Lección 6

**a.** Reflexive verbs have a special pronoun, called a reflexive pronoun, to indicate that the subject and object of the verb refer to the same person or thing:

**lavar*se*, dormir*se*, acostar*se***

**b.** Some Spanish reflexive verbs have nonreflexive English equivalents:

**levantarse** *to get up,* **divertirse** *to have fun,* **acostarse** *to go to bed*

**c.** Different subjects require different reflexive pronouns:

| | |
|---|---|
| **yo *me* visto** | **nosotros *nos* vestimos** |
| **tú *te* vistes** | |
| **Ud., él, ella *se* visten** | **Uds., ellos, ellas *se* visten** |

**d.** In Spanish reflexive constructions, the definite article is used instead of the possessive adjective with parts of the body or wearing apparel:

**Tú te lavas *la* cara.** *You wash your face.*

**e.** The reflexive pronoun normally stands directly before the verb:

**Yo me acuesto temprano.**
**Tú no te vistes rápido.**

The reflexive pronoun follows the verb and is attached to it in affirmative commands and when the reflexive verb is used as an infinitive:

**Levántate. Levántese. Levántense.**
**No queremos levantarnos.**

## Lección 7

**a.** The preterite tense of regular verbs is formed by dropping the **-ar, -er,** or **-ir** ending of the infinitive and adding preterite endings:

| | | -AR verbs | | -ER and -IR verbs |
|---|---|---|---|---|
| **yo** | | **é** | | **í** |
| **tú** | | **aste** | **com** | **iste** |
| **Ud., él, ella** | **habl** | **ó** | **sal** | **ió** |
| **nosotros** | | **amos** | | **imos** |
| **Uds., ellos, ellas** | | **aron** | | **ieron** |

b. **Dar** takes **-ER** verb endings in the preterite tense: **di, diste, dio, dimos, dieron.**

c. **-AR** and **-ER** verbs with stem changes in the present tense (**e** to **ie** and **o** to **ue**) have regular stems in the preterite:

| | PRESENT TENSE | PRETERITE |
|---|---|---|
| **pensar (ie)** | **pienso, piensas, piensa . .** | **pensé, pensaste, pensó . . .** |
| **volver (ue)** | **vuelvo, vuelves, vuelve . . .** | **volví, volviste, volvió . . .** |

**-IR** verbs with stem changes in the present tense (**e** to **ie, o** to **ue,** and **e** to **i**) change **e** to **i** in the third person singular and plural of the preterite:

| | PRESENT TENSE | PRETERITE |
|---|---|---|
| **sentir (ie)** | **siento, sientes, siente . . .** | **sentí sentiste, s*i*ntió, sentimos, s*i*ntieron** |
| **dormir (ue)** | **duermo, duermes, duerme . . .** | **dormí dormiste, d*u*rmió, dormimos, d*u*rmieron** |
| **servir (i)** | **sirvo, sirves, sirve . . .** | **serví, serviste, s*i*rvió, servimos, s*i*rvieron** |

d. Many Spanish verbs have irregular preterite forms. **Estar, hacer, poder, poner, querer, tener,** and **venir** have irregular stems and irregular endings common to all these verbs:

| | |
|---|---|
| **yo estuv** | ***e*** |
| **tú hic** | ***iste*** |
| **Ud. pud** | ***o*** |
| **él / ella pus** | ***o*** |
| **nosotros quis** | ***imos*** |
| **Uds. tuv** | ***ieron*** |
| **ellos / ellas vin** | ***ieron*** |

The preterite stem of **hacer** changes **c** to **z** in the third person singular to keep the original sound: **hizo.**

e. **Ser** and **ir** share the same irregular forms in the preterite. Only the context makes the meaning clear: **fui, fuiste, fue, fuimos, fueron.**

f. Verbs ending in a vowel + **-er** or **-ir** change **i** to **y** in the third person singular and plural. In the other forms, the **i** has an accent:

**leer: le*í*, le*í*ste, le*y*ó, le*í*mos, le*y*eron**

g. **Decir** and **traer** have irregular preterite tense forms:

| | | |
|---|---|---|
| **yo** | | **e** |
| **tú** | **dij** | **iste** |
| **Ud., él, ella** | **traj** | **o** |
| **nosotros** | | **imos** |
| **Uds., ellos, ellas** | | **eron** |

## Lección 8

a. The imperfect of regular verbs is formed by dropping the **-ar, -er,** and **-ir** ending of the infinitive and adding imperfect endings:

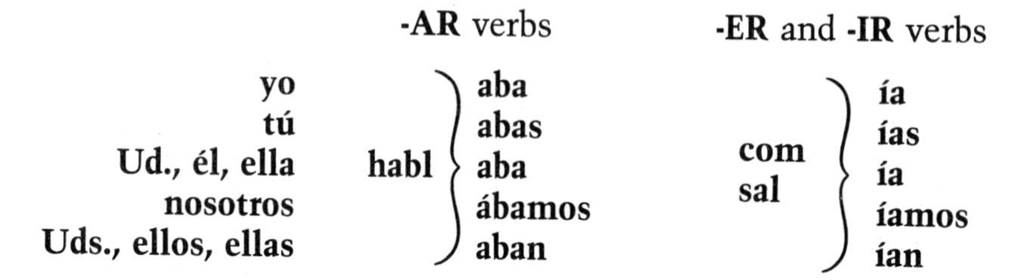

| | -AR verbs | | -ER and -IR verbs | |
|---|---|---|---|---|
| **yo** | | **aba** | | **ía** |
| **tú** | | **abas** | **com** | **ías** |
| **Ud., él, ella** | **habl** | **aba** | **sal** | **ía** |
| **nosotros** | | **ábamos** | | **íamos** |
| **Uds., ellos, ellas** | | **aban** | | **ían** |

b. There are only three verbs with irregular forms in the imperfect tense:

| | **ir** | **ser** | **ver** |
|---|---|---|---|
| **yo** | **iba** | **era** | **veía** |
| **tú** | **ibas** | **eras** | **veías** |
| **Ud., él, ella** | **iba** | **era** | **veía** |
| **nosotros** | **íbamos** | **éramos** | **veíamos** |
| **Uds., ellos, ellas** | **iban** | **eran** | **veían** |

## Lección 9

a. Uses of the preterite and the imperfect tenses:

| IMPERFECT | PRETERITE |
|---|---|
| Describes repeated or habitual actions (equivalent to English *used to*): | Describes specific events that are not habitual: |
| ***Iba* al cine todos los sábados.** | ***Fui* al cine el sábado pasado.** |
| Describes an ongoing or continuous action (equivalent to English *was* (*were*) + . . . *ing*): | Describes a particular action that happened while another action was in progress: |
| **Miguel *dormía* profundamente** | **cuando Jorge *llegó* a su casa.** |

Describes circumstances and conditions (time, dates, weather, attitudes, age, physical descriptions) that happened over an unspecified amount of time:

***Eran*** **las siete y ya *hacía* sol.**
**Un joven que *llevaba* gafas, *quería* hablar con mi mamá.**

Describes an action that started and ended at a specific point in time:

***Me desperté*** **y *me vestí.***
***Llamé*** **a mi mamá y ella *vino* a la puerta.**

**b.** **Saber** is irregular in the preterite tense: **supe, supiste, supo, supimos, supieron.** **Saber** and **conocer** have different meanings in the imperfect and the preterite tenses:

**¿*Conocías* a Rosario?**
*Did you know Rosario?*
**Sí, la *conocí* en la fiesta.**
*Yes, I met her at the party.*

**¿*Sabías* que Rosa estaba aquí?**
*Did you know that Rosa was here?*
**Sí, *supe* que llegó ayer.**
*Yes, I found out that she arrived yesterday.*

### Lección 10

**a.** Demonstrative adjectives:

| | |
|---|---|
| **este, esta** *this* | **estos, estas** *these* |
| **ese, esa** *that* | **esos, esas** *those* |
| **aquel, aquella** *that* | **aquellos, aquellas** *those* |

**b.** Demonstrative pronouns:

| | |
|---|---|
| **éste, ésta** *this one* | **éstos, éstas** *these* |
| **ése, ésa** *that one* | **ésos, ésas** *those* |
| **áquel, áquella** *that one (over there)* | **áquellos, áquellas** *those (over there)* |

## ACTIVIDADES

**A.** Here are nine pictures showing what Pepito did yesterday morning. Following the clues given, complete the sentence under each picture and then number the sentences so that they follow the correct order of his activities:

Salió del baño y ______________.

y ______________.

______________________

Después de vestirse ______________ y fue a desayunar.

y entró al baño a ______________.

Después del desayuno

______________,

______________ «Adiós» a su

mamá y ______________ de la casa.

Ayer Pepito ______________ a las seis.

______________ de la cama inmediatamente

**B. Buscapalabras.** Hidden in the puzzle are the names of 11 sports and 5 pieces of equipment needed for sports. Circle the words from left to right, right to left, up or down, or diagonally:

| | | | | | | | | | |
|---|---|---|---|---|---|---|---|---|---|
| A | B | U | K | A | R | A | T | E | Í |
| L | E | T | A | B | U | E | N | U | L |
| O | Ñ | L | N | É | F | R | Q | O | U |
| B | A | O | A | I | V | S | L | O | C |
| T | T | B | T | S | E | L | O | M | H |
| E | E | T | A | B | S | B | B | S | A |
| U | U | Ú | C | O | A | P | I | I | L |
| Q | Q | F | I | L | S | N | L | L | I |
| S | A | L | Ó | B | E | B | O | C | B |
| Á | R | N | N | T | P | L | V | I | R |
| B | O | X | E | O | C | S | A | C | E |

**C.** These people used to do different things during the summer. Complete the sentence under each picture, using the imperfect of the appropriate verb:

1. Rosa ________________________________________.

2. Juanita y Julia ________________________________________.

3. El Sr. Gómez ________________________________________.

4. Tú ________________________________________.

5. Uds. ________________________________________.

6. Jorge ________________________________________.

7. Nosotros ________________________________________.

8. Yo ______________________________________________.

**D.** Doña Matilda, the fortune teller, has told you some things about your past and your future. The problem is that she didn't say when the things happened or will happen. Use the secret numbers to break the code and find out what she saw in her crystal ball. The numbers tell you which letters to put above the lines. Then complete the sentences following the clues given:

| CLAVE | | | | | |
|---|---|---|---|---|---|
| $A_{1}$ | $B_{2}$ | $C_{3}$ | $CH_{4}$ | $D_{5}$ | $E_{6}$ |
| $F_{7}$ | $G_{8}$ | $H_{9}$ | $I_{10}$ | $J_{11}$ | $K_{12}$ |
| $L_{13}$ | $LL_{14}$ | $M_{15}$ | $N_{16}$ | $\tilde{N}_{17}$ | $O_{18}$ |
| $P_{19}$ | $Q_{20}$ | $R_{21}$ | $S_{22}$ | $T_{23}$ | $U_{24}$ |
| $V_{25}$ | $W_{26}$ | $X_{27}$ | $Y_{28}$ | $Z_{29}$ | |

1. ___ ___ ___ ___ ___ ___ ___ ___ ___ ___ ___ ___ ___ ___
23 24 7 1 15 10 13 10 1 14 6 8 18 1

___ ___ ___ ___ ___ ___ ___ ___ ___ ___ ___ ___ ___ ___
6 22 23 6 19 1 10 22 9 1 3 6

___ ___ ___ ___ ___ .

2. ___ ___ ___ ___ ___ ___ ___ ___ ___ ___ ___ ___ ___ ___
6 13 25 6 21 1 16 18

___ ___ ___ ___ ___ ___ ___ ___ ___ ___ ___ ___ ___ .
7 24 10 22 23 6 1 13 3 1 15 19 18

3. ___ ___ ___ ___ ___ ___ ___ ___ ___ ___ ___ ___

___ ___ ___ ___ ___ ___ ___ ___ ___ ___ ___
25 1 22 1 9 1 3 6 21 24 16

___ ___ ___ ___ ___ ___ ___ .
3 21 24 3 6 21 18

**4.** ___ ___ ___ ___ ___ ___ ___ ___

23 24 25 10 22 23 6 24 16

6 27 1 15 6 16 5 10 7 10 3 10 13 .

**5.** ___ ___ ___ ___ ___ ___ ___ ___ ___ ___ ___ ___

25 1 22 1 22 1 2 6 21 20 24 6

16 18 23 1 22 1 3 1 22 23 6 .

**6.** 5 6 9 18 28 ___ ___ ___ ___ ___ ___ ___ ___

___ ___ ___ ___ 25 1 1 3 1 15 2 10 1 21

23 24 25 10 5 1 .

**E.** Do you enjoy a challenge? Transform one word into another, by changing one letter at a time, using words you know:

EJEMPLO: C A S A

___ ___ ___ ___ C O S A

___ ___ ___ ___ R O S A

R O P A

| CUENTO | NOCHE | TODO |
|---|---|---|
| ___ ___ ___ ___ ___ ___ | ___ ___ ___ ___ | ___ ___ ___ ___ |
| ___ ___ ___ ___ ___ ___ | ___ ___ ___ ___ | ___ ___ ___ ___ |
| ___ ___ ___ ___ ___ ___ | ___ ___ ___ ___ | ___ ___ ___ ___ |
| DIENTE | CAMA | BOCA |

**F.** **¿Es Ud. un buen testigo?** You are walking down the street when a thief races out of a store and gets into a waiting car, which then speeds away. You have seen the whole incident and are asked to describe what you saw. Examine the following picture very carefully for one minute. Then cover the picture and try to answer the questions correctly:

1. ¿Qué hora era?
2. ¿Cómo era el carro?
3. ¿Cuál era el número de la placa?
4. ¿Tenía el ladrón la cara cubierta?
5. ¿Tenía barba o bigote?
6. ¿Llevaba sombrero?
7. ¿Cuántas personas había en el carro?
8. ¿En qué mano llevaba el ladrón lo que robó?
9. ¿Tenía pistola?
10. ¿Cuántas personas había en la calle? ¿Dónde estaban?

## G. Crucigrama

HORIZONTALES

1. Quitarse la ropa.
7. El día antes de hoy.
9. Adjetivo demostrativo.
10. Defienden a las víctimas.
13. Imperfecto de encontrar.
14. Pronombre reflexivo.
17. El primero en los deportes.
21. Pretérito de **dar.**
22. Imperativo de **leer.**
23. Pretérito de **caer.**
24. Pretérito de **poner.**
25. ______, no allí.
27. Pretérito de **llevar.**
30. Pretérito de **pasar.**
31. Pretérito de **ir.**
32. Pronombre reflexivo.
34. La comida de la mañana.
36. Adjetivo demostrativo.

VERTICALES

1. Yo ______ porque estaba cansado.
2. Presente de **ser.**
3. Pretérito de **sacar.**
4. Tiempo infinito.
5. Pretérito de **traer.**
6. No tiene dudas. Está ______.
7. Doce meses.
8. Imperfecto de **responder.**
11. Imperfecto de **dar.**
12. Contrario de **con.**
15. Ayuda al ladrón.
16. Pretérito de **lavarse.**
18. Posesivo.
19. Imperfecto de **poder.**
20. El ladrón dejó una ______.
23. Sirve para guardar joyas.
26. Pretérito de **querer.**
28. Pretérito de **estar.**

HORIZONTALES

**38.** Pretérito de **saber.**
**39.** Parte de la pierna.
**42.** Imperfecto de **cantar.**
**43.** Imperativo de **salir.**
**44.** Parte del brazo.
**45.** Hace frío. Tienes que ______ el abrigo.

VERTICALES

**29.** Pronombre demostrativo.
**33.** Adjetivo demostrativo.
**34.** Oficina.
**35.** En este momento.
**37.** Contrario de **fuerte.**
**40.** Pretérito de **decir.**
**41.** Me ______ Luisa.

## H. ¿Quién encontró la solución del crimen? To find the answer, identify the objects in the pictures, then write the letters indicated in the blanks below:

**1.**

| ___ | ___ | ___ | ___ | ___ | ___ | ___ | ___ | ___ | ___ |
|---|---|---|---|---|---|---|---|---|---|
| | | | 1 | | 2 | | 3 | 4 | |

| ___ | ___ | ___ | ___ | ___ | ___ | ___ |
|---|---|---|---|---|---|---|
| | 5 | 6 | 7 | | | |

**2.**

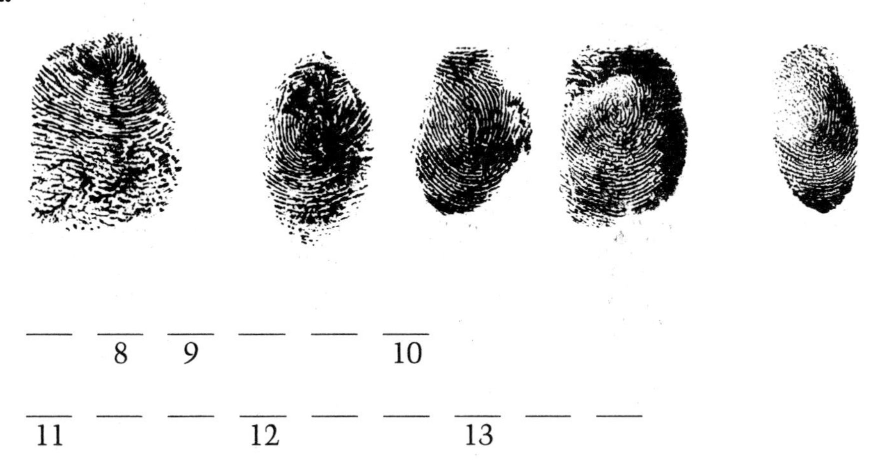

| ___ | ___ | ___ | ___ | ___ | ___ |
|---|---|---|---|---|---|
| | 8 | 9 | | | 10 |

| ___ | ___ | ___ | ___ | ___ | ___ | ___ | ___ | ___ |
|---|---|---|---|---|---|---|---|---|
| 11 | | | 12 | | | 13 | | |

3.

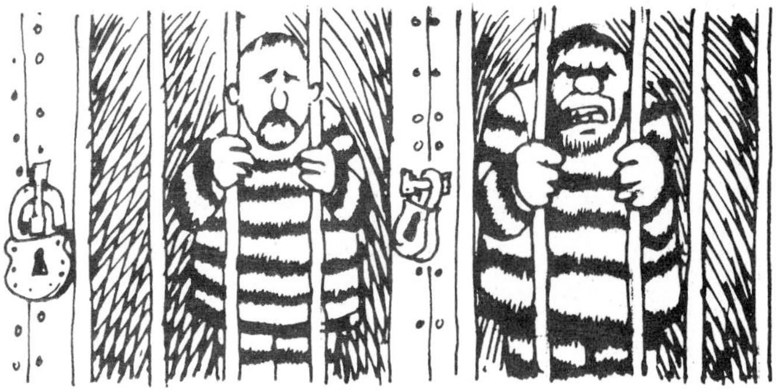

___ ___ ___ ___ ___ ___
14 15 16

4.

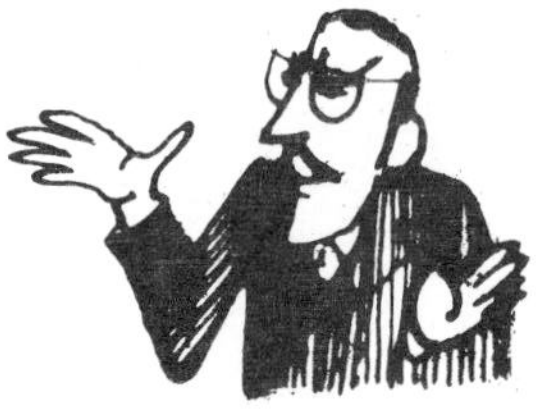

___ ___ ___ ___ ___ ___ ___ ___ ___ ___ ___ ___ ___ ___ ___
17 18 19 20 21 22

5.

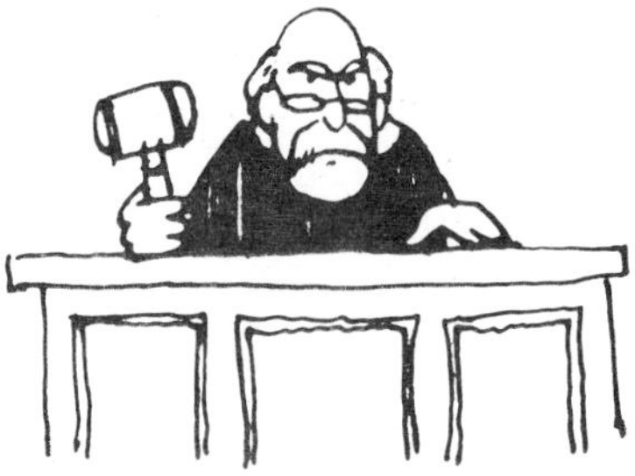

___ ___ ___ ___
23 24

6.

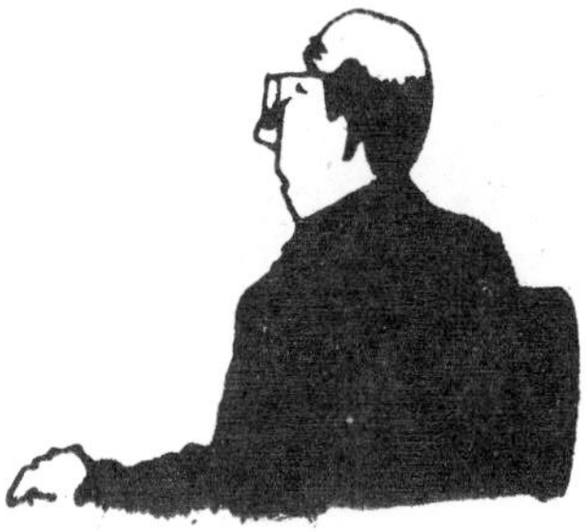

___ ___ ___ ___ ___ ___ ___
25 26 27

**Solución:** ___ ___ ___ ___ ___ ___ ___ ___ ___ ___ ___
24 6 26 22 11 2 25 12 4 8 19

___ ___ ___ ___ ___ ___ ___ ___ ___ ___
1 14 23 10 17 20 5 18 21 13

___ ___ ___ ___ ___ ___ .
16 15 7 27 9 3

**I.** Write a short story in Spanish about the situation you see in the picture:

______________________________________________

______________________________________________

______________________________________________

______________________________________________

______________________________________________

______________________________________________

# Achievement Test I (Lessons 1–10)

## Listening Comprehension [5 points]

Listen to your teacher read twice in succession a situation in Spanish. Then your teacher will pause while you circle the letter of the best suggested answer:

1. **a.** Buena suerte, señor.
   **b.** ¿Tiene Ud. mucha hambre?
   **c.** ¿Tiene tacos de pollo?
   **d.** Quiero volver a casa.

2. **a.** Mire mi reloj.
   **b.** Meta un dedo en el oído.
   **c.** Abra la boca.
   **d.** Cierre los ojos.

3. **a.** Un anillo de oro.
   **b.** Un truco.
   **c.** Un casco precioso.
   **d.** Una joyería.

4. **a.** Las noticias.
   **b.** La sección deportiva.
   **c.** Los anuncios clasificados.
   **d.** El artículo de fondo.

5. **a.** Remar en el lago.
   **b.** Pescar en el río.
   **c.** Descansar en el campo.
   **d.** Nadar en el mar.

## Vocabulary [10 points]

**¿Qué es esto?** Label the following pictures in Spanish:

1. 

______________________

2. 

______________________

3.

7.

4.

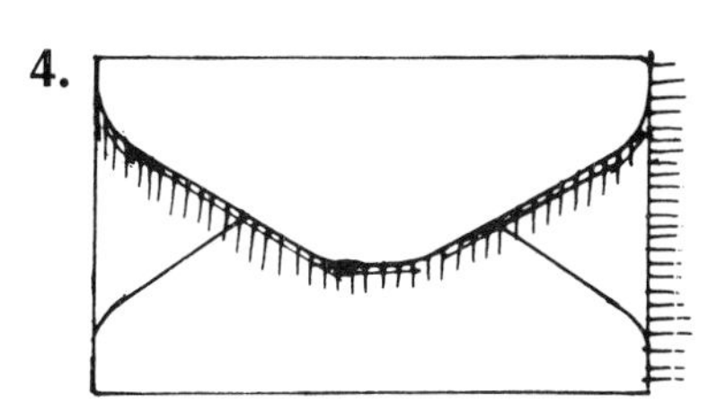

8.

5.

9.

6.

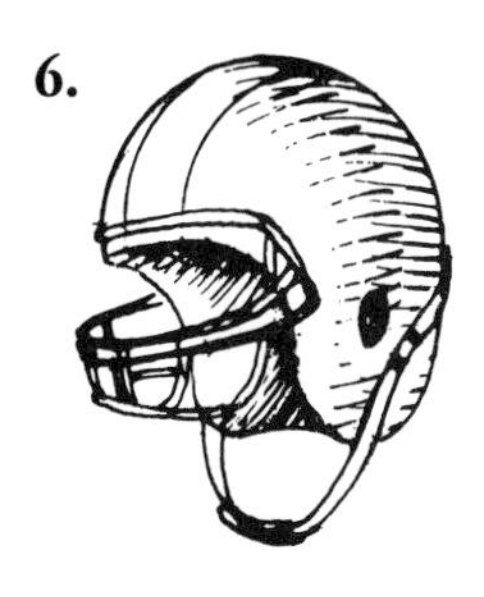

10.

## Structures [70 points]

**a.** Interrogatives [5 points]

Write a question for each of the following answers:

**1.** Mi profesor de español es el señor Pérez.

2. Mi número de teléfono es el 54-3210.

_______________

3. La ciudad de Los Ángeles está en California.

_______________

4. En las vacaciones voy a la playa.

_______________

5. Tengo cinco dólares en el bolsillo.

_______________

**b.** Stem-changing verbs [5 points]

Complete the following sentences with the correct present-tense form of the verb in parentheses:

1. (pensar) ¿Qué _______________ Ud. de mi coche nuevo?
2. (poder) Yo no _______________ ir al cine esta noche.
3. (cerrar) Nosotros siempre _______________ la puerta por la noche.
4. (perder) Yo _______________ la paciencia frecuentemente.
5. (repetir) Tú siempre _______________ lo que yo digo.

**c. Saber** and **conocer** [5 points]

Listen to the cue, then check whether you use **Yo sé** or **Yo conozco** to start the sentence:

| | **Yo sé** | **Yo conozco** |
|---|---|---|
| 1. | _______________ | _______________ |
| 2. | _______________ | _______________ |
| 3. | _______________ | _______________ |
| 4. | _______________ | _______________ |
| 5. | _______________ | _______________ |

**d.** Shortened adjectives [5 points]

Choose the correct form of the adjective to complete the sentence:

1. Mi (tercer, tercero, tercera) clase del día es inglés.

2. Simón Bolívar y Jorge Wáshington fueron (grandes, grande, gran) hombres.
3. Mañana es mi (primero, primer, primera) día de clases.
4. El Sr. Gómez es un profesor muy (buen, buena, bueno).
5. Nueva York es una ciudad (gran, grande).

**e.** Adverbs [5 points]

Write the adverb that best completes the sentence:

1. Ellos no bailan mal; por el contrario, bailan ______________.
2. A Josefa no le gusta comer mucho; ella come ______________.
3. Los Pérez no viven lejos; ellos viven ______________.
4. Ellos nunca llegan temprano; siempre llegan ______________.
5. ¿Quieres salir ahora o ______________?

**f.** Negatives [5 points]

Answer the following questions negatively:

1. ¿Viste algún programa de televisión anoche?

   ______________________________

2. ¿Quién te llamó esta mañana?

   ______________________________

3. ¿Hablas chino o ruso?

   ______________________________

4. ¿Qué quieres comer ahora?

   ______________________________

5. ¿Cuándo vas a pescar?

   ______________________________

**g.** Commands [5 points]

You are in a large department store with your little brother Carlitos and two of his friends. Complete the following commands with the correct form of the verbs in parentheses:

1. (poner, salir) Carlitos, ¡______________ ese juguete en su lugar y ______________ de ahí!

2. (tener, mirar) ¡__________ Uds. cuidado con la gente y __________ por dónde van!

3. (venir, ser) Carlitos, ¡__________ aquí, no __________, tonto!

4. (ir, correr) ¡__________ Uds. a mi lado y no __________!

5. (hacer, cerrar) Carlitos, ¡__________ lo que te digo, y Uds. dos, __________ ya la boca!

**h.** Reflexive verbs (10 points)

Describe what you did yesterday:

| **Por la mañana** | **Por la noche** |
|---|---|
|  |  |
| __________ | __________ |
|  |  |
| __________ | __________ |
|  |  |
| __________ | __________ |

**Por la mañana** | **Por la noche**

______________________ ______________________

______________________ ______________________

**i.** Preterite and imperfect tenses [20 points]

Complete the following story with the correct form of the preterite or imperfect of the verbs in parentheses:

Me llamo Susana. Como ayer ______ (1 hacer) buen tiempo, mi amiga Dolores y yo ______ (2 ir) a la playa. Yo ______ (3 poner) unos sandwiches en mi bolso y Dolores ______ (4 comenzar) a comer muy pronto porque ______ (5 tener) hambre. En la playa ______ (6 ver) a Carlos. Él ______ (7 estar) con otros amigos, pero él ______ (8 decir) que ______ (9 querer) entrar en el agua con nosotras. Yo no ______ (10 saber) que Carlos

__________ 11 (ser) tan simpático. Carlos, Dolores y yo __________ 12 (estar)

en la playa todo el día. Por la noche, nosotros __________ 13 (decidir)

comer en un restaurante que Carlos __________ 14 (conocer). Dolores

__________ 15 (pedir) solamente una ensalada, pero yo __________ 16 (pedir)

una comida completa. Naturalmente que no __________ 17 (poder)

terminar de comer todo. Cuando nosotros __________ 18 (salir)

del restaurante, __________ 19 (llover) fuertemente y __________ 20 (tener)

que coger un taxi.

**j.** Demonstrative adjectives and pronouns [5 points]

Complete the following sentences in Spanish:

1. (This, that one over there) __________ flor es bonita, pero __________ no me gusta.
2. (These, those) Quiero __________ zapatos, no __________.
3. (That one, this one) __________ cuesta diez dólares, __________ cuesta solamente cinco.
4. (That over there, this one) Juan vive en __________ edificio, yo vivo en __________.
5. (Those, those) __________ papas fritas y __________ postres son deliciosos.

## 4 Reading comprehension [5 points]

Below the following story there are five questions. For each, choose the expression that best answers the question according to the meaning of the story and circle its letter:

Su bicicleta roja está lista. Pero Joselito Torres, el joven ciclista, no puede dormirse. Es la noche antes de la gran carrera y Joselito está muy nervioso. Durante una semana entera él va a hacer todo lo posible por ganar el trofeo y el título de campeón. Comienza a pensar . . . .

El locutor deportivo grita por el micrófono: «Ya llegan los primeros ciclistas. López está a la cabeza y Torres lo sigue muy de cerca. En tercer lugar viene Rivera. Pero, ¿qué veo? Señores y señoras, ¡un accidente! López está en el suelo. No puede continuar la carrera. Los otros ciclistas lo pasan. Ahí están. ¿Quién va a la cabeza? ¡Es Torres! Joselito Torres ganó la carrera. Todo el mundo grita histéricamente. Su mamá le da un abrazo. Una chica le da unas flores y después Joselito recibe el trofeo, ¡el trofeo de campeón!»

Joselito se despierta cuando su mamá le grita: «Joselito, levántate. La competición va a comenzar dentro de dos horas».

¿Un sueño? Quizás, pero Joselito sabe ahora que va a ganar.

**1.** ¿Cómo se siente Joselito antes de la carrera?

**a.** Seguro de sí mismo.
**b.** Lleno de preocupaciones.
**c.** Con sueño.
**d.** Sin preocupaciones.

**2.** ¿Cuánto tiempo dura la carrera?

**a.** Siete días.
**b.** Cinco días.
**c.** Un día entero.
**d.** Dos semanas.

**3.** ¿Qué le pasó a López?

**a.** Se cansó.
**b.** Se cayó de la bicicleta.
**c.** No quiso continuar.
**d.** Se paró en el suelo.

**4.** ¿Qué ganó Torres?

**a.** Muchas flores.
**b.** Mucho dinero.
**c.** El campeonato.
**d.** Una bicicleta.

**5.** ¿Cómo sabe Ud. que Torres no ganó una carrera en realidad?

**a.** Su mamá dijo algo.
**b.** Su mamá soñó.
**c.** Tuvo un accidente.
**d.** López llegó el primero.

## Slot completion [5 points]

In the following passage, there are five blank spaces numbered 1 through 5. Each blank space represents a missing word. For each blank space, four possible completions are provided. Only one makes sense:

Hoy es el cumpleaños de la señora Campos y su marido quiere darle un regalo muy lujoso. ¿Qué puede comprar? El problema es que él no __(1)__. ¿__(2)__ puede pedir consejo? Decide hablar con su mejor amiga, Josefina. Josefina menciona varias posibilidades, entre ellas __(3)__ — un collar, un broche o una pulsera. ¡Qué buena idea! El señor Campos va inmediatamente a una joyería y compra un magnífico brazalete de oro y diamantes. __(4)__ regresa a su casa y le dice a su mujer: « __(5)__ el regalo que te traje». Cuando ella ve el brazalete, grita: «Eres el mejor marido del mundo. Te adoro».

(1) **a.** conoce
**b.** piensa
**c.** sabe
**d.** comprende

(2) **a.** A quién
**b.** A qué
**c.** Quién
**d.** A cuál

(3) **a.** comida
**b.** ropa
**c.** joyas
**d.** dinero

(4) **a.** Después
**b.** Pronto
**c.** Ya
**d.** Ahora

(5) **a.** Mire
**b.** Mira
**c.** Vea
**d.** Ven

## Visual stimulus (5 points)

Write five sentences in Spanish to tell a short story about the situation suggested in the picture:

______________________________

______________________________

______________________________

______________________________

______________________________

# Tercera Parte

# 11 En la tienda de ropa

## Direct Object Pronouns

### Vocabulario

## ACTIVIDADES

**A.** You need to buy some clothes and you go shopping with your mother. What would you buy in this store? Make a list of at least eight items:

1. ______________________  5. ______________________

2. ______________________  6. ______________________

3. ______________________  7. ______________________

4. ______________________  8. ______________________

**B.** You are writing a story and have four characters in mind. Here are their descriptions. What clothes would you have them wear? Use the new words and those you already know. Here are some more helpful expressions:

**de manga corta** *short-sleeved*
**de manga larga** *long-sleeved*
**sin mangas** *sleeveless*
**el algodón** *cotton*
**la lana** *wool*
**ancho** *wide*
**la tela** *fabric, material*
**a rayas** *striped*
**a cuadros** *check, plaid*
**el cuello** collar
**ultramoderno** *ultramodern*
**estrecho** *narrow*

Tomás: Un joven de 20 años. Toma clases en la universidad. Tiene ideas muy modernas y originales. Quiere ser actor.

Mario: Un muchacho de 23 años. Trabaja para un abogado. Es serio, inteligente y práctico. Quiere ganar mucho dinero.

Dolores: Una chica de 21 años. Es refinada y elegante. Quiere ser modelo. Le gusta la música moderna.

Sarita: Una chica de 19 años. Trabaja de secretaria de día y toma cursos en la universidad de noche. Quiere ser científica. Es alegre, simpática y estudiosa.

Tomás lleva ____________________

____________________

____________________

Mario lleva ____________________

____________________

____________________

Dolores lleva ____________________

____________________

____________________

Sarita lleva ____________________

____________________

____________________

## Un vestido de fiesta

Let's read a story about a special party dress and a girl's good luck. Pay special attention to the words in bold type:

Liliana acaba de recibir el regalo de Navidad de sus padres — ¡cien dólares en efectivo! ¿Qué va a hacer con tanto dinero? Pues hay una fiesta de año nuevo en casa de Blanquita. Sí, con el dinero que tiene puede comprar un vestido magnífico. Va a ser la chica más elegante de la fiesta. Necesita un vestido especial, y sabe exactamente en qué tienda **lo** puede comprar — la boutique francesa Chez Fifí. Cuando entra en la tienda, una vendedora **la** saluda:

**acabar de** *to have just*
**en efectivo** *in cash*
**saludar** *to greet*

VENDEDORA: Buenas tardes, señorita. ¿En qué puedo servirle?
LILIANA: Necesito un vestido de fiesta de talla siete para un baile de año nuevo.
VENDEDORA: ¿Qué le parece este vestido de raso rojo?
LILIANA: No me gusta. Me parece muy ordinario.
VENDEDORA: Este conjunto de blusa blanca de encaje y mini-falda de terciopelo negro es muy popular ahora. Sólo vale cien dólares.
LILIANA: No está mal. Pero yo prefiero algo más original, más sofisticado.
VENDEDORA: Ajá. Entiendo perfectamente. Aquí tiene un vestido de seda azul que es justamente para Ud. Es único. No hay otro igual.
LILIANA: Oh, me encanta. ¿Puedo probárme**lo**?
VENDEDORA: Sí, claro. Síga**me,** señorita.

**la talla** *size*
**el raso** *satin*
**el conjunto** *set*
**el encaje** *lace*
**el terciopelo** *velvet*
**la seda** *silk*
**justamente** *precisely*
**me encanta** *I love it*
**probarse** *to try on*

Liliana se **lo** prueba. Está encantada.

VENDEDORA: El vestido le va muy bien. Es además muy chic y muy de moda.
LILIANA: **Lo** compro. ¿Cuánto cuesta?
VENDEDORA: Para Ud., solamente 200 dólares.
LILIANA: Pero tengo sólo cien dólares. ¡Qué pena! Entonces me llevo la blusa con mini-falda.

**ir bien** *to fit*
**de moda** *fashionable*
**qué pena** *what a shame*

La noche de la fiesta, Liliana entra en casa de Blanquita y ve a sus tres amigas, Conchita, Lolita y Panchita. Las tres tienen la cara triste y están vestidas exactamente igual — ¡con un vestido de seda azul!

LILIANA: ¿Qué pasó, chicas? **Las** veo tristes. ¿Cómo es que llevan el mismo vestido?
CONCHITA: ¿No te gusta mi vestido «muy chic»?
LOLITA: Sí, es único. No hay otro igual en el mundo.
PANCHITA: Cuando vea a la vendedora de Chez Fifí, **la** mato.

**matar** *to kill*

## ACTIVIDAD

**C.** Conteste con frases completas:

1. ¿Cuánto dinero recibió Liliana?

_______________

2. ¿Qué tipo de fiesta hay en casa de Blanquita?

_______________

3. ¿Qué quiere comprar Liliana?

_______________

4. ¿En qué tienda piensa encontrar el vestido que busca?

_______________

5. ¿Por qué no le gusta a Liliana el vestido rojo?

_______________

6. Según la vendedora, ¿cómo es el vestido de seda azul?

_______________

7. ¿Por qué no compra Liliana el vestido azul?

_______________

8. ¿Qué ropa compra Liliana para la fiesta?

_______________

9. ¿Cómo se llaman las tres amigas de Liliana?

_______________

10. ¿Por qué están tristes?

_______________

3 What do you think of these sentences in English?

I have a Spanish book. I find my Spanish book very useful. I read my Spanish book, study my Spanish book, and refer to my Spanish book before taking a test.

Pretty repetitious! How about this version:

I have a Spanish book. I find it very useful. I read it, study it, and refer to it before taking a test.

Much better, isn't it? What have we done? We have substituted an object pronoun (*it*) instead of repeating the same noun (*Spanish book*).We can do the same thing in Spanish. Look at these sentences from the story:

**Ella necesita un vestido especial y sabe dónde *lo* puede comprar.**
*She needs a special dress, and she knows where she can buy it.*

**Cuando la chica entra en la tienda, una vendedora *la* saluda.**
*When the girl enters the store, a saleswoman greets her.*

Which noun in the first sentence is replaced by **lo?** ____________. What is the gender of **el vestido?** ____________. Which noun in the second sentence is replaced by **la?** ____________. What is the gender of **la chica?** __________.

**Lo** and **la** are direct object pronouns; **lo** replaces a masculine singular noun, and **la** replaces a feminine singular noun. **Lo** and **la** have the plural forms **los** and **las**. **Lo, la, los,** and **las** may refer to people or things.

Look at these other examples:

**¿Compras el impermeable? Sí, *lo* compro.**
*Are you buying the raincoat? Yes, I'm buying it.*

**¿Ves a la vendedora? No, no *la* veo.**
*Do you see the saleswoman? No, I don't see her.*

**¿Recibiste los libros? Sí, *los* recibí.**
*Did you receive the books? Yes, I received them.*

**¿Venden batas aquí? No, no *las* venden.**
*Do they sell robes here? No, they don't sell them.*

Where do **lo, la, los,** and **las** stand in relation to the verb? ________________. Right, contrary to English, the Spanish object pronoun comes directly before the verb.

## ACTIVIDADES

**D.** Substitute a direct object pronoun for the word in bold type:

EXAMPLE: Necesito el libro.
***Lo* necesito.**

1. El doctor examina **los ojos.**

_______________

2. Ellos traen **un vaso.**

_______________

3. No veo **la pizarra.**

_______________

4. No escribimos **las cartas.**

_______________

5. El maestro explica **la lección.**

_______________

6. ¿Compras **los periódicos?**

_______________

7. La señora no vende **frutas.**

_______________

8. Tenemos **el abrigo** aquí.

_______________

**E.** You are going on a trip and your mother wants to know what you are taking with you. Answer her questions:

EXAMPLE: ¿Llevas la camisa de seda?
**Sí, *la* llevo.**

1. ¿Llevas los pantalones negros?

_______________

2. ¿Llevas el impermeable?

_______________

3. ¿Llevas la bufanda azul?

_______________

4. ¿Llevas las botas de piel?

_______________

5. ¿Llevas ese sombrero viejo?

_______________

6. ¿Llevas la bata de casa?

_______________

7. ¿Llevas las pantuflas?

_______________

8. ¿Llevas los suéteres nuevos?

_______________

**F.** You are giving a party and your best friend wants to know who is going and what foods you will serve. Answer his questions:

EXAMPLE: ¿Invitaste a Juan?
**Sí, *lo* invité.**

1. ¿Invitaste a Rosa?

_______________

2. ¿Invitaste a los hermanos Gómez?

_______________

3. ¿Invitaste a Manuel?

_______________

4. ¿Trae Manuel a su hermana?

_______________

5. ¿Invitaste a Julia y a María?

_______________

6. ¿Compraste los helados de chocolate?

_______________

7. ¿Preparaste sandwiches de queso?

_______________

8. ¿Hizo tu mamá la torta?

_______________

9. ¿Tienes bastantes sodas?

_______________

10. ¿Compraste el pastel que me gusta?

_______________

**G.** Carmen has just met Andrés at a party. They discover that they have a lot in common:

EXAMPLE: Carmen: Yo hago las tareas por la noche.
Andrés: **Yo también *las* hago por la noche.**

1. Carmen: Yo tomo el autobús para ir a la escuela.

   Andrés: _______________

2. Carmen: Yo tengo amigos mexicanos.

   Andrés: _______________

3. Carmen: Yo estudio matemáticas.

   Andrés: _______________

4. Carmen: Yo toco el piano muy bien.

   Andrés: _______________

5. Carmen: Yo escucho música clásica todos los días.

   Andrés: _______________

How can you tell your best friend in Spanish that you saw him? How do you ask him if he saw you? Look at this short dialog:

| | |
|---|---|
| Tú: | **Ayer *te* vi por la calle con tus padres.** |
| Tu amigo: | **¿Sí? ¿*Nos* viste? ¿Por qué no *nos* saludaste?** |
| Tú: | **Uds. estaban muy lejos. ¿No *me* viste tú?** |
| Tu amigo: | **No, no *te* vi.** |

Here's a complete table of the Spanish direct object pronouns:

| | |
|---|---|
| **me** | *me* |
| **te** | *you* (familiar) |
| **lo** | *you* (formal), *him, it* (masculine) |
| **la** | *you* (formal), *her, it* (feminine) |
| **nos** | *us* |
| **los** | *them, you* (masculine plural) |
| **las** | *them, you* (feminine plural) |

## ACTIVIDADES

**H.** Express the following in Spanish:

1. Your friends visit you (familiar) often.

_______________________________________________

2. My mother called me an hour ago.

_______________________________________________

3. Our grandparents always take us to the movies.

_______________________________________________

4. You (formal singular) saw her this morning.

_______________________________________________

5. I invited them (feminine) to the party.

_______________________________________________

6. ¿Did you (plural) see us at the baseball game?

_______________________________________________

7. My parents don't understand me.

_______________________________________________

8. ¿Do your parents understand you (familiar)?

_______________________________________________

**5** We saw that the direct object pronouns come before the verb. There are some situations, however, in which they take a different position. Look at these examples:

| | |
|---|---|
| **Compra el libro. Cómpra*lo*.** | *Buy the book. Buy it.* |
| **Abre la ventana. Ábre*la*.** | *Open the window. Open it.* |
| **Escriba Ud. las cartas. Escríba*las*.** | *Write the letters. Write them.* |
| **Visita a tus abuelos. Visíta*los*.** | *Visit your grandparents. Visit them.* |

Are these commands affirmative or negative? ________________. Where is the direct object pronoun in these commands? ________________________.

Here's the easy rule: In affirmative (but NOT negative) commands, the direct object pronoun follows the verb and is attached to it. Also, an accent mark is on the stressed vowel to keep the original stress.

## ACTIVIDAD

**I.** Repeat the following commands, replacing the noun by a direct object pronoun:

**1.** Aprende la lección.

________________________

**2.** Estudia los verbos.

________________________

**3.** Cierra la puerta.

________________________

**4.** Compra las revistas.

________________________

**5.** Llama a Juan.

________________________

**6.** Despierta a tu hermana.

________________________

**7.** Escucha al profesor.

________________________

**8.** Lee esos capítulos.

________________________

**9.** Haz las tareas.

________________________

**10.** Prepara la comida.

________________________

**6** Now look at these sentences:

| I | II | |
|---|---|---|
| **Quiero *verte* hoy.** | ***Te quiero* ver hoy.** | *I want to see you today.* |
| **Pedro va a *llamarme*.** | **Pedro *me va* a llamar.** | *Peter is going to call me.* |
| **Él viene a *visitarnos*.** | **Él *nos viene* a visitar.** | *He is coming to visit us.* |
| **Voy a *comprarlos*.** | ***Los voy* a comprar.** | *I'm going to buy them.* |

How many verbs are in each Spanish sentence? ______. Which form does the second verb have? ______________. Where is the direct object pronoun in column I? ______________________________.

Is it attached to the infinitive? __________. Where is the direct object pronoun in column II? ______________________________.

Here's the rule: When a direct object pronoun is used with an infinitive, it may follow and is attached to the infinitive, or it may precede the conjugated form of the other verb.

## ACTIVIDADES

**J.** Your mother tells you to do some things and you answer that you will do them:

EXAMPLE: lavar los platos
Madre: **Lávalos.**
Ud.: **Voy a lavarlos.**

1. hacer las tareas

   Madre: ______________

   Ud.: ______________

2. lavar el carro

   Madre: ______________

   Ud.: ______________

3. leer el artículo

   Madre: ______________

   Ud.: ______________

4. comer las legumbres

   Madre: ______________

   Ud.: ______________

5. abrir la ventana

   Madre: ______________

   Ud.: ______________

6. llamar al doctor

   Madre: ______________

   Ud.: ______________

7. comprar los zapatos

   Madre: ______________

   Ud.: ______________

8. servir la comida

   Madre: ______________

   Ud.: ______________

9. escribir las cartas

   Madre: ______________

   Ud.: ______________

10. traer el pan

    Madre: ______________

    Ud.: ______________

**K.** You are talking on the phone with a friend. Answer the questions, using a direct object pronoun in each sentence:

1. ¿Escuchaste las noticias hoy?

_______________

2. ¿Viste el video nuevo que salió?

_______________

3. ¿Leíste el periódico esta mañana?

_______________

4. ¿Viste a Gloria y a Clara en el concierto?

_______________

5. ¿Quieres visitar a Raúl?

_______________

6. ¿Terminaste la tarea de biología?

_______________

7. ¿Miraste el partido de béisbol en la televisión?

_______________

8. ¿Vas a comprar las entradas para el cine?

_______________

9. ¿Conociste a la nueva profesora?

_______________

## PREGUNTAS PERSONALES

1. ¿Cómo te vistes para ir a una fiesta elegante?

_______________

2. ¿Cómo te vistes para ir a la escuela?

_______________

3. ¿Qué ropa recibiste en tu último cumpleaños?

_______________

4. ¿Compras ropa a menudo?

_______________

5. ¿Qué compraste la última vez que fuiste de compras?

_______________

## DIÁLOGO

You go into a department store to buy some presents:

## INFORMACIÓN PERSONAL

Your parents just gave you $200 to buy clothes. How would you spend them? Make a list of at least five things you would buy, in what colors, material, and so on:

1. ______________________________

2. ______________________________

3. ______________________________

4. ______________________________

5. ______________________________

# CÁPSULA CULTURAL

## Trajes tradicionales

People in Spain and Latin America wear, in general, the same types of clothes as here in the United States. There is a tendency to be more formal in dressing, but you will find that teenagers love to wear jeans and sport shirts or T-shirts.

Some traditional clothes remain in many regions, linked to folk costumes and dances. Have you heard of the gaucho, the Argentinian cowboy? His typical dress consists of a woolen poncho, long, baggy pants (**bombachas**) gathered at the ankles and covering the tops of high leather boots. And speaking of ponchos, do you know what they are and where they come from? Ponchos are originally from the South American Indians, who hand-loomed brightly colored woolen cloths, cut them into squares, and opened a hole in the middle for the head.

You have, of course, seen the Mexican sombrero: A broad-brimmed hat of felt or straw whose brim can be as much as two feet wide. Why so big? Well, the word sombrero comes from **sombra** (*shade*).

And the bullfighter? What does he wear? A short jacket, waistcoat, knee-length, skin-tight pants of silk and satin, all richly embroidered in gold, silver, and silk, heavy silk stockings, and flat black slippers.

Do you know any other typical Spanish or Latin American clothes? What are they?

# 12 ¡Viva el automóvil!

## Indirect Object Pronouns

### 1 Vocabulario

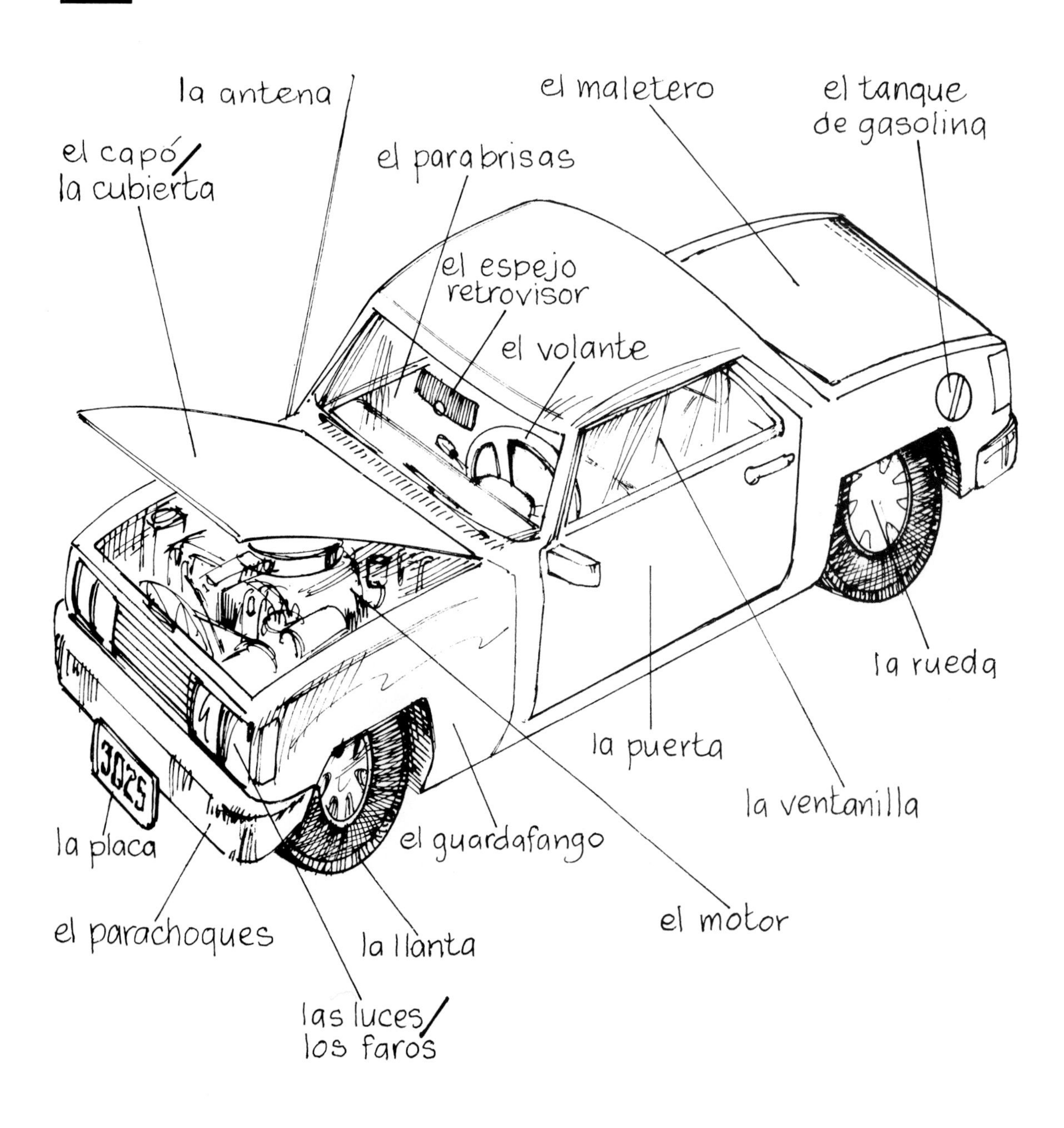

## ACTIVIDAD

**A.** Here are some important traffic signs (**señales de tránsito**). Can you figure out what they mean?

1. ______________________

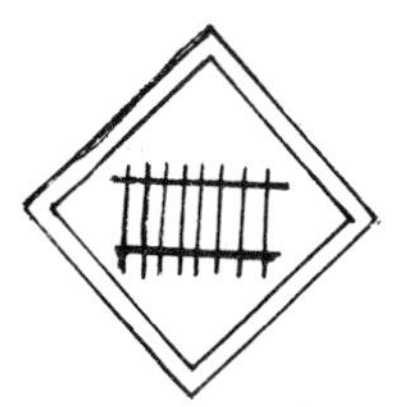

2. ______________________

3. ______________________

4. ______________________

5. ______________________

6. ______________________

## Pepita aprende a manejar

You have already learned the direct object pronouns. Pay attention now to other pronouns you will find in this story:

Los padres de Pepita **le** van a regalar un carro deportivo rojo para su cumpleaños. Antes de comprarlo, el papá decidió dar**le** unas clases de manejar a Pepita. Ella tiene hoy su primera clase y está muy nerviosa porque su padre no deja de hablar**le.**

**manejar** *to drive*
**dejar de** *to stop*

Él **le** dice: «Maneja muy despacio, por favor».
Él **le** muestra todo: «Aquí están el freno y el acelerador».
Él **le** repite: «Así se arranca el motor».

**el freno** *brake*
**arrancar** *to start*

Por fin **le** da el volante. Pepita maneja bastante bien. Sin embargo, su papá no deja de gritar**le:** «Presta atención a las señales de tránsito. Maneja más despacio. Tienes una parada en esa esquina. Mira los otros carros. Ten cuidado. Presta atención a los peatones, en especial a los niños». Y por la ventanilla del carro **les** grita a los otros choferes: «¡Cuidado! Mi hija está aprendiendo a manejar».

**prestar atención** *to pay attention*
**la parada** *stop*
**la esquina** *corner*
**el peatón** *pedestrian*

Al final de la clase Pepita está completamente rendida y más nerviosa que al principio. Está muy contenta de ser pasajera otra vez. Su padre echa un suspiro de alivio porque Pepita no chocó el carro, coge el volante y **le** dice: «Antes de compra**rte** el carro, tengo que da**rte** muchas clases más. Tienes mucho que aprender».

**al final** *at the end*
**rendido** *exhausted*
**el suspiro** *sigh*
**el alivio** *relief*
**chocar** *to crash*

De repente, oyen la sirena de un carro de la policía que está detrás de ellos. Después de pararlos, el policía se acerca y **les** dice: «Señor, ¿no vio Ud. la luz roja? Lo siento, pero tengo que poner**le** una multa. Me parece que Ud. necesita algunas clases de manejar. ¿No está Ud. de acuerdo, señorita?»

**acercarse** *to come near*
**lo siento** *I'm sorry*
**la multa** *fine, ticket*

## ACTIVIDADES

**B.** Conteste con frases completas:

1. ¿Qué regalo va a recibir Pepita?

______________________________

2. ¿Qué decidió su papá antes de comprarlo?

______________________________

3. ¿Cómo está Pepita antes de la clase? ¿Por qué?

______________________________

4. ¿Qué le muestra su padre?

______________________________

5. ¿Cómo maneja Pepita?

______________________________

**6.** ¿A quiénes debe prestar atención Pepita?

______________________________________________

**7.** ¿Qué grita el padre por la ventanilla del carro?

______________________________________________

**8.** ¿Cómo está Pepita al final de la clase?

______________________________________________

**9.** ¿Por qué paró el policía al padre?

______________________________________________

**10.** ¿Qué hace el policía?

______________________________________________

**C.** You are buying a used car, a real bargain (**una ganga**), but it needs some parts before you can drive it away. Identify the missing parts:

**1.** ____________________ **4.** ____________________

**2.** ____________________ **5.** ____________________

**3.** ____________________

**3** Look at these sentences:

| | |
|---|---|
| **Ella dio un regalo *a su madre*.** | *She gave her mother a present.* |
| **Ella dio un regalo *a sus amigos*.** | *She gave her friends a present.* |

What is the subject in both Spanish sentences? ______________________

the verb? __________ the direct object? ______________. What are

**a su madre** and **a sus amigos?** ____________________. Right, they are indirect objects. An indirect object indicates *to whom* or *for whom* the action is done.

Now look at these sentences:

| | |
|---|---|
| **Ella *le* dio un regalo.** | *She gave her a present.* |
| **Ella *les* dio un regalo.** | *She gave them a present.* |

Which word has replaced **a su madre** in the first sentence? _____ Which

word has replaced **a sus amigos** in the second sentence? _____. **Le** and **les** are indirect object pronouns. They stand before the verb and may refer to either masculine or feminine nouns. Here are some more examples:

| | |
|---|---|
| **Doy un reloj *a mi hermano*.** | *I give my brother a watch.* |
| ***Le* doy un reloj.** | *I give him a watch.* |
| **Presto un disco *a Ud*.** | *I lend you a record.* |
| ***Le* presto un disco.** | *I lend you a record.* |
| **Él presta libros *a Uds*.** | *He lends you books.* |
| **Él *les* presta libros.** | *He lends you books.* |
| **Doy un regalo *a mis hermanas*.** | *I give a present to my sisters.* |
| ***Les* doy un regalo.** | *I give them a present.* |

Note that indirect object pronouns stand before the verb.

## ACTIVIDAD

**D.** Substitute an indirect object pronoun for the expression in bold type:

EXAMPLE: Presto dinero **a mi hermano.**
***Le* presto dinero.**

**1.** La maestra enseña la lección **a los alumnos.**

______________________________________________

**2.** El Sr. Pérez da flores **a su esposa.**

______________________________________________

3. El policía pone una multa **al chofer.**

______________________________

4. José hace una pregunta **a las muchachas.**

______________________________

5. Muestro mi carro nuevo **a mis amigos.**

______________________________

6. Mi papá compró un regalo **a mi mamá.**

______________________________

7. El abuelo cuenta historias **a los niños.**

______________________________

8. Mi hermano presta su bicicleta **a su amigo.**

______________________________

9. La vendedora vendió un vestido **a Mercedes.**

______________________________

10. Ud. da trabajo **a los jóvenes.**

______________________________

**4** Where do the direct object pronouns stand in affirmative commands?

______________________________ in sentences with an infinitive?

______________________________ or

______________________________.

Well, the same rules apply to the indirect object pronouns:

| | |
|---|---|
| **Escriba una carta a sus padres.**<br>*Write your parents a letter.* | ***Escríbales*** **una carta.**<br>*Write them a letter.* |
| **Trae la comida a tu hermanito.**<br>*Bring the food to your brother.* | ***Tráele*** **la comida.**<br>*Bring him the food.* |

**Quiero** ***preguntarle*** **algo.**

or

***Le quiero*** **preguntar algo.**

*I want to ask him (her, you) something.*

## ACTIVIDADES

**E.** You are on a trip with your parents and your mother is trying to decide what presents to buy and what postcards to send. You are helping her:

EXAMPLE: ¿Mando esta tarjeta a Pablo? **Sí, mándale esta tarjeta.**

1. ¿Compro esa bufanda a mi hermana?

 ______________________________

2. ¿Mando esa tarjeta a tus abuelos?

 ______________________________

3. ¿Compro esos discos a mis amigos?

 ______________________________

4. ¿Escribo esas tarjetas a los Gómez?

 ______________________________

5. ¿Mando aquella tarjeta a José?

 ______________________________

6. ¿Compro este juguete a tu hermanito?

 ______________________________

**F.** Your brother always wants to do what you do:

EXAMPLE: Tú dices: Quiero dar flores a mamá.
Él dice: **Yo también quiero darle flores.**

1. Necesito hablar de mis planes a mis padres.

 ______________________________

2. Quiero escribir una carta al presidente.

 ______________________________

3. Debo servir refrescos a mis amigos.

 ______________________________

4. Voy a prestar mi bicicleta a Juan.

 ______________________________

5. Quiero dar unos discos a Juan y a Tomás.

 ______________________________

6. Voy a hacer una pregunta a la profesora.

 ______________________________

5 In Spanish, the indirect object pronoun is normally used even when the indirect object noun is expressed:

***Les* digo la verdad *a mis padres.***
***Le* sirvo el café *a Juan.***

## ACTIVIDAD

**G.** Your mother is a wonderful cook and likes to prepare special dishes for each person in the family:

EXAMPLE: mi papá / arroz con pollo
**A mi papá le prepara arroz con pollo.**

1. mis hermanos / carne con papas

_______________________________________________

2. mi abuela / flan

_______________________________________________

3. mis tías / camarones

_______________________________________________

4. mi hermana / una torta

_______________________________________________

5. mi abuelo / gazpacho

_______________________________________________

6 Look at these sentences:

**Mis padres *me* regalaron un carro deportivo.**
*My parents gave me a sports car.*

**¿Qué *te* dieron de regalo de cumpleaños?**
*What did they give you as a birthday present?*

**La profesora *nos* preparó una sorpresa.**
*The teacher prepared a surprise for us.*

What object pronouns do you recognize in these sentences? ______, ______, and ______. In Spanish, **me, te,** and **nos** are both direct and indirect object pronouns.

## ACTIVIDAD

**H.** A friend asks you these questions. What are your answers?

1. ¿Me prestas tus patines?

_______________

2. ¿Qué tareas nos pusieron hoy?

_______________

3. ¿Me ayudas con la tarea de español?

_______________

4. ¿Me explicas lo que dijo la profesora?

_______________

5. ¿Quién te regaló esa bicicleta?

_______________

6. ¿Te dan dinero tus padres?

_______________

7. ¿Quién nos dijo que la profesora estaba enferma?

_______________

8. ¿Quién te lava la ropa?

_______________

Here's a table of the indirect object pronouns:

| | |
|---|---|
| **me** | *(to, for) me* |
| **te** | *(to, for) you* |
| **le** | *(to, for) you* (formal), *him, her* |
| **nos** | *(to, for) us* |
| **les** | *(to, for) you* (plural), *them* |

## ACTIVIDADES

**I.** You are writing a letter to a friend. Complete it with the appropriate indirect object pronouns:

Querida Rosario:

Hoy fui de compras. A mi mamá ______ compré un suéter muy bonito y a mis hermanos ______ compré juguetes. No ______ escribí antes porque estuve muy ocupada. Ayer ______ mandé tarjetas a todos los chicos de la clase. A José, por supuesto, ______ escribí una larga carta. El viaje ______ gusta mucho; el guía ______ prometió a mis padres y a mí una excursión para mañana. Bueno, ya ______ conté muchas cosas. ¡Escríbe______ pronto!

**J.** You are telling your friend Pablo what happened last night at a restaurant. Express the following in Spanish:

1. The waiter (**el mesero**) brought us the menu.

______________________________________________

2. My mother told him: "Bring me a sandwich."

______________________________________________

3. The waiter answered her: "I'm sorry, but at this hour I can not serve you (plural) sandwiches."

______________________________________________

4. "¿What can you serve us?," my mother asked him.

______________________________________________

5. We didn't like anything on the menu.

______________________________________________

6. We left and my mother said to my father: "I told you (familiar) that this restaurant is bad."

______________________________________________

## PREGUNTAS PERSONALES

1. ¿Sabes manejar un carro? ¿Cuándo aprendiste a hacerlo?

______________________________________________

2. ¿Crees que los automóviles son necesarios? ¿Por qué?

______________________________________________

3. ¿Qué marca de automóvil prefieres? ¿Por qué?

______________________________________________

4. ¿Hay mucho tráfico en la ciudad donde vives?

______________________________________________

5. ¿Qué opción tienes si no quieres usar el carro? ¿Hay otros medios de transporte?

______________________________

## INFORMACIÓN PERSONAL

Describe your or your parents' car. Point out or explain some of its features:

1. ______________________________
2. ______________________________
3. ______________________________
4. ______________________________
5. ______________________________

## COMPOSICIÓN

You are a used-car salesperson and are trying to sell an old car to a customer. Say that the car is very good, that it doesn't use a lot of gas or oil, that the motor is new and the trunk is large, that it has four doors and is very comfortable, that the brakes and the lights work, and that it has an excellent radio with antenna. Here are some useful expressions if you want to offer more incentives to your customer:

**el aceite** *oil*
**funcionar** *to work*
**el carburador** *carburetor*
**el arranque** *starter*
**la batería** *battery*

______________________________
______________________________
______________________________
______________________________
______________________________
______________________________
______________________________
______________________________

## DIÁLOGO

You are teaching your brother how to drive:

# CÁPSULA CULTURAL

## Un viaje por las costas de España

Would you like to spend your vacation at a beach in Spain? If you do, the next question is which one? There are almost 200 resorts along the Spanish coast, since Spain forms part of a peninsula and has a coastline that stretches for hundreds of miles.

In order to narrow down the area and pinpoint the location of particular bathing areas on the map, the Spaniards have divided their coastline into six different **costas:**

There is the **Costa Brava** (Wild Coast), a rugged stretch of the Spanish Mediterranean coast extending to the French border. Next comes the **Costa Dorada** (Golden Coast), with its gently sloping beaches of golden sand extending along the coastal strip of Barcelona. Then the **Costa del Azahar** (Orange Blossom Coast), with its large, flat beaches, stretches past Valencia. It is followed by the **Costa Blanca** (White Coast), which offers a very mild winter season. Finally, the last coast on the Mediterranean is the popular **Costa del Sol** (Sunshine Coast), which faces North Africa.

There are two more coasts on the Atlantic Ocean: On the south is the **Costa de la Luz** (Coast of Light), which extends to the Portuguese border. The North Atlantic coast is called the **Costa Verde** (Green Coast) because of the abundant green vegetation that borders it.

Why not pay a visit to all of them?

# 13 *En la farmacia*

## Double Object Pronouns

## 1 Vocabulario

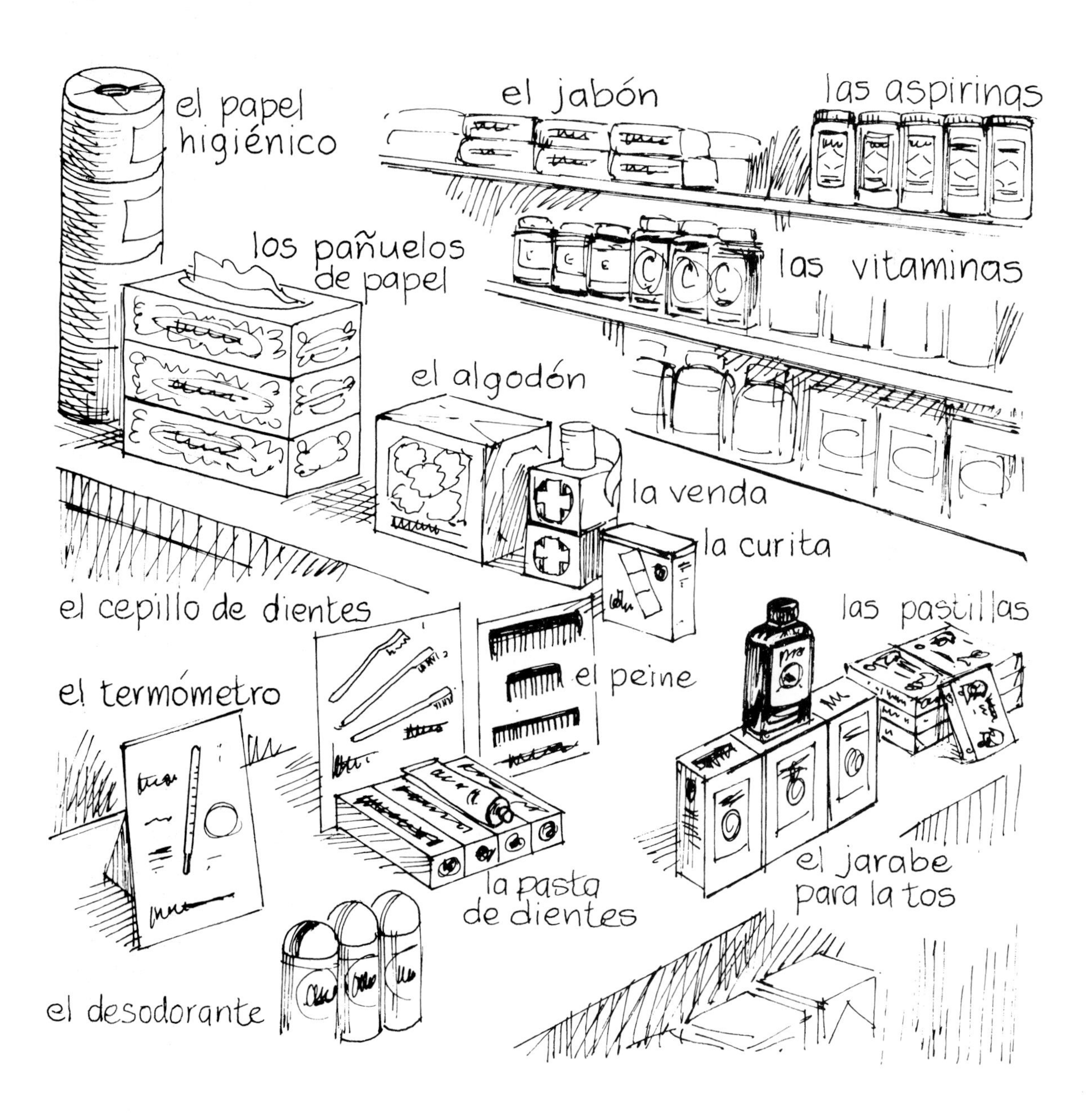

You have learned the names of certain things you can buy in a drugstore. Let's read a conversation between Isabel and a pharmacist. Isabel's little brother is sick and her mother has sent her to the drugstore to buy some things:

FARMACÉUTICO: ¿En qué puedo servirle?
ISABEL: Mi hermanito está enfermo y mi mamá dice que necesita varias medicinas y un termómetro.
FARMACÉUTICO: ¿Tiene fiebre su hermanito?
ISABEL: Creo que sí. Pero no tenemos termómetro para medírsela.
FARMACÉUTICO: ¿Qué más necesita?
ISABEL: Mi hermanito también tose y estornuda mucho. Le duelen la cabeza y la garganta.
FARMACÉUTICO: Es seguro que tiene gripe o un catarro muy fuerte. Dele estas aspirinas cada cuatro horas. Aquí tiene también un jarabe para la tos y unas pastillas para la garganta.
ISABEL: Gracias. Como mi hermanito estornuda mucho, siempre tiene que sonarse las narices. Deme una caja de pañuelos de papel y un paquete de chicle, por favor.
FARMACÉUTICO: Aquí está todo. Pero no comprendo por qué su mamá necesita chicle para su hermano.
ISABEL: El chicle no es para mi hermano. ¡Es para mí!

**la fiebre** *fever*
**medir (i)** *to measure*
**toser** *to cough*
**estornudar** *to sneeze*
**la gripe** *flu*
**el catarro** *cold*
**sonarse las narices** *to blow one's nose*
**la caja** *box*
**el paquete** *pack*

## ACTIVIDADES

**A.** Your mother has sent you to the drugstore with a shopping list. What does she want you to buy?

**1.** ______________________

**3.** ______________________

**2.** ______________________

**4.** ______________________

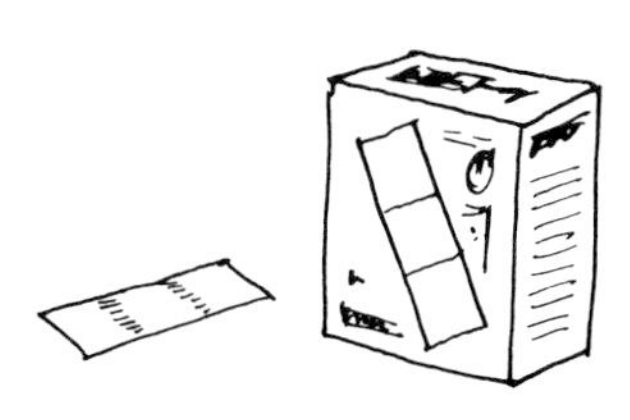

5. ______________________________

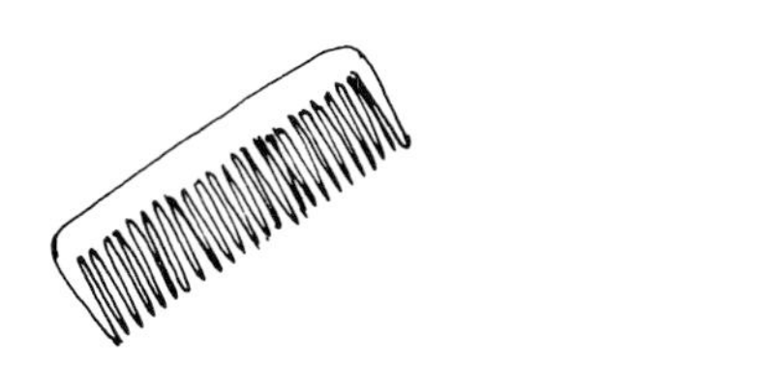

6. ______________________________

7. ______________________________

8. ______________________________

**B.** You are the pharmacist in the neighborhood drugstore. The people in the pictures below seem to be suffering from something. What do they need? (Some people may need more than one item!)

1. ______________________________

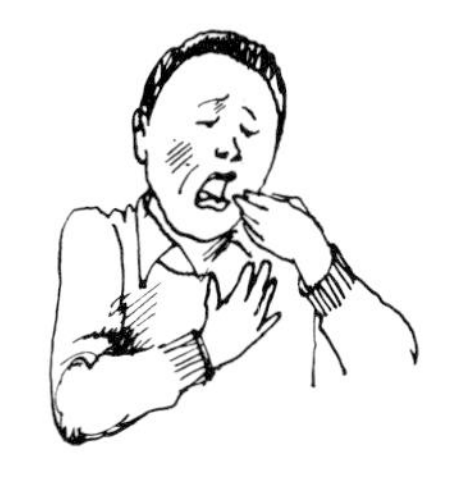

2. ______________________________

3. ______________________________

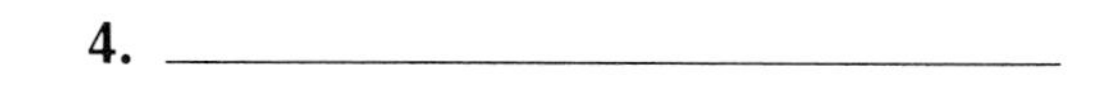

4. ______________________________

5. ______________________________

6. ______________________________

## Los anuncios comerciales

Do you think that advertisements influence your life? Let's read a story about them:

No podemos evitar la influencia de los anuncios comerciales. Están en todas partes — en los periódicos, en las revistas, en la televisión, en los buses y en carteleras por las carreteras. Para bien o para mal, son una parte importante de nuestra cultura y de nuestra vida diaria. Ellos nos dicen qué debemos comer, beber, llevar y comprar para vivir bien. ¿Tiene Ud. dolor de cabeza? Sólo cierta marca de aspirina puede ayudarle. ¿Va Ud. a una cita importante? Entonces necesita cierto desodorante o jabón para «estar seguro». Muchos niños aprenden de memoria las melodías y la letra de los anuncios comerciales antes de aprender a leer y a escribir. A continuación hay varios anuncios comunes. ¿Reconoce algunos?

**evitar** *to avoid*
**la cartelera** *billboard*
**la carretera** *highway*
**la cita** *appointment*
**de memoria** *by heart*
**la letra** *lyrics*

\- - - - - - - - - - - - -

¡Sea diferente!

¿Lo mira la gente, tratando de no reírse, cuando Ud. pasa con su carro? Si piensa que no puede ser la envidia de sus amigos y conocidos, está equivocado. Por sólo unos dólares más, Ud. puede manejar el carro del futuro. ¡No hay otro como él! Nuestros ingenieros diseñaron un automóvil de líneas aerodinámicas que incluye todos los adelantos de la tecnología moderna. Vaya hoy mismo a uno de nuestros distribuidores. ¡Siéntese detrás del volante de la maravilla del siglo!

**tratando** *trying*
**el conocido** *acquaintance*
**equivocado** *wrong, mistaken*
**diseñar** *to design*
**incluir** *to include*
**el adelanto** *advance*

\- - - - - - - - - - - - -

¿Le gusta escuchar música?

Imagínese en la playa, por las calles, en el parque con sus amigos escuchando las canciones más populares. ¿Le gusta la idea? Entonces estamos seguros de que nuestro sistema estereofónico es el que Ud. necesita. Su sonido es único. No sólo puede Ud. escuchar sin problemas sus estaciones de radio favoritas; Ud. puede grabar la música que le gusta. Y, además . . . puede ver sus programas de televisión en cualquier parte. El equipo es portátil. Acérquese a nuestros almacenes para una demostración.

**imaginarse** *to picture oneself*
**el sonido** *sound*
**grabar** *to record*
**portátil** *portable*
**el almacén** *store*

\- - - - - - - - - - - - -

¡Yo tenía miedo de sonreír!
Iba por el mundo con la boca cerrada. No quería mostrar mis dientes amarillentos, manchados de tabaco. Me sentía tímido y extraño. Luego descubrí la pasta de dientes «Dentiblanc» y con ella el secreto de los dientes blancos y limpios. «Dentiblanc» está basada en una fórmula europea secreta de doble acción que deja los dientes brillantes y el aliento agradable. Compre un tubo hoy, y si no queda completamente satisfecho, puede devolvérnoslo. Le enviamos de regreso el dinero que pagó por él. «Dentiblanc» le permite sonreír con confianza otra vez!

**manchado** *stained*
**dejar** *to leave*
**el aliento** *breath*
**devolver** *to return*

## ACTIVIDAD

**C.** Conteste en frases completas:

**1.** ¿Dónde hay anuncios comerciales?

______________________________

**2.** ¿Qué nos dicen los anuncios?

______________________________

**3.** ¿Qué aprenden muchos niños?

______________________________

**4.** ¿Cómo es el automóvil que ofrece el anuncio?

______________________________

**5.** ¿Adónde debe ir para verlo o comprarlo?

______________________________

**6.** ¿Qué sistema le ofrece el anuncio? ¿Cómo es su sonido?

______________________________

**7.** ¿Por qué lo puede escuchar en cualquier parte?

______________________________

**8.** ¿Por qué iba el hombre del anuncio por el mundo con la boca cerrada?

______________________________

**9.** ¿Qué hace la fórmula secreta de la pasta de dientes?

______________________________

**10.** ¿Compra Ud. alguna pasta de dientes especial?

______________________________

**4** You have already learned the direct and indirect object pronouns. There are many times when you need to use them together. Look at the following sentences:

| | |
|---|---|
| **Ella *me* da *la pasta de dientes*.** | *She gives me the toothpaste.* |
| **Ella *me la* da.** | *She gives it to me.* |
| **Tu mamá *te* compró *el peine*.** | *Your mother bought the comb for you.* |
| **Tu mamá *te lo* compró.** | *Your mother bought it for you.* |
| **Juan *nos* prestó *los discos*.** | *John lent us the records.* |
| **Juan *nos los* prestó.** | *John lent them to us.* |

When you use two object pronouns together in Spanish, where do they stand in relation to the verb? ________________. Which pronoun comes first? ________________. Which pronoun comes directly before the verb? ________________. In Spanish, contrary to English, the indirect object pronoun comes before the direct object pronoun and both stand before the verb.

## ACTIVIDAD

**D.** Your little sister is always asking questions. Answer them:

EXAMPLE: ¿Me prestas tu raqueta de tenis?
**Sí, te la presto.**

1. ¿Me compras un helado?
________________
2. ¿Me traes un vaso de agua?
________________
3. ¿Te enseña ella el español?
________________
4. ¿Te compró papá los zapatos?
________________
5. ¿Te vendieron las pastillas para la tos?
________________
6. ¿Me cuentas un cuento?
________________
7. ¿Me prestas tu abrigo?
________________
8. ¿Nos dijo mamá la verdad?
________________
9. ¿Me muestras esos libros?
________________
10. ¿Nos presta tu amigo la bicicleta?
________________

Now study the following examples:

| | |
|---|---|
| **Pablo *le* dio *el peine* a María.** | *Paul gave the comb to Mary.* |
| **Pablo *se lo* dio.** | *Paul gave it to her.* |
| **Yo *le* compré *unos pañuelos* a papá.** | *I bought some handkerchiefs for dad.* |
| **Yo *se los* compré.** | *I bought them for him.* |
| **Mario *les* prestó *las vendas* a ellos.** | *Mario lent them the bandages.* |
| **Mario *se las* prestó.** | *Mario lent them to them.* |
| **Yo *les* digo *la verdad* a Uds.** | *I am telling you the truth.* |
| **Yo *se la* digo.** | *I am telling it to you.* |

Look at the first two sets of examples. What happened to the indirect object pronoun **le** when it was used together with the direct object pronoun **lo** or **los?** ______________________________.

Now look at the last two sets of examples. What happened to the indirect object pronoun **les** when it was used with the direct object pronoun **la** or **las**?

______________________________.

Here's the easy rule: **Se** replaces **le** and **les** before the direct object pronouns **lo, la, los,** and **las**:

**Yo *se lo* (*la*) escribí.**
- *I wrote it to you.*
- *I wrote it to him.*
- *I wrote it to her.*
- *I wrote it to you* (plural).
- *I wrote it to them.*

As you can see, the pronoun **se** can have many meanings. Therefore, the indirect object is normally used together with **se,** either for clarification, for emphasis, or for reinforcement:

| | |
|---|---|
| **¿A quién le diste el periódico?** | *To whom did you give the newspaper?* |
| ***Se* lo di *a mi papá*.** | *I gave it to my father.* |
| **¿*Se* lo diste *a tu papá*?** | *Did you give it to your father?* |
| **Sí, *se* lo di *a él*.** | *Yes, I gave it to him.* |
| **Ella les mostró las fotos a sus amigos.** | *She showed the pictures to her friends.* |
| **Ella *se* las mostró *a ellos*.** | *She showed them to them.* |

## ACTIVIDADES

**E.** You and your friend are playing a game describing what different people do. Confirm your friend's statements:

EXAMPLE: Un médico da medicinas a los pacientes.
**Sí, *se las* da.**

1. Un cartero lleva las cartas a la gente.

______________________________

2. Un ladrón roba las joyas a las mujeres.

______________________________

3. Un mesero sirve la comida a los clientes.

______________________________

4. Una vendedora vende ropa a mi hermana.

______________________________

5. Una profesora enseña el español a la clase.

______________________________

6. Un banco presta dinero a mi papá.

______________________________

7. Una abuela lee historias a los niños.

______________________________

8. Un consejero da consejos al alumno.

______________________________

9. Un policía pone multas a los choferes.

______________________________

10. Un turista escribe tarjetas a los amigos.

______________________________

**F.** Your mother wants to know if you did certain things. Respond negatively:

EXAMPLE: ¿Escribiste la carta a tus abuelos?
**No, no *se la* escribí.**

1. ¿Compraste los cepillos de dientes a tus hermanos?

______________________________

2. ¿Explicaste tu problema al profesor?

______________________________

3. ¿Diste el dinero a Manuel?

______________________________

4. ¿Prestaste tus discos a tus amigos?

______________________________

5. ¿Serviste el café a tu papá?

______________________________

6. ¿Mandaste la tarjeta a tus tíos?

______________________________

7. ¿Escribiste la nota al director?

______________________________

8. ¿Diste las vitaminas a tu hermanita?

______________________________

**G.** Your teacher wants to know if you gave certain things to your classmates. Respond affirmatively:

EXAMPLE: el cuaderno / Rosa
**Sí, se lo di a Rosa.**

1. el libro / Manuel

______________________________

2. los ejercicios / Ud.

______________________________

3. el examen / Juan y Javier

______________________________

4. los lápices / los alumnos

______________________________

5. la regla / Mercedes

______________________________

6. las plumas / todos

______________________________

**6** Do you remember where the single object pronoun stands in affirmative commands? ______________________________

In sentences with an infinitive? ______________________________

or ______________________________.

The same rules apply to double object pronouns:

| | |
|---|---|
| **Dígame la verdad.**<br>**Díga*mela*.** | *Tell me the truth.*<br>*Tell it to me.* |
| **Cuéntele un cuento a Juan.**<br>**Cuénte*selo*.** | *Tell a story to John.*<br>*Tell it to him.* |
| **Quiero escribirle una tarjeta a Josefina.** | *I want to write a postcard to Josefine.* |
| **Quiero escribír*sela*.**<br>or<br>***Se la* quiero escribir.** | *I want to write it to her.* |

The double object pronoun (first the indirect, then the direct) follows an affirmative command and may also follow an infinitive. When the double object pronoun follows and is attached to a command or an infinitive, an accent mark is required on the stressed syllable.

## ACTIVIDADES

**H.** Your friend tells you what she wants to do. Encourage her to do it:

EXAMPLE: Quiero mandarle un regalo a Mercedes.
**Mándaselo.**

1. Necesito comprarme un jarabe para la tos.

_______________

2. Voy a escribirle una carta al director.

_______________

3. Quiero mostrarles esas fotos a mis amigos.

_______________

4. Voy a leerte este artículo.

_______________

5. Necesito darle el dinero a la maestra.

_______________

6. Quiero hacerte varias preguntas.

_______________

7. Voy a contarte mi problema.

_______________

8. Quiero comprarme unos pañuelos de papel.

_______________________________________________

## I.

You are going shopping for holiday presents with a friend. Respond to your friend:

EXAMPLE: Voy a comprarle ese disco a José.
**Sí, debes comprárselo.**

1. Voy a comprarle esa bufanda a mi mamá.

_______________________________________________

2. Voy a comprarme ese radio.

_______________________________________________

3. Voy a comprarles esos juguetes a mis hermanos.

_______________________________________________

4. Voy a comprarte ese casete.

_______________________________________________

5. Voy a comprarle aquel reloj a mi papá.

_______________________________________________

6. Voy a comprarles esos dulces a mis amigos.

_______________________________________________

7. Voy a comprarle esas pantuflas a mi abuela.

_______________________________________________

8. Voy a comprar helado.

_______________________________________________

## J.

Express the following conversation between two friends in Spanish:

1. I need a new bicycle.

_______________________________________________

2. Why don't you buy it?

_______________________________________________

3. I don't have enough money to buy it.

_______________________________________________

4. Your parents can buy it for you.

_______________________________________________

5. They say that I don't need it.

______________________________________________

6. They don't want to give me the money.

______________________________________________

7. My grandparents can buy it for me.

______________________________________________

8. If they buy it for you, can you lend it to me?

______________________________________________

## PREGUNTAS PERSONALES

1. ¿Crees los anuncios comerciales? ¿Por qué?

______________________________________________

2. ¿Tienen los anuncios algún valor? ¿Cuál?

______________________________________________

3. ¿Compras productos que ves en los anuncios de la televisión?

______________________________________________

4. ¿Tienes un equipo estereofónico? ¿Cómo es?

______________________________________________

5. ¿Qué compras en una farmacia cuando tienes gripe?

______________________________________________

## INFORMACIÓN PERSONAL

Write five sentences in Spanish about things you do for other people. Then rewrite the sentences using object pronouns:

EXAMPLE: **Le sirvo el café a mi mamá.**
**Se lo sirvo.**

1. a. ______________________________________________

   b. ______________________________________________

2. a. ______________________________

   b. ______________________________

3. a. ______________________________

   b. ______________________________

4. a. ______________________________

   b. ______________________________

5. a. ______________________________

   b. ______________________________

## COMPOSICIÓN

You are being interviewed for a job in an advertising agency. You are asked to compose a sample advertisement for any product you want (soda, toothpaste, deodorant, and the like) to see how imaginative you are:

______________________________

______________________________

______________________________

______________________________

______________________________

______________________________

______________________________

______________________________

______________________________

______________________________

______________________________

______________________________

______________________________

## DIÁLOGO

An announcer is interviewing you about a particular product:

## CÁPSULA CULTURAL

### Hispanos en los Estados Unidos

Have you ever taken a subway in New York City or driven through Miami, Los Angeles, or San Antonio? If you have, then you have seen many advertisements in Spanish. Why in Spanish and not in English? Depending on your sources, there are between fifteen and twenty million Hispanics in the United States. They are concentrated in certain areas, and the concentration is so high in some cities that Hispanics represent more than half the population. Hispanics in the United States come from different places. In the Southwest, most Hispanics are of Mexican origin. Known as Chicanos or Mexican-Americans, they have the deepest roots in this country.

Americans of Cuban origin represent the majority of Hispanics in Florida. These are fairly recent immigrants, though there have been Hispanic communities in Central and South Florida since the region was discovered by a Spanish conqueror in the sixteenth century.

In New York, Puerto Ricans represent the largest percentage of the Hispanic population. Puerto Ricans have been United States citizens since 1917. There are also large numbers of immigrants from the Dominican Republic, Colombia, and Nicaragua.

How about trying to express your favorite commercial in Spanish for the Hispanic population?

# 14 Un test psicológico

## Personal Pronouns as Objects of Prepositions

**1** ¿Qué tipo de persona es Ud.? ¿Se lleva bien con sus compañeros o pelea con ellos frecuentemente? ¿Es Ud. tímido o agresivo? ¿Tiene confianza en sí mismo? Lea Ud. las situaciones siguientes e indique sus reacciones a ellas. Luego sume los puntos que están al lado de cada respuesta para revelar su carácter.

**pelear** *to fight*

**1** Es sábado por la noche y Ud. quiere ir al cine. Sus amigos quieren ir a otro lugar que a Ud. no le interesa. ¿Qué hace Ud.?
(a) Va al cine sin ellos. ☐ 5
(b) Hace lo que ellos quieren. ☐ 1
(c) Propone otra alternativa que les gusta a todos. ☐ 3

**2** Ud. está en un restaurante. El mesero le da la cuenta y Ud. encuentra un error. Cobraron demasiado. ¿Qué hace Ud.?
(a) Le dice cortésmente al mesero que hay un error en la cuenta. ☐ 4
(b) Paga la cuenta sin decir nada. ☐ 1
(c) Le dice al mesero, «Ud. no sabe sumar». ☐ 5

**cobrar** *to charge*
**demasiado** *too much*

**3** Una persona de importancia le cuenta un chiste que Ud. ya conoce. ¿Qué hace Ud.?
(a) Le interrumpe y le dice que Ud. ya conoce el chiste. ☐ 5
(b) No dice nada. Escucha todo el chiste, pero sólo sonríe. ☐ 2
(c) Piensa que el chiste es bobo, pero se ríe histéricamente al final. ☐ 1

**el chiste** *joke*
**bobo** *silly*

**4** Una amiga acaba de comprar un vestido nuevo. A Ud. no le gusta. Su amiga le pide su opinión. Ud. le dice:
(a) Yo no salgo contigo si llevas esa ropa horrible. ☐ 5
(b) No sé. No soy experto(a) en esas cosas. ☐ 3
(c) Me gusta mucho. Te va muy bien. ☐ 1

**5** Ud. tiene una cita con alguien a las dos. La persona llega a las dos y media y no ofrece ninguna excusa. ¿Qué hace Ud.?
(a) Mira su reloj y pregunta: «¿Qué pasó?» ☐ 4
(b) Saluda sin mencionar el retraso. ☐ 1
(c) Se enoja y le dice a la persona que es maleducada. ☐ 5

**el retraso** *delay*
**enojarse** *to get angry*
**maleducado** *ill-mannered, rude*

**6** Ud. está en una fiesta. Una persona muy aburrida lo atrapa en un rincón y no para de hablar. ¿Qué hace Ud.?
(a) Le dice: «Perdón, pero tengo que ir al baño». ☐ 4
(b) Escucha lo que dice la persona, pero piensa en otra cosa. ☐ 3
(c) Trata de mostrar mucho interés en la conversación. ☐ 2

**atrapar** *to trap*

**7** Alguien le ofrece un puesto en una oficina. El trabajo ofrece buen sueldo y muchas oportunidades. Pero Ud. no tiene ninguna experiencia. ¿Qué hace?
(a) Acepta el puesto sin decir nada. ☐ 5
(b) Explica que no tiene la preparación necesaria. ☐ 3
(c) No acepta el puesto. ☐ 1

**el puesto** *job*
**el sueldo** *salary*
**la preparación** *training*

**8** Sus padres le dicen que no puede salir el fin de semana con sus amigos. ¿Qué hace Ud.?
(a) Sale con ellos sin permiso. ☐ 5
(b) Trata de resolver el asunto con sus padres. ☐ 4
(c) Acepta lo que dicen sus padres. ☐ 2

**tratar de** *to try to*
**el asunto** *matter*

**9** Un compañero de clase le pide prestados cinco dólares. Ud. sabe que él generalmente no devuelve el dinero que pide prestado. ¿Qué hace Ud.?
(a) Le presta un dólar y le dice: «No llevo más dinero conmigo». ☐ 2
(b) Le presta los cinco dólares. ☐ 1
(c) No le da nada. ☐ 5

**pedir prestado** *to borrow*

**10** Ud. hace una cita para ir a un juego de pelota por la noche. Pero al volver a casa se acuerda de que tiene un examen importante al día siguiente y tiene que estudiar. ¿Qué hace Ud.?
(a) Trata de estudiar todo lo posible antes del juego. ☐ 1
(b) Llama al amigo y le dice que está enfermo y no puede salir. ☐ 2
(c) Llama al amigo y le explica que tiene un examen y que no va a salir porque tiene que estudiar. ☐ 4

**acordarse (ue)** *to remember*

Interpretación del test:

39–48 puntos: Tiene un carácter fuerte e independiente. Está muy seguro de sí mismo. Es una persona muy decidida, directa e impulsiva. Muchas veces no es diplomático y puede ofender a la gente. Ud. cree que es honesto, pero la gente puede creer que Ud. es arrogante o antipático.

**decidido** *determined*
**antipático** *unpleasant*

27–38 puntos: Ud. es amable y simpático y generalmente se lleva bien con todo el mundo. Es paciente y sabe tratar a la gente. Tiene un carácter bastante fuerte pero es diplomático cuando es necesario.

**amable** *kind, nice*
**tratar** *to treat*

12–26 puntos: Ud. es reservado y un poco tímido. Muchas veces tiene miedo de decir la verdad. Nunca ofende a nadie. Trate de ser más dinámico y de tener más confianza en sí mismo.

## ACTIVIDADES

**A.** Conteste con frases completas:

1. ¿Qué tipo de test es éste?

______________________________

2. ¿Qué revela este test?

______________________________

3. ¿Qué hay al lado de cada respuesta?

______________________________

4. ¿Qué hay que hacer con los puntos?

______________________________

5. ¿Qué carácter tiene una persona que recibe más de 39 puntos?

______________________________

6. ¿Qué problemas puede tener esa persona?

______________________________

7. Según el test, ¿cómo es la persona que recibe 30 puntos?

______________________________

8. ¿Qué problemas puede tener una persona tímida?

______________________________

9. ¿Qué necesita una persona tímida?

______________________________

10. ¿Cuántos puntos recibió Ud.? ¿Refleja el test su personalidad?

______________________________

**B.** Using the adjectives found in the test, write one that, in your opinion, best describes the following people:

1. Su profesor(a) de español ______________
2. Su mamá ______________
3. Su papá ______________
4. Su hermano(a) ______________

5. El director de la escuela ______
6. El Presidente de los Estados Unidos ______
7. El alumno o la alumna que se sienta delante de Ud. ______
8. El alumno o la alumna que se sienta detrás de Ud. ______
9. Su mejor amigo(a) ______
10. Ud. ______

**C.** Different people like to do different things. Here is a list of activities. Check **Sí** for those you like and **No** for those you don't. Then compare your answers with those of your classmates. Be prepared to explain the reasons for your answers!

| | Sí | No |
|---|---|---|
| 1. Escuchar la radio | ____ | ____ |
| 2. Mirar la televisión | ____ | ____ |
| 3. Ir al cine | ____ | ____ |
| 4. Ayudar en casa | ____ | ____ |
| 5. Ir de compras a las tiendas | ____ | ____ |
| 6. Leer revistas | ____ | ____ |
| 7. Salir con los amigos / las amigas | ____ | ____ |
| 8. Ir a fiestas | ____ | ____ |
| 9. Practicar deportes | ____ | ____ |
| 10. Comer en restaurantes | ____ | ____ |
| 11. Hablar mucho por teléfono | ____ | ____ |
| 12. Dormir hasta mediodía | ____ | ____ |
| 13. Quedarse solo(a) en casa | ____ | ____ |
| 14. Manejar un carro | ____ | ____ |
| 15. Estudiar los fines de semana | ____ | ____ |

You have been learning about personal pronouns that are direct or indirect objects of the verb. Other personal pronouns are used after prepositions. You already know most of them. First, let's recall the most common prepositions in Spanish:

**a** *to*
**cerca de** *near*
**con** *with*
**contra** *against*
**de** *of, from*
**debajo de** *under, beneath*
**delante de** *in front of*
**detrás de** *behind*
**en** *in, on, at*
**hacia** *toward*
**hasta** *as far as; up to; until*
**lejos de** *far from*
**para** *for*
**por** *for*
**sin** *without*
**sobre** *on, over*

Now look at these sentences:

| | |
|---|---|
| **Juan vive *cerca de nosotros.*** | *John lives near us.* |
| **Voy a salir *sin ellos* (*ellas*).** | *I am going to go out without them.* |
| **La casa está *lejos de Ud.* (*Uds.*).** | *The house is far from you.* |
| **Tú vas de compras *con él* (*ella*).** | *You go shopping with him (her).* |

What do you notice about the pronouns that follow the prepositions?

__________________________________________________.

Right, they are the same as the subject pronouns.

## ACTIVIDAD

**D.** Replace the expression in bold type by an appropriate pronoun:

EXAMPLE: Les llevo la comida a **Jorge y a Juan.**
**Les llevo la comida a *ellos.***

1. Yo estudio con **María.**

________________________________________

2. ¿Quieres trabajar para **mi padre?**

________________________________________

3. Siempre hablan de **Elisa y de Juana.**

________________________________________

4. No salgas sin **tu hermana.**

________________________________________

5. Enrique se sienta detrás de **Josefina.**

________________________________________

6. El gato está debajo de **la cama.**

_______________

7. El avión vuela sobre **los edificios.**

_______________

8. Mi hermana quiere vivir lejos de **mis padres y yo.**

_______________

**3** Did you notice in Section 2 that we did not use the pronouns **yo** and **tú?** That's because they are the only ones that change after a preposition:

| | |
|---|---|
| **Este vestido es para *ti*.** | *This dress is for you.* |
| **No puedes salir sin *mí*.** | *You can't go out without me.* |

Furthermore, when used with the preposition **con, mi** and **ti** form a new word:

| | |
|---|---|
| **Venga Ud. *conmigo*.** | *Come with me.* |
| **El director quiere hablar *contigo*.** | *The principal wants to speak with you.* |

## ACTIVIDADES

**E.** You went shopping and your mother is trying to guess for whom you bought presents:

EXAMPLE: El suéter es para Luis, ¿verdad?
**Sí, es para él.**

1. La blusa es para Ana, ¿verdad?

_______________

2. Los dulces son para tu hermano y para ti, ¿verdad?

_______________

3. Esa camisa es para ti, ¿verdad?

_______________

4. Los pantalones son para tu papá, ¿verdad?

_______________

5. Los chocolates son para papá y para mí, ¿verdad?

_______________

6. Este regalo es para tus padres, ¿verdad?

_______________

**F.** You are in a contrary mood today. Your father is trying to convince you to go out and do something:

EXAMPLE: Los muchachos van a jugar al fútbol.
**No quiero jugar con ellos.**

1. Elena va a ir al parque.

_______________

2. Tu hermano va a jugar al tenis.

_______________

3. Tu mamá y yo vamos a ir al cine.

_______________

4. Yo voy a ir al supermercado.

_______________

5. Gloria y María van a nadar.

_______________

6. Tus amigos van a jugar al béisbol.

_______________

**G.** Answer your little sister's questions, using prepositional pronouns:

1. ¿Vas a salir con Mónica el sábado por la noche?

_______________

2. ¿Puedo salir con Uds.?

_______________

3. ¿Quién se sienta delante de ti en la clase?

_______________

4. ¿Puedo ir contigo a la escuela?

_______________

5. ¿Quieres ir conmigo al cine?

_______________

6. ¿Puedes devolver este libro a la biblioteca por mí?

_______________

7. ¿Compraste esa camiseta para ti?

_______________

8. ¿Vas a salir sin mí?

______________________________

## PREGUNTAS PERSONALES

1. ¿Crees que los tests psicológicos tienen valor? ¿Por qué?

______________________________

2. ¿Tomaste un test psicológico alguna vez? ¿Cuándo?

______________________________

3. ¿Dices siempre la verdad? ¿Cuándo no la dices?

______________________________

4. ¿Piensas que una persona debe ser agresiva? ¿Por qué?

______________________________

5. ¿Crees que es necesario llevarse bien con todo el mundo?

______________________________

## INFORMACIÓN PERSONAL

Write six adjectives that describe your character:

______________________________

______________________________

## COMPOSICIÓN

You have been assigned to construct a personality test that will determine a person's ability to get along with others. Make up five questions for the test:

1. ______________________________

2. ______________________________

3. ______________________________

4. ______________________________

5. ______________________________

## DIÁLOGO

You have gone to the guidance counselor for advice. Here are his answers. Complete the dialog:

# CÁPSULA CULTURAL

## ¿Cómo somos?

We tend to have stereotyped ideas about cultures and peoples we don't know too well. How many times, for example, have we seen Mexicans represented as peasants with large sombreros, walking with a burro or sleeping the siesta, or Spaniards as bullfighters or Flamenco dancers? The reality is different: Within each country, people's characters change from region to region and are affected as well by their cultural backgrounds.

An American can recognize most of the time where another American comes from, the South, the West, the East, and so on. The same thing happens in Spain and Latin America. Geography affects people's characters: those who live in the high elevations of the Andes, for example, tend to be quieter, slower, more reserved and melancholic than the people in the coastal regions. Coastal people are generally more open, dynamic, gregarious, impulsive, and they speak faster. The people who live in the large plains of South America are known for their independence and self-reliance. There's a Venezuelan song that represents their philosophy of life. Some of the lyrics say: **"Sobre mi caballo yo, sobre yo mi sombrero y sobre mi sombrero Dios."**

In Mexico and Central America, there are also great differences in attitude between the people of the "interior" and those of the coastal regions. In Spain, people from Andalucía (where the flamenco comes from) reflect their Mediterranean, Moorish, and gypsy roots. The people from Madrid are more formal. The Basques and the people from Cataluña are proud and independent and have tried to maintain their own languages.

All these differences are reflected in their music and in their art. That's why there is such a great variety of both.

# 15 En la mueblería

## Cardinal and Ordinal Numbers

### 1 Vocabulario

## ACTIVIDADES

**A.** Does this kitchen look all right to you? There are at least eight items you don't normally find in a kitchen. What are they?

1. ______________________  5. ______________________

2. ______________________  6. ______________________

3. ______________________  7. ______________________

4. ______________________  8. ______________________

**B.** You have just won a prize offered by a furniture store, and you can choose ten items to furnish your home. Which ten would you choose?

1. ______________________  6. ______________________

2. ______________________  7. ______________________

3. ______________________  8. ______________________

4. ______________________  9. ______________________

5. ______________________  10. ______________________

## ¡Qué precios!

Let's read a story about a couple who goes shopping for furniture. See if you can figure out how much money they spend:

ANITA: Ricardo, me da pena invitar a alguien al apartamento. Todos nuestros muebles son tan viejos . . . ¡Vamos a comprar muebles nuevos!

RICARDO: Está bien. Pero hoy en día todo es muy caro. No quiero gastar una fortuna en cosas innecesarias.

**caro** *expensive*
**gastar** *to spend (money)*

ANITA: Para mí una casa bonita es una necesidad. Además, hay una venta especial de verano en «La Casa Elegante», la mueblería más grande de la ciudad.

**la venta** *sale*

RICARDO: Bueno, vamos a ver qué hay.

Un poco más tarde, la pareja llega a la mueblería. En el primer piso están los muebles de dormitorio.

ANITA: Me encanta ese juego de dormitorio. Es muy moderno.

**el juego** *set*

RICARDO: Pero mira el precio, quinientos cincuenta dólares.

ANITA: ¿Qué importa? Es un sueño.

**el sueño** *dream*

En el segundo piso hay muebles de sala.

ANITA: Vamos a comprar ese sofá blanco, las dos butacas y la mesita.

RICARDO: Ay, no, mujer. Cuestan un ojo de la cara — casi seiscientos dólares.

**costar un ojo de la cara** *to cost a small fortune*

ANITA: Para eso tenemos dinero, mi cielo, para gastarlo.

En el tercer piso están los muebles de comedor.

ANITA: Quiero esa mesa con las seis sillas lujosas.

RICARDO: Pero, el precio, el precio . . . No haces caso del precio, mi amor. Cuestan casi setecientos dólares.

**hacer caso** *to pay attention*

ANITA: Amorcito, no seas tacaño.

**tacaño** *stingy*

Al final, Anita hace una lista de todos los muebles que quiere y se la muestra a un vendedor.

VENDEDOR: Bueno, señora. El precio de todo con el impuesto del seis por ciento y menos el descuento del veinte y cinco por ciento es de mil trescientos ochenta y nueve dólares.

**el impuesto** *tax*
**por ciento** *percent*

RICARDO: ¡Casi mil cuatrocientos dólares! ¡No puedo gastar tanto dinero, no soy millonario! Con esos precios, prefiero vivir con mis muebles viejos.

VENDEDOR: Señor, es evidente que Ud. es un hombre inteligente y muy prudente. Por eso, podemos llegar a un acuerdo. Les propongo un trato especial a Ud. y a su encantadora mujer. No tiene que pagarme sino quinientos dólares por lo pronto. El resto lo puede pagar a plazos, en pequeños pagos mensuales.

**el trato** *deal*
**por lo pronto** *for now*
**a plazos** *in installments*
**mensual** *monthly*

RICARDO: Claro, eso ya es otra cosa. Deme el contrato para firmarlo. Tú ves, Anita, hay que pensar antes de hacer una compra. Así se ahorra dinero.

**firmar** *to sign*
**ahorrar** *to save*

Al salir de la tienda, Anita lee el contrato: quinientos dólares de contado y después setenta dólares al mes durante diez y ocho meses.

**de contado** *cash down*

ANITA: Oh, sí, Ricardo. ¡Ahorraste mucho dinero!

## ACTIVIDAD

**C.** Conteste en frases completas:

**1.** ¿Por qué quiere Anita comprar muebles nuevos?

______________________________

**2.** ¿Dónde hay una venta especial?

______________________________

**3.** ¿En qué piso están los muebles de dormitorio?

______________________________

**4.** ¿Cuánto cuesta el juego de muebles que le gustó a Anita?

______________________________

**5.** ¿Qué hay en el segundo piso?

______________________________

**6.** ¿Qué quiere comprar Anita allá?

______________________________

7. ¿Qué quiere Anita para el comedor?

_______________

8. ¿Cuál es el precio de todo lo que compran?

_______________

9. ¿Cuánto tiene que pagar Ricardo de contado?

_______________

10. ¿Cuánto paga Ricardo por los muebles con el trato especial del vendedor?

_______________

You have already learned the numbers to 100. Do you remember them?

1 **uno**
2 **dos**
3 **tres**
4 **cuatro**
5 **cinco**
6 **seis**
7 **siete**
8 **ocho**
9 **nueve**
10 **diez**
11 **once**
12 **doce**
13 **trece**
14 **catorce**
15 **quince**
16 **diez y seis**
17 **diez y siete**
18 **diez y ocho**
19 **diez y nueve**
20 **veinte**
21 **veinte y uno**
30 **treinta**
32 **treinta y dos**
40 **cuarenta**
43 **cuarenta y tres**
50 **cincuenta**
54 **cincuenta y cuatro**
60 **sesenta**
65 **sesenta y cinco**
70 **setenta**
76 **setenta y seis**
80 **ochenta**
87 **ochenta y siete**
90 **noventa**
98 **noventa y ocho**
100 **ciento**

Now let's learn to express numbers over 100. It's very easy:

200 **doscientos**
300 **trescientos**
400 **cuatrocientos**
500 **quinientos**
600 **seiscientos**
700 **setecientos**
800 **ochocientos**
900 **novecientos**
1.000 **mil**
100.000 **cien mil**
200.000 **doscientos mil**
1.000.000 **un millón (de)**

## ACTIVIDADES

**D.** You are a clerk in a large hotel. Several people come to check in. Tell them their room number and then write it in Spanish:

EXAMPLE: Sra. Ramírez / 118
**Sra. Ramírez, su cuarto es el ciento diez y ocho.**

1. Doctor López / 213

_______________

2. Srta. Gómez / 304

_______________

3. Sr. y Sra. Pérez / 521

_______________

4. Doctora Peláez / 417

_______________

5. Srta. Casas / 745

_______________

6. Sres. Ramos / 132

_______________

7. Sra. Montes / 866

_______________

8. Srta. Gallo / 901

_______________

9. Sr. Torres / 658

_______________

**E.** Match the numbers on the left with the numerals on the right:

| | | |
|---|---|---|
| 1. ciento ochenta y cuatro | _______ | 523 |
| 2. doscientos cincuenta y seis | _______ | 120.000 |
| 3. cuatrocientos ochenta y nueve | _______ | 10.730 |
| 4. ochocientos quince | _______ | 256 |
| 5. quinientos veinte y tres | _______ | 100.340 |
| 6. mil quinientos cincuenta | _______ | 489 |
| 7. tres mil novecientos diez | _______ | 1.550 |
| 8. diez mil setecientos treinta | _______ | 815 |
| 9. ciento veinte mil | _______ | 184 |
| 10. cien mil trescientos cuarenta | _______ | 3.910 |

**F.** Write in Spanish the year in which the following things happened:

EXAMPLE: Cristóbal Colón descubrió América en 1492.
**mil cuatrocientos noventa y dos**

1. La independencia de los Estados Unidos se declaró en 1776.

______________________________

2. Ponce de León descubrió la Florida en 1512.

______________________________

3. Jorge Washington nació en 1732.

______________________________

4. La guerra de independencia mexicana comenzó en 1810.

______________________________

5. La Organización de las Naciones Unidas se estableció en 1945.

______________________________

6. Yo nací en . . .

______________________________

**4** The numbers 200 to 900 agree in gender with the nouns they accompany:

| | |
|---|---|
| **trescient*as* mesitas** | **trescient*os* escritorios** |
| **ochocient*as* cincuenta alfombras** | **ochocient*os* cincuenta floreros** |

What happens to the number 100? Look at these examples:

| | |
|---|---|
| ***cien* lámparas** | ***cien* espejos** |
| **ciento veinte lámparas** | **ciento veinte espejos** |

***cien* mil libros**
***cien* millones de habitantes**

**Ciento** becomes **cien** before any noun, masculine or feminine, and before the numbers **mil** and **millones.**

## ACTIVIDAD

**G.** Write the numbers in Spanish for the numerals in parentheses:

1. (500) ______________________________ casas.

2. (1,400) ______________________________ alumnos.

3. (750) ______________________________ personas.

4. (100,000) ______________________________ soldados.

5. (365) ______________________________ días.

6. (872) ______________________________ páginas.

7. (680) ______________________________ camas.

8. (250,000,000) ______________________________ de norteamericanos.

Let's look again at **el número *uno***:

> **Quiero comprar *un* sofá y *una* butaca.**
> *I want to buy one sofa and one easy chair.*
> **Anoche leí *veinte y un* capítulos y escribí *treinta y una* páginas.**
> *Last night I read twenty-one chapters and wrote thirty-one pages.*

**Uno** becomes **un** before a masculine singular noun. It changes to **una** before a feminine singular noun.

## ACTIVIDADES

**H.** The teacher is making a list of materials needed for the class. Write the numbers in Spanish:

1. (21) ______________________________ libros.
2. (51) ______________________________ lápices.
3. (31) ______________________________ reglas.
4. (61) ______________________________ cuadernos.
5. (41) ______________________________ plumas.
6. (71) ______________________________ mesas.

**I.** You are the teller in the foreign-exchange division of a bank. Several people need different types of currency. Can you help them?

EXAMPLE: Sr. López / 1.120 dólares
**El Sr. López necesita mil ciento veinte dólares.**

1. Sra. Martínez / 350.100 pesos mexicanos

_______________

2. Srta. Gómez / 8.671 pesetas

_______________

3. Sr. Pérez / 989 dólares

_______________

4. Sr. Ramos / 25.500 pesos colombianos

_______________

5. Sra. Vélez / 10.431 australes

_______________

6. Doctor Villa / 5.500 pesetas

_______________

**6** Do you remember the adjectives **primero** and **tercero**? They are ordinal numbers. Ordinal numbers are used to rank people or things and put them in a certain order. Ordinal numbers are adjectives and agree in number and gender with the noun they describe:

| | | |
|---|---|---|
| **primero** | **1º** | *first* |
| **segundo** | **2º** | *second* |
| **tercero** | **3º** | *third* |
| **cuarto** | **4º** | *fourth* |
| **quinto** | **5º** | *fifth* |
| **sexto** | **6º** | *sixth* |
| **séptimo** | **7º** | *seventh* |
| **octavo** | **8º** | *eighth* |
| **noveno** | **9º** | *ninth* |
| **décimo** | **10º** | *tenth* |

After ten, cardinal numbers are normally used:

**Carlos *Quinto* fue un rey muy importante.**
*Charles the Fifth was a very important king.*
**Vivo en la calle *segunda* con avenida *cuarta.***
*I live on second street and fourth avenue.*

**Alfonso *Trece* fue un rey español.**
*Alphonso the Thirteenth was a Spanish king.*
**Él vive en la calle *doce* con avenida *diez y ocho.***
*He lives on twelfth street and eighteenth avenue.*

## ACTIVIDADES

**J.** You are going shopping in a large department store. On which floor do you find the following things?

EXAMPLE: muebles / 4º
**Los muebles están en el cuarto piso.**

1. ropa de hombre / 8º

_______________

2. ropa de mujer / 5º

_______________

3. televisores / 9º

_______________

4. cafetería / 2º

_______________

5. zapatos / 3º

_______________

6. toallas / 6º

_______________

7. sombreros / 1º

_______________

**K.** There were tryouts for the track team in your school. You are telling the order of arrival in the first race:

EXAMPLE: Rosa / 1ª
**Rosa fue la primera.**

1. Jorge / 3º

_______________

2. María / 5ª

_______________

3. Raúl / 2º

_______________

4. Mercedes / 4ª

_______________

5. Josefina / 8ª

_______________

6. Mario / 9º

_______________

7. Elisa / 7ª

_______________

8. Miguel / 6º

_______________

## DIÁLOGO

You are in a furniture store. Tell the salesman what you want:

## PREGUNTAS PERSONALES

1. ¿Qué muebles hay en la sala de tu casa?

_______________

2. ¿Crees que es mejor comprar cosas a crédito o al contado?

_______________

3. ¿Qué es un tacaño? ¿Eres tú tacaño?

_______________

4. ¿Qué por ciento pagas de impuesto cuando compras ropa?

_______________

5. ¿Qué puedes comprar con mil dólares?

_______________

## INFORMACIÓN PERSONAL

1. Voy a terminar el high school en el año _______________.
2. Tengo una radio que costó _______________.
3. El modelo de carro que más me gusta cuesta _______________.
4. Mi padre nació en el año _______________.
5. Yo nací en el año _______________.

## COMPOSICIÓN

Describe your room. Tell what kind of furniture you have, when it was bought, how much you think it cost, whether you like it or not, what color the curtains, the rug, and the walls are.

_______________

_______________

_______________

_______________

_______________

# CÁPSULA CULTURAL

## Fechas importantes

The Fourth of July and Washington's Birthday are two of the holidays celebrated in the United States. Spain and all the Latin American countries also have national holidays. Some are common to all or most countries, while others are individual to each country.

October 12, for example, is a national holiday in the whole Spanish-speaking world. It commemorates the discovery of the New World and is called **Día de la Hispanidad, Día del Descubrimiento de América,** or **Día de la Raza,** depending on the country. December 25 and January 1 are also holidays throughout the Hispanic world. Labor Day (**el Día del Trabajo**) is celebrated on May 1, except in Puerto Rico, where the American tradition is followed.

Many wars of independence in Latin America started in 1810. The actual day of celebration is different in every country. For example, in Mexico, it's September 16; in Colombia, July 20; in Chile, September 18; in the Dominican Republic, February 27.

Each country also has holidays that commemorate other special historical events (like May 5 in Mexico, a victory against the French invasion in the nineteenth century; or November 19 in Puerto Rico, the day the island was discovered). There are, in addition, many Catholic holidays because the Catholic Church has played an important role in Spain and Latin America.

Which is your favorite holiday? Why?

# Repaso III (Lecciones 11–15)

## Lección 11

**a.** Direct object pronouns:

| | |
|---|---|
| **me** *me* | **nos** *us* |
| **te** *you* (familiar) | |
| **lo** *you* (formal), *him, it* (masculine) | **los** *them, you* (masculine plural) |
| **la** *you* (formal), *him, it* (feminine) | **las** *them, you* (feminine plural) |

**b.** The direct object pronoun normally comes directly before the verb:

**Yo *te* vi ayer.** *I saw you yesterday.*
**Él no *la* llamó.** *He didn't call her.*

There are two situations, however, in which direct object pronouns take a different position:

1. In affirmative commands, the direct object pronoun follows the verb and is attached to it. An accent mark is required on the stressed syllable:

   **Llláma*me*.** *Call me.*
   **Acompáña*los*.** *Accompany them.*

2. When the direct object pronoun is used with an infinitive, it may follow and is then attached to the infinitive, or it may precede the conjugated form of the other verb:

   **Quiero comprar*la*.**
   ***La* quiero comprar.** } *I want to buy it.*

## Lección 12

**a.** Indirect object pronouns:

| | |
|---|---|
| **me** (*to, for*) *me* | **nos** (*to, for*) *us* |
| **te** (*to, for*) *you* | |
| **le** (*to, for*) *you* (formal), *him, her* | **les** (*to, for*) *you* (plural), *them* |

**b.** The indirect object pronoun normally comes before the verb:

***Te* escribo una carta.** *I write a letter to you.*

Like the direct object pronoun, the indirect object pronoun follows the verb and is attached to it in affirmative commands:

**Cómpra*le* el regalo.** *Buy him the present.*

When used with an infinitive, the indirect object pronoun may follow the infinitive and is then attached to it, or it may precede the conjugated form of the other verb:

**Quiero comprar*le* un regalo.**
***Le* quiero comprar un regalo.** } *I want to buy him a present.*

**c.** In Spanish, the indirect object pronoun is normally used even when the indirect object noun is expressed:

***Le* escribí una carta *a mi amigo*.** *I wrote a letter to my friend.*

## Lección 13

**a.** When using two object pronouns in Spanish, the indirect object pronoun comes before the direct object pronoun and both stand before the verb:

**La profesora *nos lo* dio.** *The teacher gave it to us.*

**b. Se** replaces **le** and **les** before the direct object pronouns **lo, la, los,** and **las:**

**Yo *se lo* di.** *I gave it to him / her / you / them.*

For clarification, emphasis, or reinforcement, the indirect object is normally used together with **se**:

**Yo *se* lo di *a ella*.** *I gave it to her.*

**c.** The double object pronoun (first the indirect, then the direct) follows an affirmative command and may also follow an infinitive. When the double object pronoun follows and is attached to a command or an infinitive, an accent mark is required on the stressed syllable:

**Tráe*melo*.** *Bring it to me.*
**Tengo que comprár*tela*.**
***Te la* tengo que comprar.** } *I have to buy it for you.*

## Lección 14

**a.** Common prepositions:

| | | |
|---|---|---|
| **a** *to* | **con** *for* | **de** *of, from* |
| **cerca de** *near* | **contra** *with* | **debajo de** *under* |

| | | |
|---|---|---|
| **delante de** *in front of* | **hasta** *as far as, until, up to* | **por** *for* |
| **detrás de** *behind* | **lejos de** *far from* | **sin** *without* |
| **en** *in, on, at* | **para** *for* | **sobre** *on, over* |
| **hacia** *toward* | | |

**b.** Personal pronouns used after prepositions:

| | |
|---|---|
| **mí** | **nosotros** |
| **ti** | |
| **Ud.** | **Uds.** |
| **él** | **ellos** |
| **ella** | **ellos** |

**c.** **Mí** and **ti** form a new word with the preposition **con**: **conmigo, contigo:**

**Ella fue al cine *conmigo.*** *She went to the movies with me.*

## Lección 15

**a.**

| | | | | | |
|---|---|---|---|---|---|
| 200 | **doscientos** | 600 | **seiscientos** | 1.000 | **mil** |
| 300 | **trescientos** | 700 | **setecientos** | 100.000 | **cien mil** |
| 400 | **cuatrocientos** | 800 | **ochocientos** | 200.000 | **doscientos mil** |
| 500 | **quinientos** | 900 | **novecientos** | 1.000.000 | **un millón (de)** |

The numbers 200 to 900 agree in gender with the nouns they accompany:

**El libro tiene trescientas páginas.**

**b.** **Ciento** becomes **cien** before any noun, masculine or feminine, and before the numbers **mil** and **millones:**

**Anoche leí *cien* páginas del libro.**
**La biblioteca tiene *cien* mil libros.**

**c.** **Uno** becomes **un** before a masculine singular noun. It changes to **una** before a feminine singular noun:

**Enero tiene treinta y *un* días.**
**En la clase hay cuarenta y *una* sillas.**

**d.** Ordinal numbers:

| | | | |
|---|---|---|---|
| 1° | **primero** | 6° | **sexto** |
| 2° | **segundo** | 7° | **séptimo** |
| 3° | **tercero** | 8° | **octavo** |
| 4° | **cuarto** | 9° | **noveno** |
| 5° | **quinto** | 10° | **décimo** |

After ten, cardinal numbers are normally used.

Ordinal numbers are adjectives and agree in gender and number with the noun they describe:

**Vivo en el *segundo* edificio de la avenida *quinta*.**

e. **Primero** and **tercero** drop the final **o** before a singular masculine noun:

**Terminé el *primer* capítulo.**
**Subí al *tercer* piso.**

## ACTIVIDADES

**A.** **¿Cuáles son las diferencias entre los dos carros?** There are several differences between these two cars. Can you spot at least five and write them down?

______________________________

______________________________

______________________________

______________________________

______________________________

**B.** Unscramble the words. Then unscramble the letters to find out what Carmen bought in the clothing store:

A S T I E C A M

T A R C E A R

A P Z A LL I T A S

S O B A T E D L E P I

I M A P A J

**Carmen compró un**

**C.** Find the hidden objects. Hidden in the picture, there are 10 items that you can purchase in a drugstore. Circle them in the picture and then list them below:

______________________________

______________________________

______________________________

______________________________

______________________________

**D.** Insert in the puzzle 21 adjectives that can describe a person. Each adjective starts with a different letter, from A to V. Letters at the intersections between two adjectives give further clues:

**E.** Your mother asks you to bring in one of the articles hanging on the line. Pick it out from her description. Place an X in the correct circle:

Tiene un bolsillo pequeño.
Tiene mangas.
Es una prenda de mujer.

Tiene botones.
Tiene cuello.
La tela es a rayas.

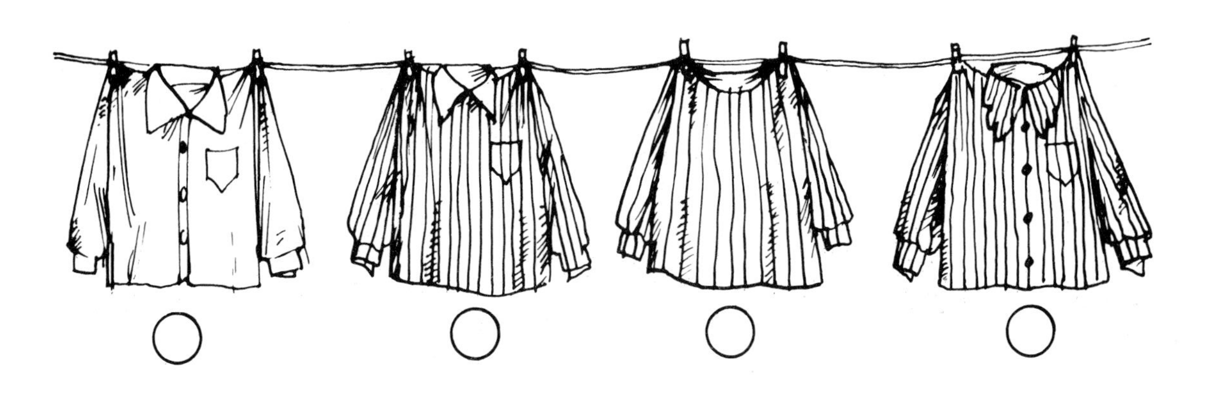

## F. Crucigrama

HORIZONTALES

1. La usas en el cuello para el frío.
4. _____ de dientes. (pl.)
9. Pronombre de complemento (*object*) directo.
10. Extensión de agua con tierra por todos los lados.
11. Automóvil.
12. La pones en la ventana.
13. La usas después de bañarte.
14. Parte superior del cuerpo.
15. En la farmacia compras jarabe para la _____.
17. Lo usas para dormir.
20. Pronombre que lleva preposición.
21. No tienen mangas y los usas sobre la camisa o la blusa.

VERTICALES

1. Las usas en los pies.
2. Lo usas para poner flores.
3. Sirve para cubrir el piso.
4. Lugar donde preparas la comida.
5. Cristal que se pone al frente del carro.
6. Está alrededor de la rueda del carro.
7. Material para hacer ropa.
8. Pones las manos en el _____ para manejar.
15. Es reservado. Tiene miedo.
16. La tienen las ambulancias y los carros de la policía.
17. Preposición.
18. Líquido transparente necesario para vivir.

HORIZONTALES

**23.** Las usas para jugar al tenis.
**25.** Lo usas para peinarte.
**26.** Imperativo de **tomar.**
**27.** En este momento.
**28.** Te lavas con agua y ____.
**31.** Negación.
**33.** Preposición.
**34.** Imperativo de **parar.**
**35.** La cuenta no está bien. Tiene un ____.
**37.** Imperativo de **ir.**
**38.** Parte del carro para protegerlo si choca.
**39.** Preposición que expresa el fin de algo.
**41.** Imperativo de **ver.**
**42.** Preposición que indica movimiento.
**43.** Terminación verbal.
**45.** Duermes en ella.
**46.** Afirmación.
**47.** Deme un ____ de agua.
**50.** Las usas en los pies dentro de la casa.
**51.** Tienda de muebles.

VERTICALES

**19.** Contrario de después.
**21.** Cuento para reírse.
**22.** Te miras en el ____.
**24.** Butacas.
**25.** Persona que va por la calle.
**29.** El carro comienza a andar.
**30.** Los ____ de gasolina.
**31.** Refrigerador.
**32.** Preposición que indica oposición.
**36.** Sobre el pijama te pones una ____.
**39.** Presente de **hacer.**
**40.** No aquí, ____.
**44.** Cualquier cosa que sirve para vestirte.
**46.** Imperativo de **ser.**
**48.** Escuchar.
**49.** Pronombre de complemento indirecto.

**G.** **¿Qué tiene que pagar el Sr. Campos?** To find the answer, identify the objects in the pictures. Then write the letters indicated in the blanks below:

**El Sr. Campos tiene que pagar** ___ ___ ___ ___ ___ ___ ___ ___
13 24 15 9 26 1 4 23

___ ___ ___ ___ ___ ___ ___ ___ ___ ___ ___ ___ ___ ___
14 17 6 27 5 21 29 12 10 7 20 3 22 25

___ ___ ___ ___ ___ ___ ___ .
19 8 16 28 11 2 18

**H.** How many of these words do you remember? Fill in the Spanish words, then read down the boxed column to find out what Mrs. Ramos bought in the furniture store:

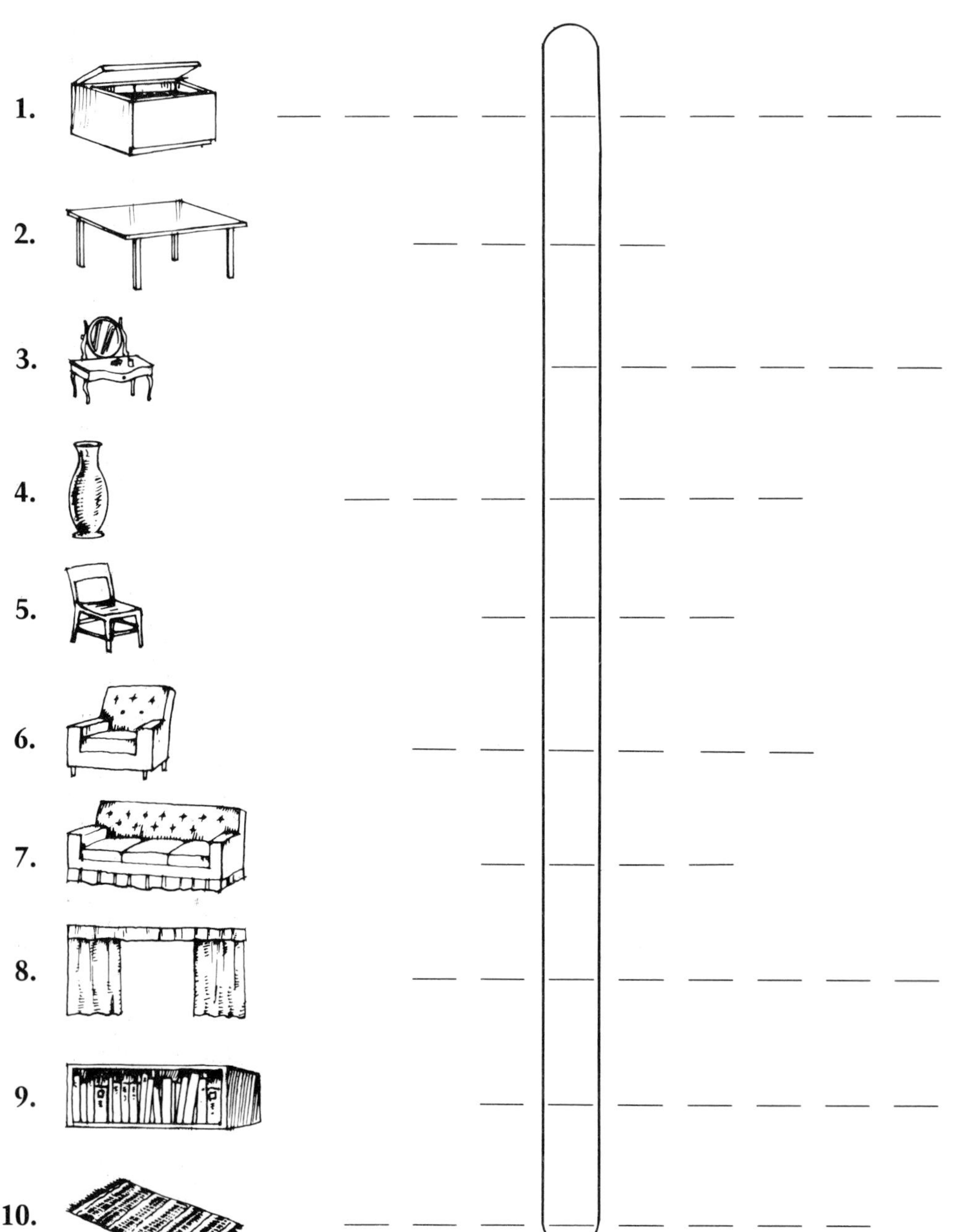

**I.** Picture Story. Can you read this story? Whenever you come to a picture, read it as if it were a Spanish word:

Hoy sale Carlos de viaje para . Ayer puso todas sus , , , y sobre la para decidir qué llevaba. Como no sabe si va a , decidió llevar también su y sus . Lleva también dos , sus y una . Del sacó el , un , un un tubo de , un y un y los puso sobre la . Su mamá le dijo: «Lleva también , y unas Y no olvides llevar una y un para ponerte si vas a una o a un .» Ahora su lo llama desde la y los dos salen en el . Dentro del , Carlos y su padre se ponen el de seguridad y abren las . El viaje al

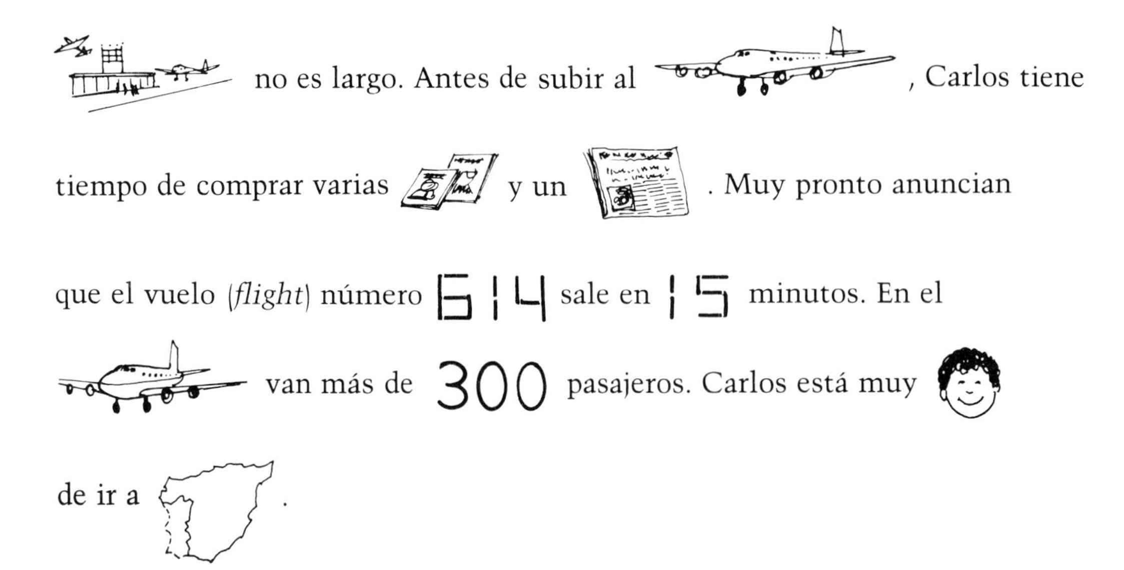

no es largo. Antes de subir al
, Carlos tiene
tiempo de comprar varias
y un
. Muy pronto anuncian
que el vuelo (*flight*) número
514
sale en
15
minutos. En el
van más de
300
pasajeros. Carlos está muy
de ir a
.

# Cuarta Parte

# 16 La superstición

## Spelling-Changing Verbs

### Vocabulario

## ACTIVIDADES

**A.** Match the statements in column A with a related expression in column B. Write the matching letter in the space provided:

| A | | B |
|---|---|---|
| **1.** Los astros (*stars*) influencian nuestras vidas. | ______ | **a.** la fantasía |
| **2.** Según la superstición, el día trae mala suerte. | ______ | **b.** la bruja |
| **3.** Una creación de la imaginación. | ______ | **c.** la pesadilla |
| **4.** Lo que trae romper un espejo. | ______ | **d.** el fantasma |
| **5.** Hombre que posee poderes mágicos. | ______ | **e.** la mala suerte |
| **6.** Mujer con poderes sobrenaturales. | ______ | **f.** el viernes trece |
| **7.** Un mal sueño. | ______ | **g.** el mago |
| **8.** El espíritu de un muerto, que anda por el mundo. | ______ | **h.** la astrología |

**B.** Now have fun identifying these pictures:

1. ______________________________

3. ______________________________

2. ______________________________

4. ______________________________

5. ______________________ 7. ______________________

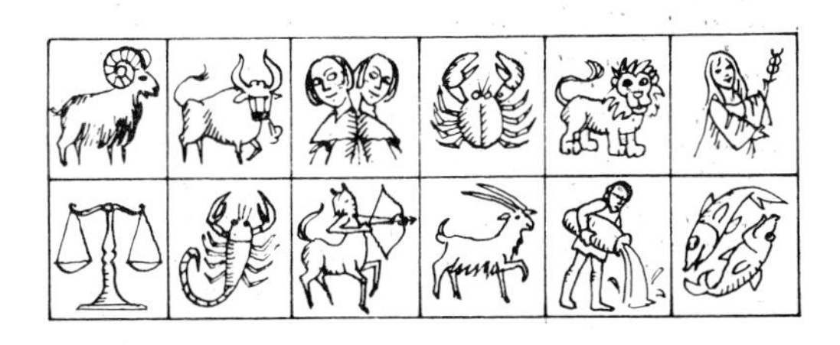

6. ______________________ 8. ______________________

## Las supersticiones

Are you superstitious? Read this story about superstitions and see if you believe in any of them. Pay attention to the spelling of some verbs:

**Acérquese** Ud. Quiero preguntarle algo. ¿Es Ud. una persona supersticiosa? ¡Claro que no! La idea es ridícula. Ud. es una persona inteligente, moderna, lógica, que no cree ni en los agüeros ni en la mala suerte. La superstición es para los viejos y los ignorantes.

**el agüero** *omen*

Y sin embargo, . . . dígame, ¿Qué hace Ud. si un gato negro le pasa por delante, si tiene que pasar por debajo de una escalera, si rompe un espejo, si alguien abre un paraguas dentro de su casa o si Ud. derrama accidentalmente sal en la mesa? ¿Toca madera? ¿Cruza los dedos? ¿Echa sal sobre el hombro izquierdo?

**el paraguas** *umbrella*
**derramar** *to spill*
**el hombro** *shoulder*
**izquierdo** *left*

¿Qué piensa Ud. cuando se levanta y ve que es viernes trece? (A propósito, ¿sabe Ud. si en los aviones hay asientos con el número trece o si los edificios tienen pisos con ese número?)

Como ve, el mundo está lleno de supersticiones. Muchos científicos afirman que la superstición es una creencia basada en la ignorancia y en el temor a lo desconocido. No obstante, algún tipo de superstición guía ciertos actos de nuestra vida diaria. Muchas de estas supersticiones son universales y se encuentran en casi todos los países. Otras son propias de ciertas culturas solamente. Entre los hispanos, por ejemplo, se considera de mala suerte casarse o embarcar un martes, más aún si es trece; probarse un vestido de novia antes del día de la boda; o atropellar a un gato.

**la creencia** *belief*
**el temor a** *fear of*
**lo desconocido** *the unknown*
**no obstante** *all the same*
**propio de** *peculiar to*
**la novia** *bride*
**atropellar** *to run over*

Por el contrario, si Ud. sueña con toros es porque va a ganar la lotería; si ve a tres curas juntos, va a recibir un regalo; si derrama vino en la mesa o si bebe la última copa de la botella de vino, va a tener buena suerte. Hay además objetos que se consideran amuletos de buena suerte: una pata de conejo, un trébol de cuatro hojas, una estatua de un elefante blanco . . . Y si tiene visita aburrida en la casa, **coloque** una escoba detrás de una puerta: la visita se va pronto.

**el cura** *priest*
**la copa** *glass*
**el amuleto** *charm*
**la pata** *animal foot*
**el conejo** *rabbit*
**el trébol** *clover*
**la visita** *visitors*
**colocar** *to place*
**la escoba** *broom*

¿Está convencido ahora? Entonces, **siga** todas las supersticiones y así **busque** el modo de evitar la mala suerte. **Toque** madera, **cruce** los dedos, no **llegue** de viaje el día trece. El único problema es que muchas veces las supersticiones tienen significados opuestos en distintos lugares del mundo. La vida es complicada, ¿verdad?

## ACTIVIDAD

**C.** Conteste con frases completas:

1. ¿Existen los malos agüeros para una persona lógica?

_______________________________________________

2. ¿Quiénes creen en la superstición?

_______________________________________________

3. ¿Qué hace una persona supersticiosa si tiene que pasar por debajo de una escalera?

_______________________________________________

4. ¿Por qué no abre una persona supersticiosa un paraguas dentro de su casa?

_______________

5. ¿Cuándo cruza los dedos una persona supersticiosa?

_______________

6. Según mucha gente, ¿qué número trae mala suerte?

_______________

7. ¿En qué está basada la superstición?

_______________

8. Según los hispanos, ¿qué día no debe uno viajar o casarse?

_______________

9. ¿Qué objetos se consideran amuletos de buena suerte?

_______________

10. ¿Por qué no se pueden creer todas las supersticiones?

_______________

## 3

Did you notice these sentences in the story?

| | |
|---|---|
| **Toque madera.** | *Knock on wood.* |
| **No llegue de viaje el trece.** | *Don't arrive from a trip on the thirteenth.* |
| **Cruce los dedos.** | *Cross your fingers.* |

What are the infinitives of these verbs?

**toque** _______________

**llegue** _______________

**cruce** _______________

What happened to the **c** in **tocar?** _______________

What happened to the **g** in **llegar?** _______________

What happened to the **z** in **cruzar?** _______________

Right. The **c** changed to **qu,** and **g** changed to **gu,** and the **z** changed to **c**. Here's the easy rule: Verbs ending in **-car, -gar,** and **-zar** change their spelling in the first person (**yo**) of the preterite and in the formal commands in order to maintain the original sound of the infinitive:

| | |
|---|---|
| c to **qu**<br>g to **gu**<br>z to **c** | before **e** |

Here are more examples:

| | | |
|---|---|---|
| **expli*car*:** | **Yo *expliqué* la lección.**<br>***Explíquela* Ud. ahora.** | *I explained the lesson.*<br>*(You) Explain it now.* |
| **ju*gar*:** | **Yo ya *jugué* con ese juego.**<br>***Jueguen* Uds. con él.** | *I already played with that game.*<br>*(You) Play with it.* |
| **almor*zar*:** | **Gracias, yo ya *almorcé*.**<br>***Almuerce* Ud. sin mí.** | *Thanks, I already had lunch.*<br>*Have lunch without me.* |

Note that some verbs with spelling changes also have stem changes: **jugar (ue), almorzar (ue), comenzar (ie), empezar (ie),** and others.

## ACTIVIDADES

**D.** What did you do yesterday?

EXAMPLE: pescar en el lago
**Yo *pesqué* en el lago.**

1. buscar un libro en la biblioteca

_______________

2. sacar una buena nota en el examen

_______________

3. tocar la guitarra

_______________

4. explicar las tareas a mi hermanito

_______________

5. acercarse a la escuela por la tarde

_______________

**E.** Give the following commands:

EXAMPLE: empezar a trabajar ya (Uds.)
***Empiecen* a trabajar ya.**

1. almorzar en la cafetería (Ud.)

_______________

2. cruzar la calle con cuidado (Uds.)

_______________

3. comenzar a hacer las tareas (Ud.)

_______________

4. pagar la cuenta del gas (Ud.)

_______________

5. no jugar en la sala (Uds.)

_______________

6. llegar temprano a la casa (Uds.)

_______________

**F.** Answer the following questions:

1. ¿A qué hora almorzaste ayer?

_______________

2. ¿Con quién jugaste el sábado pasado?

_______________

3. ¿Qué nota sacaste en el último examen de español?

_______________

4. ¿A qué hora comenzaste a ver televisión anoche?

_______________

5. ¿Cruzaste muchas calles para llegar a la escuela?

_______________

6. ¿A qué hora llegaste a casa ayer por la tarde?

_______________

7. ¿Tocaste a la puerta?

_______________

8. ¿Buscaste palabras en el diccionario para la tarea de español?

_______________

Other verbs undergo different spelling changes to maintain the original sound of the infinitive. Look at these examples:

| | | |
|---|---|---|
| **recog*er*:** | **Yo *recojo* los juguetes.** | *I pick up the toys.* |
| | ***Recoja* Ud. su ropa.** | *Pick up your clothes.* |
| **dirig*ir*:** | **Yo *dirijo* la obra de teatro.** | *I direct the play.* |
| | ***Dirija* Ud. el coro.** | *Direct the choir.* |

What happened to the **g** *in* **recoger** and **dirigir?** ______________________

Right, the **g** changed to **j** in the first person (**yo**) singular of the present tense and in the formal commands. The rule is easy: Verbs ending in **-ger** or **-gir** change the **g** to **j** before the vowels **a** and **o** to keep the original sound of the infinitive. Some **-ger** and **-gir** verbs also have stem changes: **corregir (i)** *to correct* and **elegir (i)** *to elect.*

## ACTIVIDAD

**G.** Give the following commands:

EXAMPLE: recoger los platos sucios (Ud.)
***Recoja* los platos sucios.**

1. corregir los errores en la composición (Uds.)

______________________________________________

2. proteger a los animales (Uds.)

______________________________________________

3. escoger una película cómica (Ud.)

______________________________________________

4. coger la pelota (Ud.)

______________________________________________

5. elegir al presidente de la clase (Uds.)

______________________________________________

6. dirigir el coro en la clase de música (Ud.)

______________________________________________

Finally, verbs ending in **-guir** undergo a spelling change in the first person (**yo**) singular of the present tense and in the formal commands:

| | | |
|---|---|---|
| **seg*uir*:** | **Yo *sigo* un curso de inglés.** | *I am taking a course in English.* |
| | ***Sigan* a ese señor.** | *Follow that man.* |

In these sentences, **gu** changes to ______ before ______ and ______ to maintain the original sound of the infinitive. Note that some verbs with spelling changes also have stem changes: **seguir (i)** *to follow,* **perseguir (i)** *to pursue,* and **conseguir (i)** *to obtain, get.*

## ACTIVIDADES

**H.** Answer the following questions:

1. ¿Escoges a tus maestros en la escuela?

 ______________________________

2. ¿Sigues algún curso de arte?

 ______________________________

3. ¿Recoges los platos sucios después de la comida?

 ______________________________

4. ¿Consigues siempre entradas para los conciertos que quieres ver?

 ______________________________

5. ¿Proteges a los animales?

 ______________________________

6. ¿Diriges algún proyecto en la escuela?

 ______________________________

**I.** Here are some statements you heard from some political candidates. Express them in Spanish:

1. I follow the advice of the people.

 ______________________________

2. I knocked on every door in the neighborhood.

 ______________________________

3. I embraced (**abrazar**) a hundred babies.

 ______________________________

4. I do not protect criminals. I pursue them.

 ______________________________

5. I do not choose friends for political jobs.

 ______________________________

6. I arrived in this city twenty years ago.

_______________

7. I always say to the people: "Look for and elect the best candidate."

_______________

8. I correct my mistakes.

_______________

## PREGUNTAS PERSONALES

1. ¿En qué supersticiones crees?

_______________

2. En tu opinión, ¿cuál es la superstición más ridícula?

_______________

3. ¿Tuviste mala suerte el año pasado? ¿Qué pasó?

_______________

4. ¿Tienes algún objeto que te sirve de amuleto de buena suerte?

_______________

5. ¿Te gustan los cuentos de hadas o de brujas?

_______________

## INFORMACIÓN PERSONAL

Write five things about yourself, using the verbs **conseguir, tocar, recoger, comenzar,** and **seguir:**

1. _______________

2. _______________

3. _______________

4. _______________

5. _______________

## DIÁLOGO

Your friend Francisco (a very superstitious person) is always a nervous wreck when he walks down the street. You are trying to calm him down:

# CÁPSULA CULTURAL

## Dichos populares

Sayings and superstitions have some things in common: they are very old, they are part of the popular folklore, and they are transmitted orally from generation to generation. Many people believe that proverbs and sayings reflect the "wisdom" of the people, acquired by observation and experience, and that they are also a reflection of their culture. There are many sayings and proverbs in Spanish. Here are some of the more popular ones:

**Dime con quién andas y te diré quién eres.**
**En boca cerrada no entran moscas.**
**Más vale tarde que nunca.**
**Perro que ladra no muerde.**
**Querer es poder.**
**No todo lo que brilla es oro.**
**Más vale pájaro en mano que ciento volando.**
**El mono aunque se vista de seda, mono se queda.**

Can you find equivalent sayings in English?

# 17 Las maravillas del reino animal

## Comparing People and Things

### Vocabulario

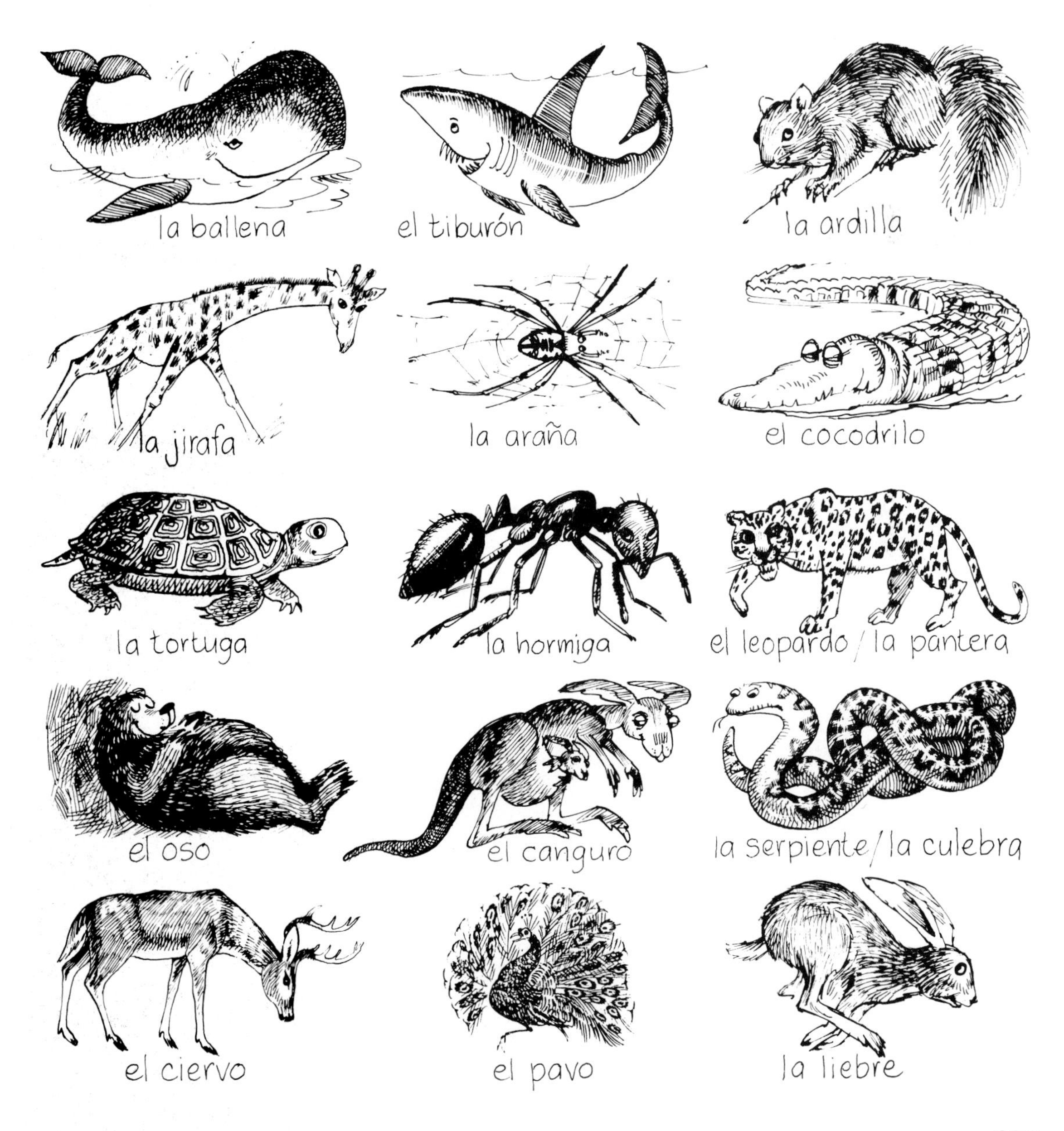

## ACTIVIDADES

**A.** Did you ever play **"¿Quién soy"?** This time we are going to play it with animals. See if you can guess the animal by what it says:

1. Me muevo despacio y vivo por mucho tiempo.

   Soy ___________________________.
2. Soy un insecto pequeño pero fuerte, que siempre trabaja.

   Soy ___________________________.
3. A la gente le gusta comerme el Día de Acción de Gracias.

   Soy ___________________________.
4. Vivo en el mar y la gente me tiene mucho miedo.

   Soy ___________________________.
5. Salto en vez de correr y vengo de Australia.

   Soy ___________________________.
6. Soy pequeña y tengo una cola larga y bonita.

   Soy ___________________________.
7. Soy muy grande y vivo en el mar.

   Soy ___________________________.
8. Tengo ocho patas y atrapo a otros insectos en mis telarañas.

   Soy ___________________________.
9. Corro rápidamente y tengo las orejas muy grandes.

   Soy ___________________________.

**B.** Here are some cages in a zoo. The names of the animals are missing. Write them in:

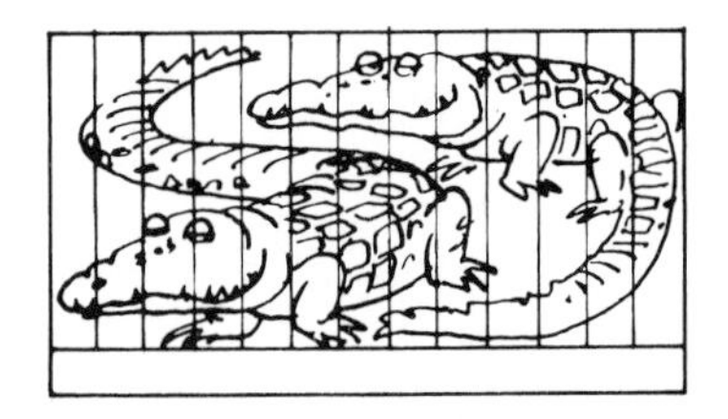
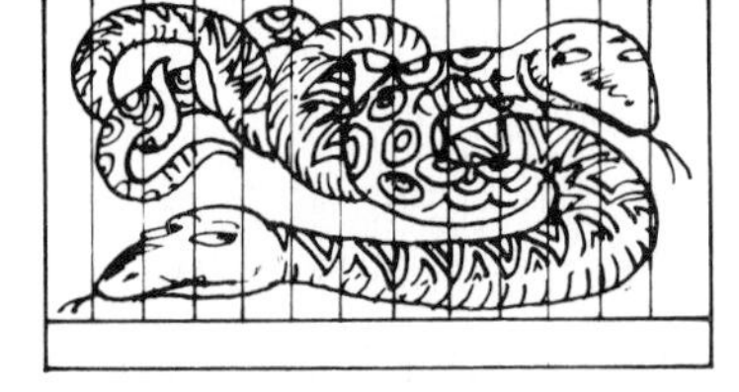
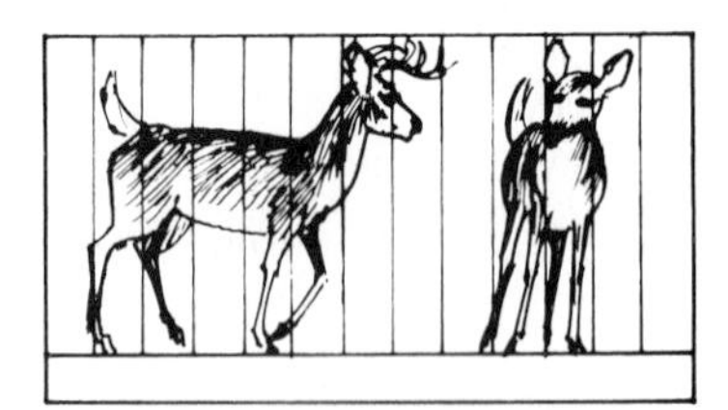

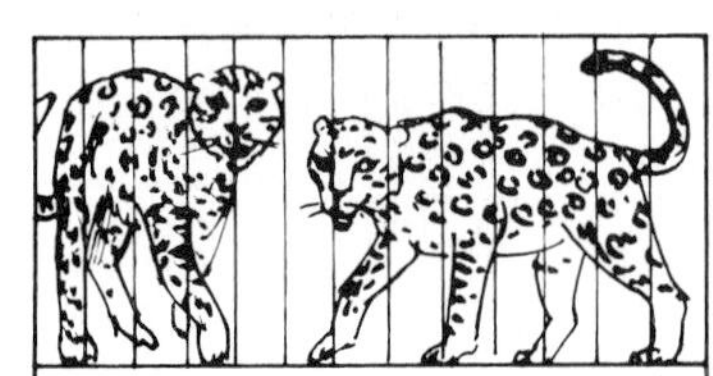
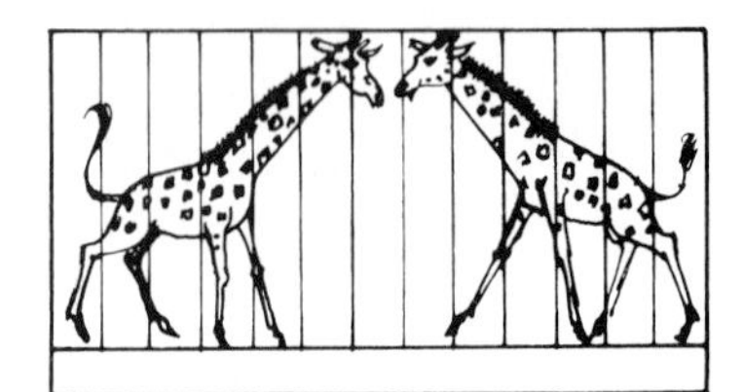

## ¡Es increíble!

Let's read a story about some world records:

En todo el mundo a la gente le gusta discutir sobre cuál es la cosa más grande, la más pequeña, la más fría, la más caliente, la más alta, la más vieja, etc. Se hacen preguntas como ¿Quién es el hombre más gordo del mundo? ¿Quién es el más rápido? ¿Quién batió el jonrón más largo? ¿Cuál es el animal más grande?

Las respuestas a todas estas preguntas, y a miles más, se encuentran en un solo libro, «El libro Guinness de los récords». La compañía Guinness produce cerveza y es la compañía más grande de Irlanda. Cuando publicó su libro por primera vez, no tenía la menor idea del éxito que iba a tener. El libro se publica hoy día en 23 lenguas y hasta ahora se han vendido más de 30 millones de ejemplares.

**la cerveza** *beer*
**menor** *least*
**el ejemplar** *copy*

Aquí tenemos algunos récords mundiales interesantes: La persona más alta: un hombre que medía 8 pies, 11 pulgadas. La persona más pequeña: una mujer que medía 23 pulgadas. La persona más gorda: un hombre que pesaba 1.069 libras. El ser humano más viejo: un japonés que murió a la edad de 120 años. El animal más grande y más pesado: una ballena azul que medía 110 pies y pesaba 195 toneladas. El animal más alto: una jirafa que medía 20 pies. El animal más veloz: el leopardo cazador que puede correr a 60–63 millas por hora. El animal terrestre más grande: un elefante africano que medía 13 pies de alto y pesaba 26.328 libras. El perro más pequeño: un chihuahua de México que pesaba 10 onzas. La serpiente más larga y más pesada: una anaconda que medía 27 pies, 9 pulgadas. El reptil más grande y más pesado: un cocodrilo que medía 27 pies y pesaba 1.100 libras. El pez marino más grande: un tiburón que medía 60 pies, 9 pulgadas y pesaba 90.000 libras. El árbol más alto: una secoya gigante de California que medía 366 pies. El árbol más viejo: un pino de los Estados Unidos que tenía 4.900 años.

**la pulgada** *inch*
**pesar** *to weigh*
**la libra** *pound*
**la edad** *age*
**la tonelada** *ton*
**el leopardo cazador** *cheetah*
**la secoya** *sequoia*

¿Le pareció interesante la información? ¿Sabe la respuesta a las preguntas siguientes? Algunas pueden parecer ridículas, pero sin embargo están en el libro oficial de récords mundiales. Las respuestas están en la página 285.

¿Cuál ha sido (*has been*) o es
(a) la pizza más grande del mundo?
(b) el mayor peso levantado por un ser humano?
(c) el maratón de besos más prolongado?
(d) el perfume más caro?
(e) la perla más grande?
(f) la iglesia más grande?
(g) el jonrón más largo?

## ACTIVIDAD

**C.** Conteste con frases completas:

1. ¿Qué le gusta discutir a la gente?

______________________________

2. ¿Cuáles son algunas preguntas que hace la gente?

______________________________

3. ¿Dónde se encuentran las respuestas a esas preguntas?

______________________________

4. ¿Qué produce la compañía Guinness?

______________________________

5. ¿En cuántas lenguas se publica el libro?

______________________________

6. Según el libro, ¿cuánto medía el hombre más alto del mundo?

______________________________

7. ¿De qué nacionalidad era el hombre más viejo?

______________________________

8. ¿De qué país viene el perro más pequeño?

______________________________

9. ¿Cuál es el animal más grande y más pesado del mundo?

______________________________

10. ¿Dónde está el árbol más alto del mundo?

______________________________

In order to arrive at the facts you read in the story, people had to make comparisons. Let's look at some examples:

| | |
|---|---|
| **El elefante medía 13 pies de alto.** | *The elephant was 13 feet tall.* |
| **La jirafa medía 23 pies de alto.** | *The giraffe was 23 feet tall.* |
| **La jirafa era *más alta que* el elefante.** | *The giraffe was taller than the elephant.* |
| **El elefante era *menos alto que* la jirafa.** | *The elephant was less tall than the giraffe.* |

In Spanish, to form a comparison stating that one thing (or person) is MORE than another, use **más** + adjective + **que**. To form a comparison stating that one thing (or person) is LESS than another, use **menos** + adjective + **que**. It's that simple. Remember, however, that the adjective has to agree in gender and number with the noun it refers to:

| | |
|---|---|
| ***María* es más estudios*a* que Juan.** | *Mary is more studious than John.* |
| ***Juan* es menos estudios*o* que María.** | *John is less studious than Mary.* |

## ACTIVIDADES

**D.** Compare the animals using the clues given:

EXAMPLE: pequeño

**El gato es más pequeño que el cochino.**

**1.** alto

______________________________

**2.** grande

______________________________

3. veloz

______________________________________________

4. inteligente

______________________________________________

5. peligroso

______________________________________________

6. feroz

______________________________________________

7. bonito

______________________________________________

8. pequeño

______________________________________________

**E.** What do you find less fun? Give you opinion of the following:

EXAMPLE: el tenis / el béisbol
**El tenis es *menos divertido que* el béisbol.**

1. una película romántica / una película de horror

_______________

2. el golf / el fútbol americano

_______________

3. un picnic / una comida en un restaurante

_______________

4. la playa / la piscina

_______________

5. la clase de español / la clase de matemáticas

_______________

6. una novela policíaca / una novela de ciencia ficción

_______________

7. viajar en avión / viajar en barco

_______________

**4** Now look at the following type of comparison:

**La serpiente es *tan larga como* el cocodrilo.**
*The snake is as long as the crocodile.*
**Yo soy *tan alto(a)* como tú.**
*I am as tall as you.*

To form a comparison of equality in Spanish, use **tan** + adjective + **como.**

## ACTIVIDAD

**F.** You are talking about your two best friends, Juan and Elisa. For you, they are both equal:

EXAMPLE: amable
**Juan es tan amable como Elisa.**

1. serio _______________

**2.** bueno ____________________

**3.** alegre ____________________

**4.** inteligente ____________________

**5.** sincero ____________________

**6.** estudioso ____________________

**7.** cortés ____________________

**8.** honesto ____________________

**5** What happens if you want to express a superlative — that is, say that something or somebody is the greatest or the most intelligent? Look at these examples:

| | |
|---|---|
| **Pablo es *el más alto de* la clase.** | *Paul is the tallest in the class.* |
| **Rosa es *la menos tímida de* la clase.** | *Rose is the least timid in the class.* |
| **Andrés y Mario son *los más pequeños del* grupo.** | *Andrew and Mario are the smallest in the group.* |
| **Elisa y Luisa son *las menos serias del* grupo.** | *Elise and Louise are the least serious in the group.* |

Which words stand before **más** and **menos** in our examples? ______, ______, ______, and ______. Which word stands after the adjectives? __________

In Spanish, the superlative is expressed as follows:

definite article **(el, la, los, las)** + **más** / **menos** + adjective + **de**
*the* + *most* / *least* + *adjective* + *in*

## ACTIVIDADES

**G.** Using the following adjectives, state who in your family is the most or the least:

EXAMPLE: estricto
**Mi papá es *el más estricto de* la familia.**
**Mi mamá es *la menos estricta*.**

**1.** alegre ____________________

____________________

**2.** serio ______________________________

______________________________

**3.** ambicioso ______________________________

______________________________

**4.** amable ______________________________

______________________________

**5.** divertido ______________________________

______________________________

**6.** generoso ______________________________

______________________________

**H.** In your opinion, which are the best and the worst in each category?

EXAMPLE: animal rápido
**El leopardo es *el más rápido.***
**La tortuga es *la menos rápida.***

**1.** película cómica ______________________________

______________________________

**2.** actor famoso ______________________________

______________________________

**3.** carro caro ______________________________

______________________________

**4.** deporte interesante ______________________________

______________________________

**5.** animal inteligente ______________________________

______________________________

**6.** programa de televisión aburrido ______________________________

______________________________

6 There are four adjectives with irregular comparative forms:

| | | |
|---|---|---|
| **bueno** *good* | **mejor** *better, best* | **Pablo es *mejor que* Jorge.** **Él es *el mejor* alumno *de* la clase.** |
| **malo** *bad* | **peor** *worse, worst* | **Ellos son *peores que* sus amigos.** **Ellos son *los peores de* la escuela.** |
| **grande** *big* | **mayor** *older, oldest* **más grande** *bigger, biggest* | **Francisco es *mayor que* yo, pero yo soy *más grande que* él.** **Él es *el mayor* y yo soy *el más grande de* los hermanos.** |
| **pequeño** *small* | **menor** *younger, youngest* **más pequeño** *smaller, smallest* | **María es mi hermana *menor* y es *la más pequeña de* la familia.** |

**Mayor** and **menor** refer to age, **más grande** and **más pequeño** refer to physical size.

## ACTIVIDADES

**I.** In your opinion, which was or is the best and the worst of these things?

EXAMPLE: novela de ciencia ficción
**La mejor novela de ciencia ficción es «El planeta desconocido».**
**La peor novela de ciencia ficción es «Noche de horror».**

1. película del año ______________________________

______________________________

2. jugador de béisbol del país ______________________________

______________________________

3. actor de televisión ______________________________

______________________________

4. equipo de fútbol profesional ______________________________

______________________________

5. carro deportivo ______________________________

______________________________

6. grupo de rock ______________________________

______________________________

7. jugador(a) de tenis profesional ______________________________

______________________________

**J.** You are writing a letter to a new pen pal in Madrid. Express the following in Spanish:

I have a brother and a sister. I am older than my brother, and my sister is the youngest of the three. I am the oldest and also the biggest. My brother is small but not as small as my sister. She is the smallest in the family. Do you have brothers and sisters? Are they older or younger than you? Are they bigger or smaller?

______________________________

______________________________

______________________________

______________________________

______________________________

______________________________

## INFORMACIÓN PERSONAL

1. La mejor película que vi el año pasado fue ______________________________.
2. El programa de televisión que más me gusta es ______________________________.
3. Creo que el deporte más peligroso es ______________________________.
4. La canción que más me gusta es ______________________________.
5. Yo soy el mejor ______________________________.

## DIÁLOGO

Your sister Carmencita is a very curious child. She's forever asking you difficult questions. Give your answers:

## PREGUNTAS PERSONALES

1. ¿Quién es el alumno más estudioso de tu clase de español?

_______________________________________________

2. ¿Crees que un libro como el «Guinness» es importante? ¿Por qué?

_______________________________________________

3. ¿Quieres batir (*break*) algún récord mundial? ¿Cuál?

_______________________________________________

4. ¿Puedes mencionar algún récord mundial?

_______________________________________________

5. ¿Tienes alguna pregunta que nadie puede contestarte? ¿Cuál es?

_______________________________________________

## COMPOSICIÓN

You are a camp counselor and have gone to the zoo with a group of small children. Write some of the questions the children ask you about the animals. For example, they want to know whether the leopard is as strong as the tiger; whether the crocodile is as dangerous as the shark; which is the longest snake in the zoo; which is the smallest animal in the zoo, and so on:

_______________________________________________

_______________________________________________

_______________________________________________

_______________________________________________

_______________________________________________

Respuestas a las preguntas de la página 276:
(a) una que medía 80 pies y pesaba 18.664 libras; (b) 6.270 libras; (c) 119 horas y 12 minutos; (d) una esencia de jazmín (*jasmine*) que cuesta más de $200 por onza; (e) una que pesó 14 libras, una onza; (f) San Pedro en Roma, con un área de 18.110 yardas cuadradas (*square*); (g) 618 pies de distancia.

# CÁPSULA CULTURAL

## Animales de los países hispanos

As long as we are learning the names of animals in Spanish, why not discover some of those that are native to Latin America?

In the higher elevations of the Andes Mountains in South America live the alpaca and the llama — hardy, domesticated animals related to the camel. The alpaca, which is smaller than the llama, is bred for its thick coat of hair, from which the finest wool is produced. The llama, about four feet tall, also has very long thick hair, but not as fine. Llamas have been very useful to the Indians throughout the centuries for food, clothing, and transportation.

The caiman is a Central and South American reptile related to the crocodile. The largest of the species is the black caiman, a dangerous animal that can grow to be 15 feet long.

The piranha (**la piraña**) is a fish living in many rivers of east and central South America. Known for their ferocity, piranhas live in groups and can detect the smell of blood. A group of piranhas can eat a large animal in a very short time.

The quetzal is a brilliantly colored bird found in Mexico and Central America. It was a sacred bird of the Aztecs and the Mayas. The quetzal's long tail feathers (3 feet) were used as a symbol of authority.

The jaguars of Mexico and Central and South America are the largest, most powerful wild cats of the Western Hemisphere. Jaguars were a symbol of strength and courage in ancient Indian civilizations.

On the other extreme, have you ever seen a Chihuahua? The smallest breed of dogs, almost like toys, Chihuahuas are originally from Mexico.

Which is your favorite animal? Do you know any other animals native to North, Central, or South America?

# 18 ¿Cuál será tu profesión?

## Future Tense of Regular Verbs

### 1 Vocabulario*

la programadora de computadores

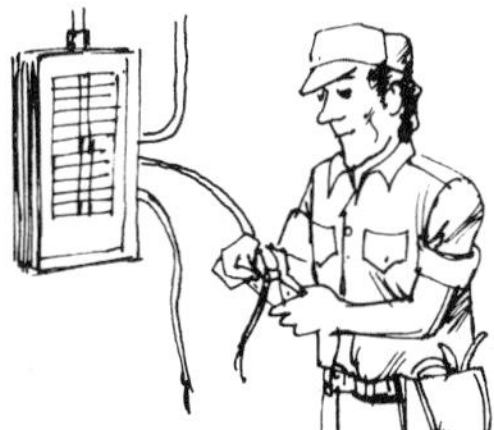

el electricista

el bombero

la veterinaria

el empleado de correos

la aeromoza/ la azafata

la fotógrafa

el carnicero

el zapatero

la empleada de banco

el piloto

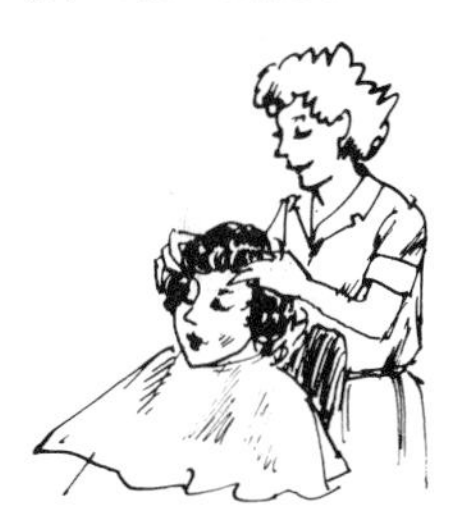

la peluquera

el entrenador

el panadero

la periodista

la gerente

*In this **Vocabulario,** we illustrate sometimes male, sometimes female professionals. Most of the professions, however, have both male and female practitioners. In the vocabulary in the back of your book, see if you can find the male or female counterparts of the professions illustrated on this page.

## ACTIVIDAD

**A.** Who does the following? Complete the sentences with the appropriate noun:

1. ______________________ corta el pelo a la gente.
2. ______________________ vende carne.
3. ______________________ prepara y vende el pan.
4. ______________________ trata a los animales cuando están enfermos.
5. ______________________ hace o arregla zapatos.
6. ______________________ vende estampillas en el correo.
7. ______________________ saca fotos artísticas.
8. ______________________ escribe programas para los computadores.
9. ______________________ entrena a los deportistas.
10. ______________________ maneja el avión.
11. ______________________ escribe en los periódicos.
12. ______________________ trabaja en el banco.
13. ______________________ combate los incendios (*fires*).
14. ______________________ ayuda a los pasajeros en el avión.
15. ______________________ dirige una compañía.
16. ______________________ conecta los cables para la electricidad.

## 2 El horóscopo

Do you want to know what will happen in your future? Astrologists say that they can predict the future from the stars. Let's read this story and see what's in the stars for you. Pay attention to the verbs in bold type:

¿No quiere Ud. saber qué **pasará** en el futuro? Los astrólogos dicen que nuestra personalidad y nuestro futuro están influenciados por los astros. Todos nacimos bajo uno de los doce signos del zodíaco, y hay personas que no toman ninguna decisión importante sin consultar antes su horóscopo. ¿Qué **traerá** el día de mañana? ¿Qué sorpresas **revelarán** las estrellas? Lea el horóscopo siguiente y **se enterará**:

**enterarse** *to find out*

**Acuario,** del 21 de enero al 18 de febrero
Ud. es una persona generosa y comprensiva, romántica y poética. Muy pronto **recibirá** una noticia de gran importancia para su felicidad. **Realizará** su sueño de hacer un viaje largo.

**comprensivo** *understanding*
**realizar** *to fulfill*

**Piscis,** del 19 de febrero al 20 de marzo
Ud. es una persona tierna, idealista y sentimental. En los próximos meses **conocerá** a alguien que **será** muy importante en su vida.

**tierno** *tender*

**Aries,** del 21 de marzo al 20 de abril
Ud. es una persona valiente y decidida. Siempre **conseguirá** lo que quiere. Le **llegarán** noticias de un amigo querido.

**valiente** *brave*

**Tauro,** del 21 de abril al 21 de mayo
Ud. tiene mucho sentido común. Es una persona práctica y realista. Este año le **sonreirá** la fortuna. **Recibirá** una herencia o un cheque inesperado.

**la herencia** *inheritance*
**inesperado** *unexpected*

**Géminis,** del 22 de mayo al 21 de junio
Ud. es impaciente e impulsivo(a). Los próximos meses **estará** muy ocupado(a) con actividades sociales. **Ganará** la admiración de una persona importante para Ud.

**Cáncer,** del 22 de junio al 22 de julio
Ud. es una persona sensible y simpática. Le gusta ayudar a los demás. Pronto **resolverá** muchos de sus problemas. El próximo año **será** muy interesante.

**sensible** *sensitive*
**resolver** *to solve*

**Leo,** del 23 de julio al 23 de agosto
Ud. es una persona segura de sí misma, con cualidades de líder. En las próximas semanas **establecerá** contactos importantes con personas que le **ayudarán** en el futuro.

**Virgo,** del 24 de agosto al 23 de septiembre
Ud. es perfeccionista. Antes de hacer algo, estudia

todos los detalles y lo piensa bien. Los resultados de un examen que Ud. **tomará serán** brillantes.

**Libra,** del 24 de septiembre al 23 de octubre
Ud. es una persona tranquila, que busca la armonía en las cosas. **Ganará** mucho dinero este año, pero tenga cuidado porque, si no, lo **gastará** pronto.

**Escorpión,** del 24 de octubre al 22 de noviembre
A Ud. le gusta trabajar y es una persona determinada que no acepta el fracaso. Ud. **tratará** de cambiar su vida este año, pero los cambios no le **traerán** satisfacción.

**el fracaso** *failure*

**Sagitario,** del 23 de noviembre al 20 de diciembre
Ud. es una persona alegre, sincera y honesta, pero necesita tener más confianza en sí misma. Los nuevos proyectos que **comenzará** pronto le **darán** prestigio.

**Capricornio,** del 21 de diciembre al 20 de enero
Ud. es independiente y ambicioso(a), pero también melancólico(a) y pesimista. Los problemas de dinero no **durarán** mucho tiempo. Este año **empezará** a trabajar en algo que le **gustará.**

**durar** *to last*

## ACTIVIDAD

**B.** Conteste en frases completas:

1. ¿Qué dicen los astrólogos?

_______________________________________________

2. ¿Qué tenemos todos en común?

_______________________________________________

3. ¿Qué hacen muchas personas antes de tomar una decisión importante?

_______________________________________________

4. ¿Qué tipo de persona es un Leo?

_______________________________________________

5. ¿Qué problema tiene un Sagitario?

_______________________________________________

**6.** Según el horóscopo, ¿qué recibirá pronto un Acuario?

______________________________

**7.** ¿Qué tipo de persona es un Cáncer?

______________________________

**8.** ¿Bajo qué signo nacieron las personas tiernas, idealistas y sentimentales?

______________________________

**3** Up to now, we have been talking in the present and the past tenses. How do we describe actions and events that will happen in the future? The horoscope in the story told you some things that will happen in the future. Let's look at some examples:

| | |
|---|---|
| **Ud. *realizará* su sueño.** | *You will fulfill your dream.* |
| **¿Qué *traerá* el día de mañana?** | *What will tomorrow bring?* |
| **Ud. *recibirá* una noticia importante.** | *You will receive important news.* |

Which are the infinitives of the three verbs used in these sentences?

______________, ______________, and ______________. What ending was added to all three infinitives? ______. It's very easy to form the future tense in Spanish. You simply add the following endings to the infinitive of most verbs:

| SUBJECT | INFINITIVE | FUTURE ENDING |
|---|---|---|
| **yo** | | **-é** |
| **tú** | **hablar-** | **-ás** |
| **Ud., él, ella** | **comer-** | **-á** |
| **nosotros** | **vivir-** | **-emos** |
| **Uds., ellos, ellas** | | **-án** |

Now try to supply the forms of the future tense for these verbs:

| | **estar** | **ser** | **abrir** |
|---|---|---|---|
| **yo** | ________ | ________ | ________ |
| **tú** | ________ | ________ | ________ |
| **Ud., él, ella** | ________ | ________ | ________ |
| **nosotros** | ________ | ________ | ________ |
| **Uds., ellos, ellas** | ________ | ________ | ________ |

Note that all endings, except for **nosotros,** have an accent.

## ACTIVIDADES

**C.** You are going to spend your vacation at the beach. What will you do there?

EXAMPLE: tomar el sol
**Yo tomaré el sol.**

1. nadar en el mar

_______________

2. correr por la playa

_______________

3. construir castillos de arena

_______________

4. comer en restaurantes

_______________

5. recoger conchas

_______________

6. jugar con mis amigos

_______________

**D.** Here's a list of things your mother will do tomorrow:

EXAMPLE: comprar carne en la carnicería.
**Ella comprará carne en la carnicería.**

1. llamar al peluquero para hacer una cita

_______________

2. llevar el gato al veterinario

_______________

3. hablar con el fotógrafo

_______________

4. leer el artículo de la periodista española

_______________

5. dar instrucciones al electricista

_______________

6. escribir al empleado del banco

_______________

**E.** You are going to spend tomorrow afternoon at a friend's house. What will you do there?

EXAMPLE: mirar la televisión
**Miraremos la televisión.**

1. estudiar para el examen

______________________________

2. terminar las tareas

______________________________

3. escribir la composición

______________________________

4. leer el periódico

______________________________

5. escuchar unos discos

______________________________

6. beber mucho café

______________________________

**F.** Your school is going to have a party. How will everyone help?

EXAMPLE: la profesora / mandar las invitaciones
**La profesora mandará las invitaciones.**

1. los muchachos / traer los discos

______________________________

2. las muchachas / escoger la música

______________________________

3. tú / servir el ponche

______________________________

4. Uds. / ayudar a decorar

______________________________

5. el director / tocar la guitarra

______________________________

6. las madres / preparar los sandwiches

______________________________

7. tú / comprar los platos de papel

_______________

8. yo / abrir la puerta

_______________

9. Ud. / recoger la basura (*garbage*)

_______________

10. todos nosotros / cantar y bailar

_______________

**G.** Next week you are going to the flea market with some friends. Write what each of you will be doing, using the suggestions:

| | |
|---|---|
| yo | estar allí temprano |
| Uds. | pasar el día allí |
| tú y yo | comprar muchas cosas |
| Carlos y Ana | vender los juguetes viejos |
| tú | comer hamburguesas |
| Roberto | gastar mucho dinero |
| todos nosotros | escoger libros de uso |

EXAMPLE: **Tú y yo pasaremos el día allí.**

1. _______________
2. _______________
3. _______________
4. _______________
5. _______________
6. _______________

You know that the future tense is used in Spanish to describe future actions or events. But look at these sentences:

| | |
|---|---|
| **¿Qué hora *será*?** | *I wonder what time it is.* |
| **No sé. *Serán* las seis.** | *I don't know. It's probably six o'clock.* |
| **¿Dónde está tu mamá?** | *Where is your mother?* |
| **No sé. *Estará* en la cocina.** | *I don't know. I guess she's in the kitchen.* |

In Spanish, the future tense is sometimes used to express wonder or probability in the present. It is then equivalent to English *I wonder, I guess, probably.*

## ACTIVIDAD

**H.** You have been told that a new Spanish teacher will join the school and you are wondering about him:

EXAMPLE: ser simpático
**¿Será simpático?**

1. ser estricto ______________________
2. dar muchos exámenes ______________________
3. estar en clase el lunes ______________________
4. hablar bien español ______________________
5. ser puntual ______________________
6. conocer a los otros maestros ______________________

## *PREGUNTAS PERSONALES*

1. ¿En qué fecha naciste? ¿Cuál es tu signo del zodíaco?

______________________

2. ¿Qué otros alumnos de tu clase nacieron bajo tu signo?

______________________

3. ¿Consultas tu horóscopo antes de tomar una decisión importante?

______________________

4. ¿Cómo es tu personalidad?

______________________

5. ¿En qué profesión piensas trabajar en el futuro?

______________________

## DIÁLOGO

You are talking with your brother, wondering about the future:

## INFORMACIÓN PERSONAL

Using the following verbs, list five things you will or will not do next weekend:

**ir** **jugar** **comenzar** **comprar** **comer**

**1.** ______________________________

**2.** ______________________________

**3.** ______________________________

**4.** ______________________________

**5.** ______________________________

# CÁPSULA CULTURAL

## Una ocupación española

Occupations change with the times. Some disappear because the social development of our society or new technologies make them obsolete, and others are created. One occupation that is disappearing slowly is typical only of Spain: **el sereno.**

**El sereno** is a night watchman who wears a long, grey dust coat and a cap. He walks around the streets in the cities and small towns making sure that everything is quiet. **El sereno** has been a part of Spanish life for centuries. Many songs and stories have been written about him, to the point where he has become part of the Spanish folklore.

The job usually remained in a family for generations when it was normal for a son to follow in his father's footsteps and each **sereno** had "his" neighborhood. He knew all the people living there and greeted everyone coming home late at night. He had the keys to all the houses and would open the doors for those who had forgotten them. A person needing him would yell **"¡Sereno!"**, and he would answer **"¡Va!"** In his rounds, he would sometimes call **"las tres y sereno"** to let people know the time and that he was there to keep the neighborhood safe.

How many professions you know have been created in this century? Can you name them in Spanish?

# 19 La exploración del espacio

## Future Tense of Irregular Verbs

### 1 Vocabulario

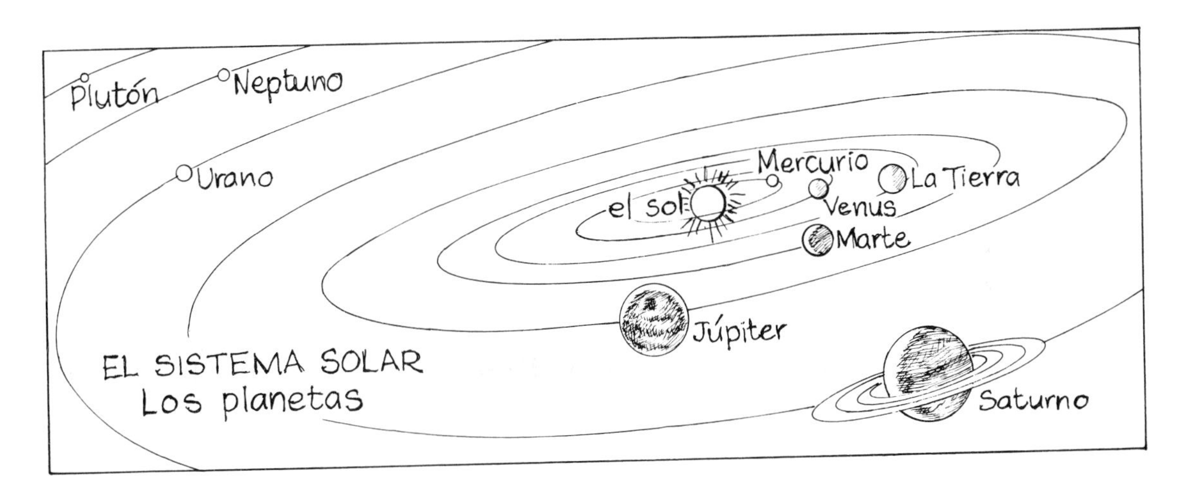

## ACTIVIDADES

**A.** Picture story. Can you read this story? Whenever you come to a picture, read it as if it were a Spanish word:

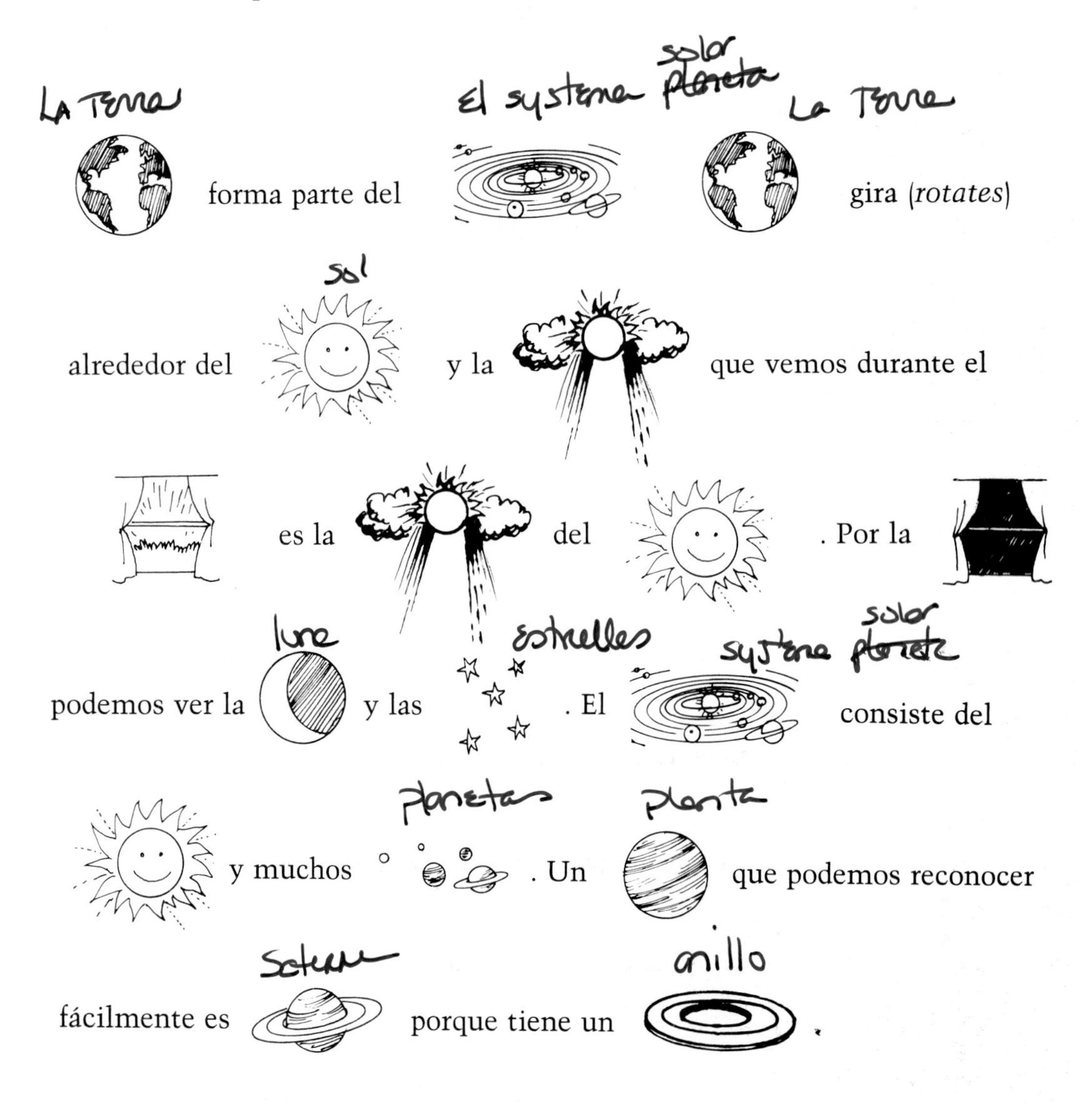

forma parte del
gira (*rotates*)
alrededor del
y la
que vemos durante el
es la
del
. Por la
podemos ver la
y las
. El
consiste del
y muchos
. Un
que podemos reconocer
fácilmente es
porque tiene un
.


**B.** Space humor. Make up a funny caption for each situation:

Mamá y Papa, esto es mi esposo
Mi amore, diga mi!

**C.** Identify the five pictures and write the names in the spaces below. Each name has a different number of letters:

| | | | | | | | |
|---|---|---|---|---|---|---|---|
| | S | O | l | | | | |
| | L | U | N | A | | | |
| T | I | E | R | R | A | | |
| J | U | P | I | T | E | R | |
| E | S | T | R | E | L | L | A |

## 2 Una aventura en el espacio

Let's read a story about an adventure in space. Pay attention to the verbs in bold type:

CONTROL: ¿Listos para despegar del satélite? — **despegar** *to take off*

ASTRONAUTA: Estaremos listos dentro de 15 minutos.

CONTROL: ¿Creen que la cápsula **podrá** aterrizar sobre el planeta XGB37 (equis, ge, be, treinta y siete)? — **aterrizar** *to land*

ASTRONAUTA: No **tendremos** ningún problema. La cuenta atrás puede comenzar en cualquier momento. — **la cuenta atrás** *countdown*

CONTROL: ¿Quiénes **harán** el primer viaje en la cápsula?

ASTRONAUTA: Paco y Flaco, nuestros dos astronautas hispanos, serán los primeros en hacer el viaje. Ellos **saldrán** de la cápsula, observarán todo muy bien y nos **dirán** qué vieron. Por fin **sabremos** si hay vida en ese planeta o no.

CONTROL: Bueno, en un minuto Uds. estarán al otro lado del planeta y no **podremos** comunicarnos más. Empiecen la cuenta atrás. ¡Adiós y buena suerte!

ASTRONAUTA: 10, 9, 8, 7, 6, 5, 4, 3, 2, 1 ¡Fuego! — **el fuego** *fire*

Paco y Flaco aterrizan en el planeta desconocido. Salen de la cápsula y sólo ven unas plantas enormes por todas partes. De repente las plantas comienzan a moverse y rodean a los dos astronautas.

**enorme** *huge*
**rodear** *to surround*

PACO: ¡Ay, Flaco, esto no me gusta nada! ¿Qué crees que **harán** estas plantas?

Una de ellas empieza a hablar.

VEGETAL: ¿Qué derecho tienen Uds. de interrumpir la paz y la tranquilidad de nuestro mundo? Uds. son seres terrestres, ¿verdad? ¿**Vendrán** otros detrás de Uds.?

**el derecho** *right*

PACO Y FLACO: Sí, pero . . .

VEGETAL: ¡Silencio! Conocemos muy bien las crueldades de su planeta. En la Tierra hacen ensaladas mixtas de nuestros hermanos. Preparan guacamole de nuestros primos, los aguacates. ¡Uds. son todos unos asesinos!

**la crueldad** *cruelty*
**el primo** *cousin*
**el aguacate** *avocado*

PACO: Seguro que hacemos eso. Pero no somos asesinos. Los aguacates son solamente vegetales.

VEGETAL: ¡Solamente vegetales! Uds. pagarán ese insulto con la vida. ¡Morirán ahora mismo! Pronto, tráiganme la sal.

FLACO: Oh, no. Los vegetales nos van a comer. ¡Qué manera tan horrible de morir!

VEGETAL: Les **pondremos** también un poco de mayonesa.

PACO: No, no quiero morir así. ¡Auxilio! ¡Socorro!

VOZ DE LA MAMÁ: Miguelito, son las once. Apaga ya el televisor. Seguro que **tendrás** pesadillas a causa de toda esa basura de ciencia ficción.

**apagar** *to turn off*

## ACTIVIDAD

**D.** Conteste en frases completas:

1. ¿Dónde está el astronauta?

______________________________

2. ¿En qué vehículo viajarán al planeta XGB37?

______________________________

3. ¿Quiénes serán los primeros en hacer el viaje?

Paco y Flaco serán los primeros en hacer el viaje

4. ¿Qué ven Paco y Flaco cuando aterrizan en el planeta desconocido?

Ven sólo unas plantas enormes

5. ¿Cómo reciben las plantas a los astronautas? ¿Están contentas de verlos?

las Plantas no reciben bien a los astronautas

6. ¿Qué opinión tienen las plantas de los seres terrestres? son crecientes

las plantas piensan que los seres terrestres

7. ¿Qué quieren hacer las plantas con Paco y Flaco?

las plantas tienen que comer Paco y Flaco

8. ¿Fue cierta la historia de los astronautas?

No la historia de los astronautas fue falso

9. ¿Qué hacía Miguel cuando le habló su mamá?

Cuando Miguel le habló su mamá, apaga ... el televisor

10. ¿Qué piensa la mamá de Miguel sobre la ciencia ficción?

la Mamá piensa que todo eso basura y Miguel tendrá pesadillas

**3** Did you pay attention to the verbs in bold type in the story? They are all in the future tense. They have regular endings, but their stem is not the infinitive:

> **¿Creen que la cápsula *podrá* aterrizar?**
> *Do you believe the capsule will be able to land?*
> **Por fin *sabremos* si hay vida en el planeta o no.**
> *Finally we will know if there is life on the planet or not.*

What are the stems of **podrá** and **sabremos**? Poder and Saber.

What are the infinitives of these verbs? Poder and Saber.

Can you figure out what happened to the infinitive to become **podr-** and **sabr-**? ______________________.

Right, **poder** and **saber** drop the **e** of the infinitive and then add the endings of the future tense. **Querer** also belongs in this category.

Can you complete the verb tables below?

| | **poder** | **querer** | **saber** |
|---|---|---|---|
| **yo** | **podré** | **querré** | **sabré** |
| **tú** | podres | querres | sabres |
| **Ud., él, ella** | podra | querra | sabra |
| **nosotros** | podremos | querremos | sabremos |
| **Uds., ellos, ellas** | podren | querren | sabren |

## ACTIVIDAD

**E.** You have invited a friend from another city to visit you and he has called to ask you some questions. Answer them:

1. ¿Podrás ir al aeropuerto a recibirme?

   Si, me gustare a Recabirse

2. ¿Querrán tus padres ir contigo?

   No. Tomaremos un taxi

3. ¿Sabrás cómo llegar al aeropuerto?

   Si. llegare a las seis de la tarde

4. ¿Sabrán Uds. en qué puerta esperarme?

   Si. Yo sabre a la puerta quince

5. ¿Podré llamar por teléfono a mis padres desde tu casa?

   Si, paro [illegible] necesitarás a darme mucho dinero

6. ¿Podremos salir el sábado por la noche?

   No podremos salir. Es muy peligrosa

7. ¿Querrá tu hermano salir con nosotros?

   No. Mi hermano querra salir con sus amigos

8. ¿Podrán tus padres prestarte el carro?

   Si, solamente si nosotros estaremos muy sympatico

Look now at these sentences from the story:

| | |
|---|---|
| **Les *pondremos* también mayonesa.** | *We will also put mayonnaise on them.* |
| **No *tendremos* ningún problema.** | *We won't have any problem.* |
| **Ellos *saldrán* de la cápsula.** | *They will leave the capsule.* |
| **¿*Vendrán* otros detrás de Uds.?** | *Will others come behind you?* |

Can you figure out how the stems of these verbs were formed?

| INFINITIVE | STEM OF FUTURE TENSE |
|---|---|
| **poner** | **pondr-** |
| **tener** | **tendr-** |
| **salir** | **saldr-** |
| **venir** | **vendr-** |

The **e** of **poner** and **tener** and the **i** of **salir** and **venir** change to **d**. Complete the following tables:

| | **poner** | **tener** | **salir** | **venir** |
|---|---|---|---|---|
| **yo** | **pondré** | **tendré** | **saldré** | **vendré** |
| **tú** | pondes | tendres | sadres | vendres |
| **Ud., él, ella** | pondra | tendra | saldra | vendra |
| **nosotros** | pondremos | tendremos | saldremos | vendremos |
| **Uds., ellos, ellas** | pondren | tendren | saldren | vendren |

## ACTIVIDADES

**F.** You are writing a letter to some friends who will come to visit you. Complete the letter with the appropriate form of the future tense:

Queridos amigos,

Yo saldré (1 salir) de la escuela temprano y podre (2 poder) ir a la estación a recibirlos. Sé que Paula y Mario querren (3 querer) ir conmigo. Como Uds. son cuatro, yo tndre (4 tener) que hacer dos viajes a la estación. Mientras yo hago un viaje, los demás ___podre___ (5 poder) esperarme en un café. Según me dicen, Uds. ___vendren___ (6 venir) en el tren de las cuatro.

**G.** You are going camping with some friends. Write what the subjects will do, using the following suggestions:

| | |
|---|---|
| yo | salir a las seis |
| mis amigos y yo | ponerse ropa cómoda |
| usted | querer ser el (la) guía |
| Roberto y Rosa | poder nadar en el lago |
| tú | tener que levantarse temprano |
| Mario | venir a visitarnos |
| ustedes | saber cómo llegar al campamento |

EXAMPLE: **Usted vendrá a visitarnos.**

1. Yo saldre a las seis
2. Mis Amigos y yo querremos ser El guia
3. Ud ~~querras~~ podras nadar en El lago
4. Roberto y Rosa pondrase ropa comoda
5. tu vendras a visitarnos
6. Mario sabra como llegar al campamento

**5** There are two more verbs with irregular future tense forms, **decir** and **hacer**:

| | |
|---|---|
| **Ellos nos *dirán* qué vieron.** | *They will tell us what they saw.* |
| **¿Quiénes *harán* el primer viaje?** | *Who will travel first?* |

The stem of the future tense of **decir** is ___dir-___. The stem of the future tense of **hacer** is ___har-___. Complete the following tables:

| | | |
|---|---|---|
| **yo** | **dir**e | **har**e |
| **tú** | diras | haras |
| **Ud., él, ella** | dira | hara |

| | | |
|---|---|---|
| **nosotros** | diremos | hacemos |
| **Uds., ellos, ellas** | diran | hacan |

## ACTIVIDADES

**H.** Using the suggested expressions, write when the following people will do certain things:

| | | |
|---|---|---|
| más tarde | el año que viene | el próximo verano |
| los fines de semana | pasado mañana | mañana |
| de hoy en quince | de hoy en ocho | el mes que viene |

EXAMPLE: mis padres / ir a Europa
**Mis padres *irán* a Europa *el próximo verano.***

1. Enrique / tener que trabajar
   Enrique tendra que trabajar mañana
2. nosotros / venir a comer
   Nosotros vendran a comer de hoy en ocho
3. tú / hacer las tareas
   Tú haras las tareas de hoy en quince
4. Uds. / querer salir
   Uds. querran salir pasado mañana
5. Marta y Rosa / hacer una torta
   Marta y Rosa haran una torta mas tarde
6. yo / salir de vacaciones
   Yo saldre de vacaciones el proximo verano
7. Ud. / poder viajar
   Ud podra viajar los fines de semana
8. tú y yo / saber hablar español
   Tú y yo sabremos hablar español el mes que viene

**I.** Your father wants to know your plans for next weekend. Answer his questions:

1. ¿Saldrás con tus amigos el sábado?
   Sí, papa. Saldre con mis amigos al cine

2. ¿A qué hora te encontrarás con ellos?

Encontraré con ellos a las seis de la tarde

3. ¿Te dirán ellos adónde quieren ir?

Si. Mi diran que ellos quierran ir al cine

4. ¿Sabrás qué bus coger?

Si cogera el numero cinco

5. ¿Querrá tu hermano ir contigo?

No. Mi hermano no quirre ir conmigo. Me destesta.

6. ¿Tendrás suficiente dinero?

No. Quierre que tomar mucho dinero.

7. ¿Qué ropa te pondrás?

Pondre la ropa roja y muy courta

8. ¿Qué harán Uds. el domingo?

El domingo, iran al iglesia

9. ¿Podrás lavar el carro?

Si tu daraone dinero, podre lavar el carro.

10. ¿Me dirás si piensas regresar muy tarde a casa?

Si. Tu dire si piense regresar muy tarde.

## PREGUNTAS PERSONALES

1. ¿Cuántos años tendrás en el año 2020?

Seguro que MURIRE ante eso ano

2. ¿Crees que en el futuro todos podremos viajar en naves espaciales?

Si creo que en el futuro viajaran en naves especiales

3. ¿Crees que es importante explorar el espacio? ¿Por qué?

No. Hay muchos problemas en terra que tendean mucho dinero

4. ¿Qué cualidades debe tener un astronauta?

Un astronauta tendra que ser muy inteligente

5. ¿Crees que hay seres vivientes en otras partes del universo?

Por supuesto. Estas personas estaran muy feos

## DIÁLOGO

You are looking at a TV science-fiction movie with a friend. Complete the dialog:

## INFORMACIÓN PERSONAL

What will you do when you graduate from high school?

Cuando me gradúe de la secundaria

1. Yo trabajare por BH
2. Yo visitare muchos locales estranos
3. 
4. 
5. 

## COMPOSICIÓN

What will your life be like when you are 25 years old? Write six sentences saying where you think you will live, what type of job you will have, how much money you will earn, whether you will be married or not, what kinds of clothes you will be wearing, and what kind of music will be in style:

I can't remember

## TURAL

ring the universe, we dream of knowing for their bravery. How many times do we ers of the fifteenth and sixteenth centuries pher Columbus (**Cristóbal Colón**) embarked no help from maps and no knowledge of what

World, but he never reached North America. It f the oldest settlement in Puerto Rico, who dis- his search for the "Fountain of Youth." Another **oronado,** explored a vast region of the southwestern es in Kansas, Texas, New Mexico, and Arizona), and **Álvar Núñez Cabeza de Vaca** spent many years in what is ... of Texas, reached Tampa Bay in Florida, and explored parts of Mississipp...

But the two best-known ...anish explorers are **Hernán Cortés** and **Francisco Pizarro.** Why? Because they conquered two Indian empires, the two most advanced Indian civilizations in the Americas. Cortés conquered the last Aztec emperor, Moctezuma, and Pizarro defeated the last Inca emperor, Atahualpa.

Do you know the names of any other Spanish explorers? Do you know who discovered the Pacific Ocean? Who were the first mariners to undertake a trip around the world?

# 20 En la aduana

## Past Participles; Present Perfect Tense

### 1 Vocabulario

el pasaporte

la visa

la declaración de aduana

el aduanero

la partida de nacimiento

la partida de matrimonio

el certificado de vacunación

el certificado de salud

la etiqueta

el equipaje

la maleta

el maletín

## ACTIVIDAD

**A.** You have just arrived from a trip abroad and are going through customs. The officer asks you some questions. What documents would you have to show? In the space provided, write the letter that corresponds to the document needed:

1. ¿Está Ud. bien de salud? ______
2. ¿Es Ud. soltero o casado? ______
3. ¿Dónde nació Ud.? ______
4. ¿Trae Ud. comida o licores? ______
5. ¿Es Ud. ciudadano norteamericano? ______
6. ¿Está Ud. vacunado? ______
7. ¿Tiene permiso para entrar en este país? ______
8. ¿Son éstas sus maletas? ______

**a.** el pasaporte
**b.** la visa
**c.** el certificado de salud
**d.** el certificado de vacunación
**e.** la etiqueta
**f.** la partida de nacimiento
**g.** la declaración de aduana
**h.** la partida de matrimonio

## Cruzando la frontera

Let's read a one-act play about a family's problems at the border. Pay attention to the verbs in bold type:

PERSONAJES: Mario Matagatos, hombre de negocios de unos 40 años de edad
Matilde, su mujer, más o menos de la misma edad
Minerva, la hija mayor, de 13 años
Maruja, la hija menor, de 8 años

**el hombre de negocios** *businessman*

ESCENA: En la frontera, la familia Matagatos espera su turno para pasar la aduana. **Han llegado** en carro y **han descargado** todo su equipaje.

**la frontera** *border*

MATILDE: Mario, **has traído** todos los documentos que vamos a necesitar?
MARIO: Creo que sí. **He traído** los pasaportes, los certificados de salud y de vacunación, las partidas de nacimiento y nuestra partida de matrimonio.

MATILDE: Bien. **Hemos viajado** mucho hoy y estoy muy cansada. No quiero problemas.

MARIO: No te preocupes, mi vida. Todo está en orden. Allí viene el inspector.

ADUANERO: Buenas tardes, señores. ¿Tienen Uds. algo que declarar?

MARIO: No señor, absolutamente nada.

ADUANERO: **¿No han comprado** comida, cigarrillos, licores, joyas u otros artículos de oro o de plata?

**el cigarrillo** *cigarette*

MARIO: **No hemos comprado** ni cigarrillos ni licor. Yo no fumo ni bebo.

**fumar** *to smoke*

MATILDE: Bueno, **hemos traído** unas pocas cosas para nuestro uso personal y regalos para unos pocos amigos. Las únicas joyas que tenemos son nuestras hijas.

ADUANERO: Veo nueve maletas. Parece que tienen muchos amigos. ¿Quiere Ud. abrir ese maletín verde, por favor?

MATILDE (a Mario): No me acuerdo de ningún maletín verde.

MARIO (a Matilde): Ni yo tampoco.

ADUANERO (abriendo el maletín): ¡Ajá! Uds. no fuman ni beben y **han comprado** sólo unas pocas cosas de uso personal. ¿Eh? ¿Cómo explican Uds. esto? Tres cartones de cigarrillos, tres botellas de coñac, dos de vino, dos relojes de oro . . .

**abriendo** *opening*

MARIO y MATILDE: ¡Ay, Dios mío!

MINERVA: Pero, papá, ese maletín no es nuestro. Miren la etiqueta con el nombre y la dirección adentro: Héctor González.

MARUJA: Yo vi el maletín en el pasillo del hotel y lo puse en el carro. Pensé que era nuestro.

**el pasillo** *lobby*

MARIO: Señor, mi hija dice la verdad. Ud. puede comprobarlo.

**comprobar** *to check*

ADUANERO: Está bien. Uds. pueden cruzar la frontera. Nosotros nos quedaremos con el maletín para devolvérselo al dueño. Pero de ahora en adelante tengan cuidado con su «joya».

**quedarse con** *to keep*
**el dueño** *owner*
**de ahora en adelante** *from now on*

## ACTIVIDAD

**B.** Conteste con frases completas:

1. ¿Qué espera la familia Matagatos?

_______________

2. ¿Quiénes son los miembros de la familia?

_______________

3. ¿Qué documentos ha traído el marido?

_______________

4. ¿Qué pregunta el aduanero?

_______________

5. ¿Qué artículos declara Mario?

_______________

6. ¿Qué dice la mujer que tienen en las maletas?

_______________

7. ¿Qué hay dentro del maletín verde?

_______________

8. ¿Quién puso el maletín en el carro? ¿Por qué?

_______________

9. ¿Dónde encontró la chica el maletín?

_______________

10. ¿Qué va a hacer el aduanero con el maletín?

_______________

**3** Look at these sentences:

| | |
|---|---|
| **El museo estaba *cerrado.*** | *The museum was closed.* |
| **El dinero está *escondido.*** | *The money is hidden.* |
| **Mi hermano está *aburrido.*** | *My brother is bored.* |

What are **cerrado, escondido,** and **aburrido** in these sentences? _______________. These adjectives are derived from the verbs **cerrar** (*to close*), **esconder** (*to hide*), and **aburrir** (*to bore*), and they are called past participles. Can you figure out how these past participles were formed?

_______________

Right. The infinitive endings **-ar, -er,** and **-ir** were replaced by **-ado, -ido,** and **-ido.**

You have been using many past participles as adjectives. Here are some that you know. From which infinitives were they derived?

| PAST PARTICIPLE | | INFINITIVE |
|---|---|---|
| **sentado** | *seated* | ________________ |
| **cansado** | *tired* | ________________ |
| **preocupado** | *worried* | ________________ |
| **vestido** | *dressed* | ________________ |
| **dormido** | *asleep* | ________________ |

Now let's try the opposite. Here are some infinitives you know. What are their past participles?

| INFINITIVE | | PAST PARTICIPLE |
|---|---|---|
| **apagar** | *to turn off* | ________________ |
| **encender** | *to turn on* | ________________ |
| **casar** | *to marry* | ________________ |
| **perder** | *to lose* | ________________ |
| **interesar** | *to interest* | ________________ |

Remember that past participles used as adjectives agree in gender and number with the noun they accompany:

***María y Juan* están *sentados* en la sala.**
***Rosa* está *sentada* en el comedor.**

## ACTIVIDAD

**C.** Complete the sentences, using the past participle of one of the following verbs:

| | | | |
|---|---|---|---|
| descansar | cansar | preocupar | encender |
| aburrir | dormir | apagar | esconder |

EXAMPLE: Manuel durmió la siesta y ahora está **descansado.**________.

1. Los muchachos corrieron diez millas y están ______________________.
2. María está sola en casa y está ______________________.
3. Mis padres oyeron malas noticias y están ______________________.
4. Ya es muy tarde y el bebé está ______________________.
5. Es de noche y las luces están ______________________.
6. Es de mañana y la luz está ______________________.
7. La verdad está ______________________.

The past participle is used to form the present perfect tense. In Spanish, the present perfect consists of two words: the present tense form of the verb **haber** (*to have*) and a past participle. Let's start by learning the present tense of **haber**:

| | |
|---|---|
| **yo** | **he** |
| **tú** | **has** |
| **Ud., él, ella** | **ha** |
| **nosotros** | **hemos** |
| **Uds., ellos, ellas** | **han** |

Do not confuse the verb **haber** with the verb **tener. Haber** is the only verb that can be used with a past participle to form the present perfect:

| | | |
|---|---|---|
| **yo** | **he** | **estudiado** |
| **tú** | **has** | **estudiado** |
| **Ud., él, ella** | **ha** | **estudiado** |
| **nosotros** | **hemos** | **estudiado** |
| **Uds., ellos, ellas** | **han** | **estudiado** |

Note that the past participle does not change in the present perfect tense; it always ends in **o**.

Look at these examples:

| | |
|---|---|
| **Esta semana ya *he ido* dos veces al cine.** | *This week I have already gone twice to the movies.* |
| **¿*Ha llamado* alguien hoy por la mañana?** | *Has anybody called this morning?* |

In Spanish, the present perfect is generally used to describe an action that happened in the past but is connected to the present.

## ACTIVIDADES

**D.** You are having a picnic in the park. How has each of these people contributed?

EXAMPLE: Ramón / comprar el pan
**Ramón ha comprado el pan.**

1. Julio y Jaime / preparan la ensalada

_______________

2. yo / encender el fuego

_______________

3. Uds. / cocinar las hamburguesas

_______________

4. Nora / buscar dónde comprar sodas

_______________

5. tú / sacar fotos

_______________

6. Ud. / decidir dónde hacer el picnic

_______________

7. Mario y yo / lavar las frutas

_______________

8. Rosa y Josefina / organizar los juegos

_______________

**E.** Answer the following questions:

1. ¿Has estudiado mucho últimamente?

_______________

2. ¿Has estado enfermo este año?

_______________

3. ¿Cuántos exámenes has tenido este semestre?

_______________

4. ¿Has salido con tus amigos este mes?

_______________

5. ¿Has sacado buenas notas hasta ahora?

_______________

**6.** ¿Has viajado mucho?

________________________________________

**5** Now look at these examples:

| | |
|---|---|
| ***Has hablado* con Juan ya?** | *Have you spoken with John already?* |
| **No, *no he hablado* con él todavía.** | *No, I haven't spoken with him yet.* |

Where does **no** stand in the second Spanish sentence? __________________.

The two words forming the present perfect cannot be separated in Spanish; **no** stands before the conjugated form of **haber.**

What happens if you use an object pronoun?

| | |
|---|---|
| ***Has comido* paella alguna vez?** | *Have you ever eaten paella?* |
| **Sí, *la he comido.*** | *Yes, I have eaten it.* |
| **No, *no la he comido* nunca.** | *No, I have never eaten it.* |

The object pronoun comes before the conjugated form of **haber**. In negative sentences, **no** comes before the object pronoun.

## ACTIVIDADES

**F.** Answer the following questions negatively:

**1.** ¿Han terminado ya las clases este año?

________________________________________

**2.** ¿Has decidido dónde pasar tus vacaciones?

________________________________________

**3.** ¿Has estado alguna vez en el Perú?

________________________________________

**4.** ¿Has montado a caballo alguna vez?

________________________________________

**5.** ¿Has visitado la Casa Blanca?

________________________________________

**6.** ¿Ha llegado la profesora tarde a clase alguna vez?

________________________________________

**G.** Answer these questions, using an object pronoun in your response:

EXAMPLE: ¿Has escuchado las noticias?
**Sí, las he escuchado.**

1. ¿Has buscado trabajo para el verano?

______________________________

2. ¿Ha preparado tu mamá la comida?

______________________________

3. ¿Ha enseñado la profesora muchas cosas nuevas?

______________________________

4. ¿Han aprendido los alumnos español?

______________________________

5. ¿Has escuchado muchos discos últimamente?

______________________________

6. ¿Has visitado a tu familia recientemente?

______________________________

**6** The past participles of **-ER** and **-IR** verbs with stems ending in a vowel have an accent mark:

| | | | | | |
|---|---|---|---|---|---|
| **caer:** | **caído** *fallen* | **leer:** | **leído** *read* | **traer:** | **traído** *brought* |
| **creer:** | **creído** *believed* | **oír:** | **oído** *heard* | | |

A few verbs have irregular past participles, and you will have to memorize these:

| | | | |
|---|---|---|---|
| **abrir:** | ***abierto*** *open(ed)* | **morir:** | ***muerto*** *died* |
| **cubrir:** | ***cubierto*** *covered* | **poner:** | ***puesto*** *put* |
| **decir:** | ***dicho*** *said* | **romper:** | ***roto*** *broken* |
| **escribir:** | ***escrito*** *written* | **ver:** | ***visto*** *seen* |
| **hacer:** | ***hecho*** *done* | **volver:** | ***vuelto*** *returned* |

Remember that compounds of these verbs also have irregular past participles:

**describir:** ***descrito*** *described*
**descubrir:** ***descubierto*** *discovered*
**devolver:** ***devuelto*** *returned*

## ACTIVIDADES

**H.** It's Sunday and you have slept till noon. Write what the other members of your family have done while you slept:

1. mi papá / leer el periódico

___

2. mi mamá / poner la mesa

___

3. mis hermanos / hacer las tareas

___

4. mis hermanas / escribir cartas

___

5. mi gato / descubrir un ratón

___

6. mi perro / romper un florero

___

7. mi tía / volver del supermercado

___

8. tú / ver un programa de televisión

___

**I.** What have these people done for your birthday party?

1. mi padre / traer los refrescos

___

2. mis amigos / decir «Feliz cumpleaños»

___

3. mi mamá / hacer una torta

___

4. mis hermanas / cubrir la torta con chocolate

___

5. tú / escribir las invitaciones

___

6. yo / abrir los regalos

______________________________________________

**J.** Describe what you and your friend Carlos have done before leaving for Spain. Use these expressions:

| | |
|---|---|
| sacar el pasaporte | pedir la visa |
| hacer las reservaciones | ir a la agencia de viajes |
| escribir a los hoteles | cambiar dólares por pesetas |
| leer las guías turísticas | oír casetes en español |
| ver al cónsul español | hacer las maletas |
| decir adiós a los amigos | devolver libros a la biblioteca |

EXAMPLE: **Carlos y yo hemos hecho las reservaciones.**

1. ______________________________________________
2. ______________________________________________
3. ______________________________________________
4. ______________________________________________
5. ______________________________________________
6. ______________________________________________
7. ______________________________________________
8. ______________________________________________
9. ______________________________________________
10. ______________________________________________

Now look at these sentences:

| | |
|---|---|
| **¿Has hablado con Darío?**<br>**Sí, *acabo de hablar* con él.** | *Have you spoken with Dario?*<br>*Yes, I have just spoken with him.* |
| **¿Dónde está Consuelo?**<br>**Ella *acaba de salir*.** | *Where is Consuelo?*<br>*She has just gone out.* |

If you want to express in Spanish the idea that something has just taken place, use the following construction:

present tense of **acabar** + **de** + infinitive

| | |
|---|---|
| **El avión acaba de aterrizar.** | *The plane has just landed.* |
| **Acabo de levantarme.** | *I just got up.* |
| **Acabamos de llegar.** | *We have just arrived.* |

**Acabar** is a regular **-AR** verb that by itself means *to finish*:

| | |
|---|---|
| **¿Cuándo vas a acabar las tareas?** | *When are you going to finish your homework?* |

## ACTIVIDAD

**K.** You want to go out, but all the friends you have called say that they are too tired. Why are they tired?

EXAMPLE: Pedro / jugar al fútbol
**Pedro acaba de jugar al fútbol.**

1. Roberto y Raúl / correr cinco millas

_______________

2. tú / limpiar tu cuarto

_______________

3. Uds. / estudiar para un examen difícil

_______________

4. Rosario / trabajar en el jardín

_______________

5. José / lavar el carro

_______________

## *PREGUNTAS PERSONALES*

1. ¿Has viajado alguna vez al extranjero (*abroad*)? ¿Adónde?

_______________

2. ¿Sabes qué documentos necesitas para viajar al extranjero?

_______________

3. Como ciudadano americano, ¿necesitas un pasaporte para viajar a Puerto Rico?

_______________

4. ¿Te han vacunado alguna vez? ¿Contra qué?

_______________

5. ¿Qué dice tu partida de nacimiento?

_______________

## INFORMACIÓN PERSONAL

List five things you haven't done up to now:

EXAMPLE: **No he visto una ópera.**

1. _______________
2. _______________
3. _______________
4. _______________
5. _______________

## COMPOSICIÓN

The customs officials have been stopping all suspicious-looking luggage. They have asked you to fill out a form describing your recent activities before they allow you to cross the border. Tell where you have been, for how long, your reasons for going there, the nature of your work; list the merchandise you have purchased abroad and any other pertinent information that will convince the customs officials that you are an honest citizen.

_______________

_______________

_______________

_______________

_______________

## DIÁLOGO

You have come back from a trip to South America and the customs official is asking the usual questions. Complete the dialog:

# CÁPSULA CULTURAL

## Pasaporte a las Américas

Do you have a passport? You will need it for the trip we are going to take to Latin America. You'll learn some interesting facts about some places. Let's start in Mexico. Did you know that Mexico City is the third-largest city in the world after Tokyo and Shanghai? In Mexico, you can also visit Taxco, the center of the country's silver industry, which even today looks like an old Spanish town. Then, if you go to Santo Domingo in the Dominican Republic, you will be visiting the oldest city in the Americas, founded in 1496. It also has the oldest university in the New World.

And how about flying to Cartagena, in Colombia? Founded in 1533, it's one of the few walled cities in the world. It still has an imposing seventeenth-century fortress, built to defend the city against pirate attacks. You could continue on to La Paz, in Bolivia. The highest capital in the world, La Paz lies at an altitude of 11,735 feet above sea level. You could then take a side trip to Lake Titicaca, the world's highest navigable lake, which lies 12,500 feet above sea level on the Peru-Bolivia border. And as long as you enter Peru, you have to visit Lima, its capital, to admire the many buildings remaining from the Spanish colonial period. A side trip to Cuzco is a must. Located at 11,207 feet above sea level, Cuzco was the capital of the former Incan empire and dates from the eleventh century.

You could try, as others have before, to conquer the peak of Mount Aconcagua between Argentina and Chile. At 22,834 feet, it is the highest mountain in the Americas. The Chilean side has become South America's most popular winter resort. Finally, you could visit the Iguazú Falls on the Argentina-Brazil border. The falls, 269 feet high and 2.5 miles wide, are one of the natural wonders of South America.

Has your interest in traveling to Latin America been aroused? Good, because there are many more places we haven't mentioned here. Do you know of any?

# Repaso IV (Lecciones 16–20)

## Lección 16

Some Spanish verbs change their spelling in certain forms to maintain the original sound of the infinitive:

**a.** Verbs ending in **-car, -gar,** and **-zar** change the **c** to **qu,** the **g** to **gu,** and the **z** to **c** before **e**:

| | | |
|---|---|---|
| **tocar:** | **Yo to*qu*é a la puerta.** | **To*qu*e Ud. ahora.** |
| **pagar:** | **Yo no pa*gu*é la cuenta.** | **Pá*gu*ela Ud.** |
| **comenzar:** | **Yo ya comen*c*é a hacer las tareas.** | **Comien*c*e Ud. también.** |

**b.** Verbs ending in **-ger** or **-gir** change the **g** to **j** before **a** and **o**:

| | | |
|---|---|---|
| **coger:** | **Yo co*j*o esta pelota.** | **Co*j*a Ud. la otra.** |
| **corregir:** | **Yo corri*j*o los ejercicios.** | **Corrí*j*anlos Uds. también.** |

**c.** Verbs ending in **-guir** change the **gu** to **g** before **a** and **o:**

| | | |
|---|---|---|
| **seguir:** | **Yo sigo su ejemplo.** | **Síganlo Uds. también.** |

## Lección 17

**a. más** + adjective + **que** are used to form a comparison stating that one thing or person is more than another:

**Ese edificio es más alto que éste.**

**menos** + adjective + **que** are used to form a comparison stating that one thing or person is less than another:

**Esta tarea es menos difícil que la otra.**

**b. tan** + adjective + **como** are used to form a comparison of equality:

**Este diccionario es tan bueno como ése.**

**c.** In Spanish, the superlative is expressed as follows:

definite article (**el, la, los, las**) + **más** / **menos** + adjective + **de**

**María es la alumna más seria de la clase.**

**d.** Four adjectives have irregular comparative forms:

| | | | |
|---|---|---|---|
| **bueno** | *good* | **mejor** | *better, best* |
| **malo** | *bad* | **peor** | *worse, worst* |
| **grande** | *big* | **mayor** | *older, oldest* |
| **pequeño** | *small* | **menor** | *younger, youngest* |

**Más grande** and **más pequeño** refer to size, **mayor** and **menor** refer to age.

## Lección 18

**a.** The future of regular verbs is formed by adding the future endings to the infinitive:

| | | |
|---|---|---|
| **yo** | | **-é** |
| **tú** | **estudiar** | **-ás** |
| **Ud., él, ella** | **aprender** | **-á** |
| **nosotros** | **escribir** | **-emos** |
| **Uds., ellos, ellas** | | **-án** |

**b.** In Spanish, the future tense is sometimes used to express wonder or probability in the present:

| | |
|---|---|
| **¿Quién llamará a esta hora?** | *I wonder who's calling at this hour.* |
| **Será Carlos.** | *It's probably Charles.* |

## Lección 19

**a. Poder, querer,** and **saber** drop the **e** of the infinitive before adding the regular endings of the future tense:

**Yo *podr*é visitarte mañana.**
**Ella *querr*á ir conmigo.**
**Mañana *sabr*emos los resultados del examen.**

**b. Poner, tener, salir,** and **venir** change the **e** and the **i** of the infinitive to **d** before adding the regular endings of the future tense:

**Tú *pondr*ás los libros en la mesa.**
**Él *tendr*á que estudiar hoy.**
**Uds. *saldr*án mañana para Europa.**
**Ellas *vendr*án temprano.**

**c. Decir** and **hacer** have irregular stems in the future tense forms:

**Ud. me *dir*á la verdad.**
**Ellos *har*án las tareas esta noche.**

## Lección 20

**a.** In Spanish, past participles are formed by dropping the **-ar, -er,** and **-ir** ending of the infinitive and adding **-ado, -ido,** and **-ido:**

**sentar:** ***sentado***
**perder:** ***perdido***
**vestir:** ***vestido***

Many past participles can be used as adjectives, agreeing in gender and number with the noun they accompany:

***Nosotros*** **estamos** ***cansados.***
***La niña*** **está** ***vestida*** **de blanco.**

**b.** The past participle is used to form the present perfect tense. The present perfect consists of the present tense form of **haber** (*to have*) and a past participle:

| | |
|---|---|
| **yo he** | **viajado** |
| **tú has** | **viajado** |
| **Ud., él, ella ha** | **viajado** |
| **nosotros hemos** | **viajado** |
| **Uds., ellos, ellas han** | **viajado** |

In the present perfect tense, the past participle always ends in **o.**

**c.** The present perfect in Spanish describes an action that happened in the past but is connected to the present:

**El correo ya ha llegado.** *The mail has already arrived.*

**d.** In Spanish, contrary to English, the two words forming the present perfect cannot be separated:

**Juan no me ha llamado todavía.** John hasn't called me yet.

**e.** The past participles of **-ER** and **-IR** verbs with stems ending in a vowel have an accent mark:

**leer:** ***leído***
**oír:** ***oído***

A few verbs have irregular past participles:

| | |
|---|---|
| **abrir:** ***abierto*** | **morir:** ***muerto*** |
| **cubrir:** ***cubierto*** | **poner:** ***puesto*** |
| **decir:** ***dicho*** | **romper:** ***roto*** |
| **escribir:** ***escrito*** | **ver:** ***visto*** |
| **hacer:** ***hecho*** | **volver:** ***vuelto*** |

f. In Spanish, the present tense of **acabar** + **de** + infinitive expresses the idea that something has just taken place:

**Acabo de terminar las tareas.** *I have just finished my homework.*

**Acabar** is a regular **-AR** verb that by itself means *to finish:*

**El electricista acabó el trabajo.** *The electrician finished the job.*

## ACTIVIDADES

**A.** Following the clues given, complete the descriptions under the pictures, using the following verbs. All statements should be in the first person singular:

| | | | | |
|---|---|---|---|---|
| almorzar | cruzar | explicar | jugar | sacar |
| llegar | pagar | perseguir | recoger | |

1. 

Ayer __________________ con Juan.

2. 

El semestre pasado __________________ muy buenas notas.

3. 

Fui a la pizarra y __________________.

4. 

__________________ $30 por

__________________ que compré.

5. 

Cuando __________________ a la esquina, un señor me dijo:

«__________________ conmigo, por favor».

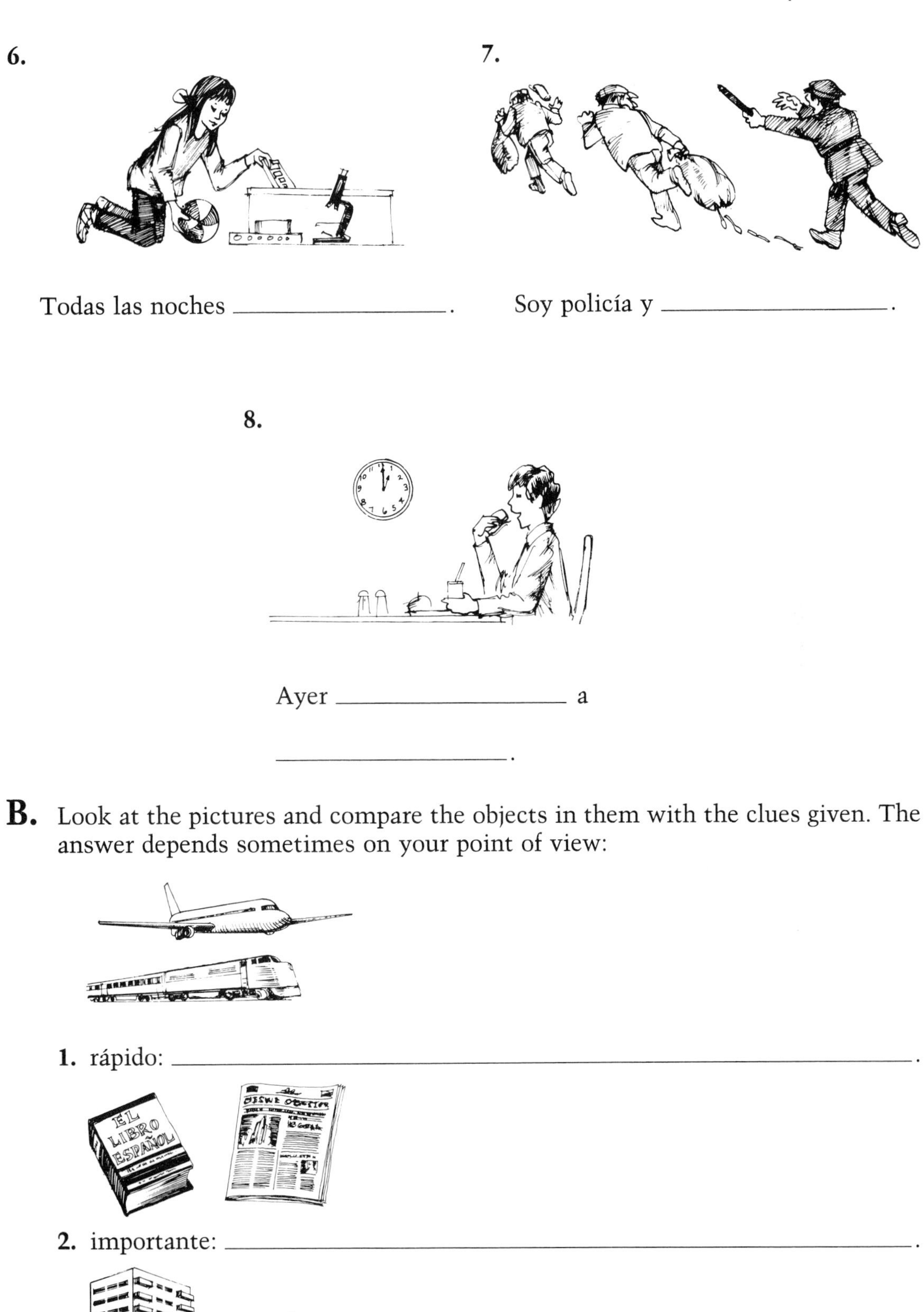


**6.** Todas las noches ____________.

**7.** Soy policía y ____________.

**8.** Ayer ____________ a ____________.

**B.** Look at the pictures and compare the objects in them with the clues given. The answer depends sometimes on your point of view:

1. rápido: ______________________________.
2. importante: ______________________________.
3. pequeño: ______________________________.

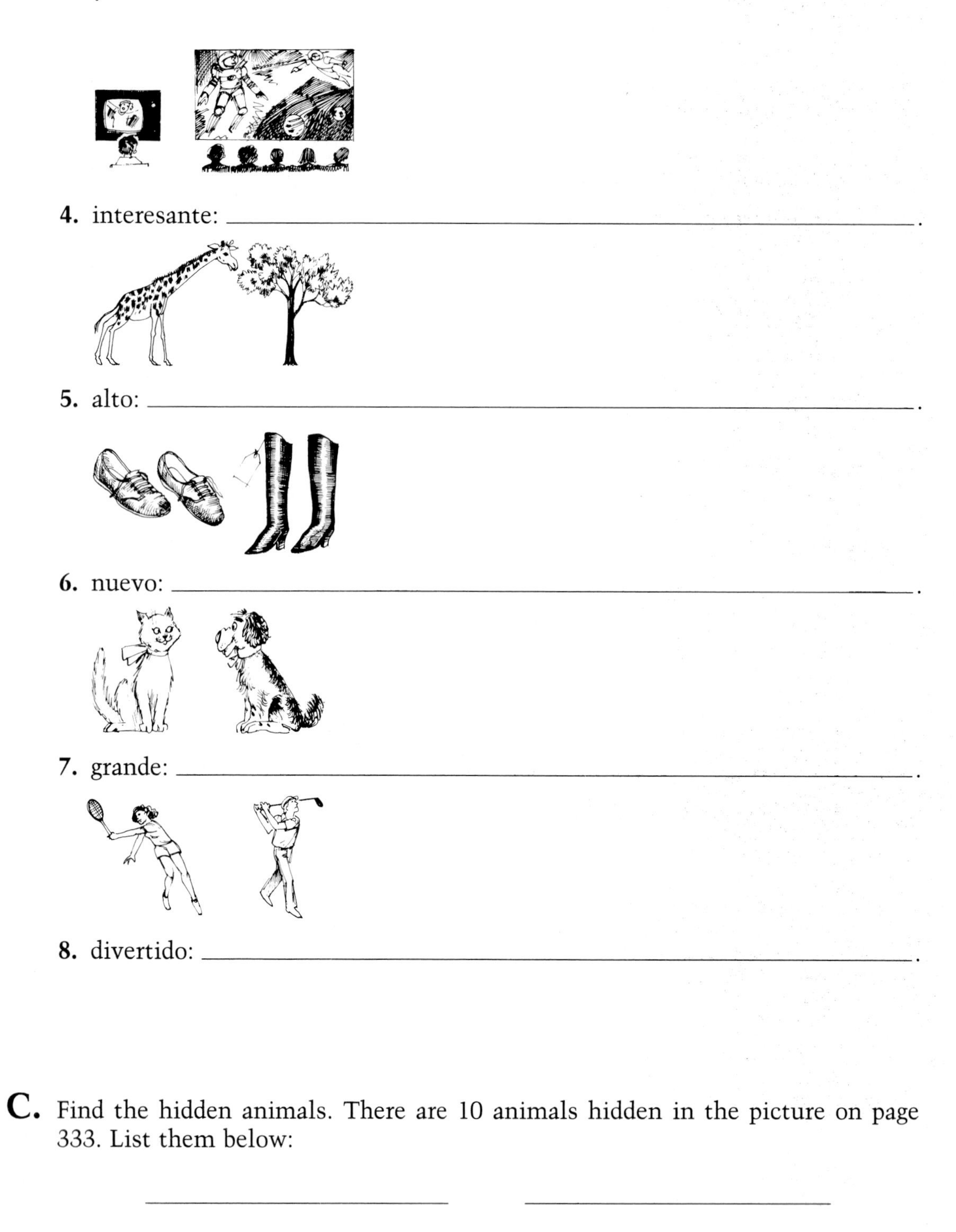

**4.** interesante: ________________________________.

**5.** alto: ________________________________.

**6.** nuevo: ________________________________.

**7.** grande: ________________________________.

**8.** divertido: ________________________________.

**C.** Find the hidden animals. There are 10 animals hidden in the picture on page 333. List them below:

____________________ ____________________

____________________ ____________________

____________________ ____________________

____________________ ____________________

____________________ ____________________

**D.** Word search. There are 16 words hidden in the puzzle. They are all related to travel, on earth and in space. Can you find them? The words may be read from left to right, right to left, up or down, or diagonally:

| | | | | | | | | | | |
|---|---|---|---|---|---|---|---|---|---|---|
| A | N | A | U | D | A | M | N | D | I | E |
| A | S | T | R | O | N | A | V | E | A | J |
| T | Q | C | R | U | S | T | T | S | E | A |
| U | N | Á | E | A | A | E | I | P | T | P |
| A | Ó | P | N | T | T | V | E | E | R | I |
| N | I | S | Í | A | É | L | R | G | O | U |
| O | V | U | T | F | L | R | R | A | P | Q |
| R | A | L | E | A | I | S | A | R | A | E |
| T | N | A | L | Z | T | Z | U | U | S | B |
| S | M | C | A | A | E | L | U | N | A | L |
| A | Q | R | M | O | T | O | L | I | P | P |

**E.** Jumble. Unscramble the words. Then unscramble the letters in the circles to find out what Juanita dreamed (or had a nightmare) about:

**A S E D A LL P I**

**T A N S A F Í A**

**G A O M**

**J U B A R S**

**Juanita soñó con**

**F.** How many of these words do you remember? Fill in the Spanish words, then read down the boxed column to find the answer to this question: **¿Cuál es la profesión de la señorita Gómez?**

1.

2.

3.

4.

5.

6.

7.

8.

9.

10.

11.

12.

**G.** You are one of a group of astronauts exploring a new planet. Report your findings:

_______________________________________________

_______________________________________________

_______________________________________________

_______________________________________________

_______________________________________________

_______________________________________________

_______________________________________________

## H. Crucigrama

HORIZONTALES

1. Documento necesario para viajar al extranjero.
5. Lo necesitas cuando llueve.
8. Presente de **ser.**
10. Pronombre reflexivo.
11. La cuenta ____.
13. Insecto pequeño que siempre trabaja.
14. El avión baja al suelo.
15. Preposición.
16. Contrario de **después.**
19. Contrario de **con.**
20. Imperativo de **reír.**
21. Negación.
22. Presente de **ser.**
24. Animal de los Andes.

VERTICALES

1. Mal sueño.
2. Lo usas en la oreja.
3. Pronombre reflexivo.
4. Nave espacial.
5. Dinero mexicano (pl.).
6. Dirige una compañía.
7. Contrario de **cerrados.**
9. Sirve para llevar ropa en un viaje.
11. Ayuda a los pasajeros del avión.
12. Expresa comparación.
13. Presente de **haber.**
17. Pronombre reflexivo.
18. Los astronautas viajan al ____.
23. Sirve para volar de un lugar a otro.
28. Pronombre de complemento directo.
29. Presente de **haber.**

HORIZONTALES

**25.** Lo prepara el panadero.
**26.** Animal que comes en noviembre.
**27.** Movimiento del mar.
**29.** Presente de **haber.**
**30.** Adjetivo demostrativo.
**31.** La ____ de aduana.
**37.** Participio de **nacer.**
**39.** Conjunto de maletas.
**42.** Pretérito de **dar.**
**43.** Pretérito de **decir.**
**45.** Participio de **cubrir.**
**46.** Adjetivo del participio de **querer.**
**48.** Participio de **hacer.**
**49.** Futuro de **poder.**
**51.** Es su casa. Ella es la ____.
**53.** Adjetivo posesivo.
**54.** Participio de **romper.**
**56.** Miedo.
**57.** ____, no aquí.
**59.** Futuro de **saber.**
**60.** Imperfecto de **ir.**
**61.** Arreglan zapatos.
**62.** Maneja el avión.

VERTICALES

**32.** Imperativo de **leer.**
**33.** Imperativo de **reír.**
**34.** Contrario de **alguien.**
**35.** Los médicos de los animales.
**36.** Mujer que corta el pelo.
**38.** Participio de **dar.**
**40.** Escribe para el periódico.
**41.** Tomas ____ para la tos.
**42.** Participio de **decir.**
**44.** Futuro de **ser.**
**47.** Número ordinal.
**48.** Futuro de **hacer.**
**50.** Número ordinal.
**52.** Utiliza.
**55.** Animales grandes y fuertes. Les gustan las frutas y la miel (*honey*).
**58.** Imperativo de **hacer.**

**I.** Here's a new challenge. Transform one word into another, by changing one letter at a time, using words you know:

EJEMPLO: P E L O

___ ___ ___ ___ P E S O

___ ___ ___ ___ P E S A

M E S A

| H A B E R | P A G A R | M A L O S |
|---|---|---|
| ___ ___ ___ ___ ___ | ___ ___ ___ ___ ___ | ___ ___ ___ ___ ___ |
| ___ ___ ___ ___ ___ | ___ ___ ___ ___ ___ | ___ ___ ___ ___ ___ |
| ___ ___ ___ ___ ___ | ___ ___ ___ ___ ___ | ___ ___ ___ ___ ___ |
| S A L A S | C O S A S | M E N O R |

**J.** It's the year 3000 and you, an inspector in the Earth's Department of Immigration, are interviewing newcomers from outer space. You have just received word to keep on the lookout for a particular creature that reproduces itself every 24 hours. You can see what a problem that would create. Spot this creature from the information given:

Lleva una forma de zapatos.
No tiene barba, pero sí bigote.
Tiene antenas en vez de orejas.
Parece estar siempre contento.
Tiene los pies muy pequeños.
Tiene dos ojos, uno muy cerca del otro.

# Achievement Test II (Lessons 11–20)

## 1 Listening Comprehension — Situations [10 points]

**a.** Listen to your teacher read twice in succession a situation in Spanish. Then your teacher will pause while you circle the letter of the best suggested answer:

1. **a.** Tengo que llevar el chaleco.
   **b.** Mejor me pongo el impermeable.
   **c.** Debo ponerme las zapatillas.
   **d.** Mejor llevo el cinturón.

2. **a.** Revisar el baúl.
   **b.** Arreglar los parachoques.
   **c.** Arreglar el volante.
   **d.** Poner faros nuevos.

3. **a.** Este suéter es muy bonito.
   **b.** ¿Tiene una alfombra roja?
   **c.** Quiero devolver esta ropa.
   **d.** Necesito una talla más grande.

4. **a.** Algodón y un peine.
   **b.** Jarabe y pañuelos de papel.
   **c.** Curitas y una venda.
   **d.** Papel higiénico.

5. **a.** Siéntese en este horno.
   **b.** Siéntese en esta cómoda.
   **c.** Siéntese en este sillón.
   **d.** Siéntese en este estante.

**b.** Listen to your teacher read twice in succession a situation in Spanish. Then your teacher will pause while you write an appropriate response to the situation in the spaces provided. Assume that in each situation you are speaking with persons who speak Spanish:

1. ______________________________

2. ______________________________

3. ______________________________

4. ______________________________

5. ______________________________

## Vocabulary [10 points]

**¿Qué es esto?** Label the following pictures in Spanish:

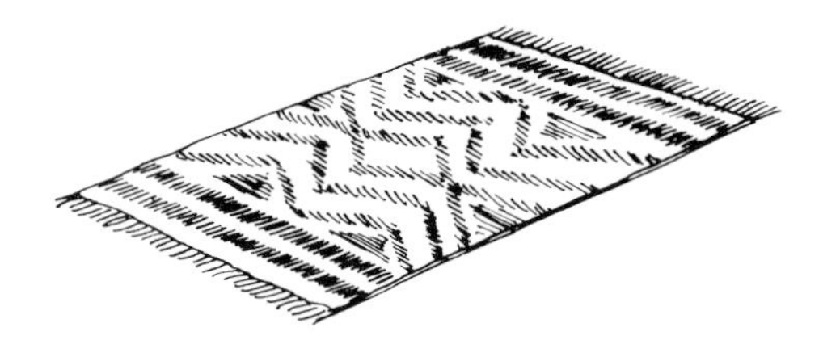

1. ______________________________

2. ______________________________

3. ______________________________

4. ______________________________

5. ______________________________

6. ______________________________

7. ______________________________

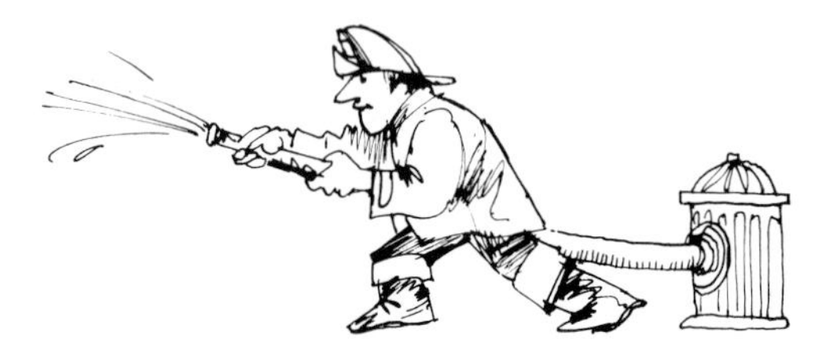

8. ______________________________

9. ______________________________

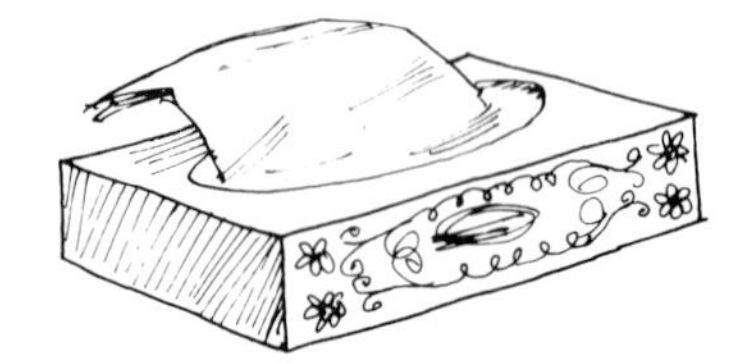

10. ______________________________

# 3 Structures [60 points]

**a.** Cardinal numbers [5 points]

Complete the sentences in Spanish:

**1.** Yo tengo (600) ____________________ estampillas en mi colección.

**2.** Los muebles pesan (271) ______________________________ libras.

**3.** Puerto Rico tiene (3,000,000) ____________________ de habitantes.

**4.** La entrada vale (51) ___________________________________ pesos.

**5.** Hay casi (100) _________________________ muchachos en el baile.

**b.** Ordinal numbers [5 points]

Complete the sentences in Spanish:

**1.** José vive en el (6°) ________________ piso de ese edificio.

**2.** Ellos llegaron al (4°) ________________ día de viaje.

**3.** La tienda queda en la avenida (7°) ________________.

**4.** Es la (2°) ______________________ vez que te escribo.

**5.** Ése es el (10°) ______________________ avión que aterriza en una hora.

**c.** Spelling-changing verbs [5 points]

Following the clues given, complete the sentences in Spanish with the correct form of the verb in parentheses:

**1.** (sacar) Yo ________________ esas fotos el verano pasado.

**2.** (pagar) ¡________________ Ud. la cuenta inmediatamente!

**3.** (empezar) Yo ________________ el trabajo ayer por la mañana.

**4.** (recoger) Yo nunca ________________ los platos de la mesa.

**5.** (seguir) ¡________________ Ud. bien las instrucciones!

**d.** Comparison of adjectives [10 points]

Complete the following sentences in Spanish:

**1.** (as big as) Ella es ______________________ su hermano.

**2.** (faster) Ese tren es ______________________ éste.

**3.** (better) Este libro es ______________________ el otro.

**4.** (as interesting) Este cuadro no es ______________________ aquél.

**5.** (worst) Ese chico es ______________________ la clase.

**6.** (less nice) Yo creo que Jorge es ______________________ Manuel.

**7.** (older) Margarita es mi hermana ______________________.

**8.** (oldest) Ese hotel es ______________________ la ciudad.

**9.** (smallest) Maritza es ______________________ la escuela.

**10.** (youngest) Ella es también ______________________.

**e.** Future tense [10 points]

What will these people do next summer? Complete the sentences with the correct future tense form of the verbs in parentheses:

**1.** (visitar) Mis padres ______________ España.

**2.** (hacer) Nosotros ______________ un viaje en barco.

**3.** (ir) Yo ______________ a la playa todos los días.

**4.** (estar) Mi hermana ______________ trabajando en una farmacia.

**5.** (venir) Mis tíos ______________ a mi casa.

**6.** (tener) Tú ______________ que trabajar.

**7.** (poder) Uds. ______________ jugar al tenis todos los días.

**8.** (querer) Mi primo ______________ ver muchas películas.

**9.** (salir) Ud. ______________ a dar caminatas.

**10.** (decir) Nosotros ______________ después lo que vamos a hacer.

**f.** Present perfect tense [10 points]

What have these people done lately? Complete the sentences with the correct present perfect tense form of the verbs in parentheses:

**1.** (trabajar) Nosotros ______________________ mucho.

**2.** (comer) La niña ______________ dos veces en un restaurante.

**3.** (decir) Yo ______________________ unas cuantas mentiras.

**4.** (hacer) Uds. ______________ reservaciones para un viaje.

**5.** (abrir) Ellos ______________________ un negocio.

**6.** (escribir) Tú ______________ los ejercicios correctamente.

**7.** (romper) Yo ______________________ tres platos nuevos.

**8.** (ver) Ud. ______________________ a sus amigos.

**9.** (volver) María ______________________ a la universidad.

**10.** (leer) Nosotras ______________ dos novelas en español.

**g.** Object pronouns [15 points]

Rewrite the following sentences, substituting object pronouns for the words in bold type:

**1.** El médico examina **al enfermo.**

______________________________________________

**2.** Ella da el dinero a **los niños.**

______________________________________________

**3.** Vivimos cerca de **María.**

______________________________________________

**4.** Nosotros hacemos **las tareas** todos los días.

______________________________________________

**5.** Él explicó **la lección a la muchacha.**

______________________________________________

**6.** Quiero decir **la verdad a mi mamá.**

______________________________________________

7. Sirva un café **a nosotros.**

______________________________

8. Ud. vende **juguetes** en la tienda.

______________________________

9. Quiero trabajar para **mi padre.**

______________________________

10. ¡Abra Ud. **el libro** y lea!

______________________________

11. Yo doy **el regalo a Pedro.**

______________________________

12. Voy a escribir una carta **a Luisa.**

______________________________

13. Venda Ud. **la casa a nosotros.**

______________________________

14. No vaya sin **mi hermano y yo.**

______________________________

15. No quiero contar **el secreto a los alumnos.**

______________________________

## 4 Slot Completion [5 points]

In the following passage, there are five blank spaces numbered 1 through 5. Each blank space represents a missing word. For each blank space, four possible completions are provided. Only one makes sense:

Acabamos de regresar de un viaje maravilloso. Comenzamos a divertirnos desde el momento en que subimos al avión. De comida, los aeromozos __(1)__ un arroz con __(2)__ muy sabroso, al estilo español. El viaje no duró mucho. Cuando __(3)__ en la isla, el sol brillaba fuertemente y un guía muy simpático nos esperaba en el aeropuerto. Él nos __(4)__ al hotel donde teníamos las reservaciones, que quedaba en

(1) **a.** pidieron
**b.** comieron
**c.** sirvieron
**d.** ordenaron

(2) **a.** caracoles
**b.** camarones
**c.** claves
**d.** culebras

una playa preciosa. Todos los días nadábamos en el mar, tomábamos el sol, montábamos a caballo y jugábamos al tenis o al golf. Todo era tan bonito y tan agradable, que ahora nos parece que vivimos __(5)__ fabuloso.

(3) **a.** bajamos
**b.** despegamos
**c.** subimos
**d.** aterrizamos

(4) **a.** llegó
**b.** llevó
**c.** llamó
**d.** llenó

(5) **a.** una pesadilla
**b.** un signo
**c.** un sueño
**d.** un dueño

## Reading Comprehension [5 points]

Below the following story there are five questions. For each, choose the expression that best answers the question according to the meaning of the story and circle its letter:

Es medianoche cuando Luis regresa de la oficina. Al salir del tren, ve que no hay nadie en el andén de la estación. Camina rápidamente por las calles desiertas y solitarias. Quiere llegar a su casa lo más pronto posible porque tiene un poco de miedo.

Por fin llega. Abre la puerta y entra. No hay nadie en casa tampoco. Sus padres están de vacaciones en la Florida. Su hermano mayor, Raúl, estudia en una universidad en Texas y no vendrá hasta fin de año. Luis está solo. Mira a su alrededor y nota que todo no está en el orden de siempre. Ve en el suelo, roto, un florero que generalmente está sobre una mesita, cerca del sofá.

Entra en la cocina. En el piso hay un plato y un vaso, ¡rotos también! «¿Qué pasó aquí?», se pregunta el muchacho. «¿Habrán entrado ladrones? ¿Estarán aquí todavía?» Luis está ahora realmente nervioso. De repente, oye un ruido que sale del sótano. Parece que hay alguien allí. Sin perder un segundo, Luis corre hacia allá. Enciende la luz y . . . ¿qué ve? Es su gato, Tigre, que corre por todas partes, tratando de atrapar a un ratón.

**1.** ¿A qué hora vuelve Luis del trabajo?

**a.** a las dos
**b.** por la tarde
**c.** al mediodía
**d.** a las doce

**2.** ¿Dónde está la familia de Luis?

**a.** en el sur
**b.** en el oeste
**c.** en el colegio
**d.** en diferentes lugares

3. ¿Cuántas cosas rotas ve en la casa?

a. tres
b. cuatro
c. dos
d. una

4. ¿Qué sospecha el muchacho?

a. Sus padres regresaron.
b. Su hermano llegó de sorpresa.
c. Alguien vino a visitarlo.
d. Alguien quiso robar la casa.

5. ¿Qué descubre al final?

a. No hay luz.
b. Un animal causó el desorden.
c. Unos animales entraron.
d. Hay ratones por todas partes.

## 6 Compositions [10 points]

a. Write a five-sentence note to your parents, persuading them to let you spend a week at a friend's house near the beach. Tell them that you need to rest because you have been studying very hard; that you got good grades last semester; that your friend's parents have invited you; that you will swim in the sea and run on the beach; and that your friend will pick you up and bring you back home.

___

___

___

___

___

___

___

___

___

___

___

**b.** Write five sentences in Spanish to tell a short story about the situation suggested in the picture:

# *Proficiency Test*

## 1. Speaking

**a.** Your teacher will award up to 10 points for your oral performance in the classroom.

**b.** Oral Communication Tasks (20 points)

Your teacher will administer a series of communication tasks. Each task requires at least four utterances on your part, for which you can earn up to 5 points of credit.

An utterance is any spoken statement that leads to accomplishing the stated task. Assume that in each situation you are speaking with persons who speak Spanish.

A. Socializing

You have a telephone conversation with a friend. Ask your friend what he/she is going to do for the day and then tell what you have planned.

B. Providing and obtaining information

You are in a clothing store. The salesclerk comes over to you and begins the conversation by asking you how he/she can help you. Tell why you are there and what you are looking for.

C. Expressing personal feelings

You are at home with your parents. Tell them about your classes and your teachers. Talk about your likes and dislikes. You begin the conversation.

D. Persuading others to adopt a course of action

You are talking with your brother or sister. Try to convince him/her to lend you some money to buy a new recording. You begin the conversation.

## 2. Listening Comprehension

**a.** Multiple Choice (English) (20 points)

Part 2a consists of 10 questions. For each question, you will hear some background information in English. Then you will hear a passage in Spanish *twice*, followed by a question in English. After you have heard the question, look at the question and the four suggested answers in your book. Choose the best suggested answer and write its number in the space provided.

**1** What is wrong with Carlos? ______

1. He's very cold.
2. He doesn't want to go to school.
3. He has no classes tomorrow.
4. He has a cold or the flu.

**2** What should you do when you hear this announcement? ______

1. Pick up your baggage at "Lost and Found."
2. Go to your departure gate.
3. Find out about the delay.
4. Buy your ticket.

**3** What will you have to study for the test? ______

1. The verb endings.
2. The past tense.
3. The structures.
4. The vocabulary.

**4** Which meal is Tomás eating? ______

1. Breakfast.
2. Lunch.
3. Supper.
4. Afternoon snack.

**5** In which season of the year are we? ______

1. Spring.
2. Summer.
3. Fall.
4. Winter.

**6** Why can't you take the scheduled bus? ______

1. None of the buses is running today.
2. Your bus has just left.
3. There is a problem on the highway.
4. Your ticket is no longer valid.

**7** What is your friend's suggestion? ______

1. To go to the movies.
2. To go to a dance.
3. To go to a concert.
4. To go to the beach.

**8** Where can these items be bought? ______

1. In a restaurant.
2. In a drugstore.
3. In a butcher shop.
4. In a supermarket.

**9** What's the good news? ______

1. You have been invited to spend your vacation in Spain.
2. Your friend has received excellent marks this term.
3. Your friend's father got a job in Madrid.
4. Your friend might spend the summer in Spain.

**10** What does your friend want you to do? ______

1. Listen to a certain radio station.
2. Go out and buy a record.
3. Buy her a radio.
4. Send her the words of a song.

**b.** Multiple Choice (Spanish) (10 points)

Part 2b consists of 5 questions. For each question, you will hear some background information in English. Then you will hear a passage in Spanish *twice,* followed by a question in Spanish. After you have heard the question, look at the question and the four suggested answers in your book. Choose the best suggested answer and write its number in the space provided.

**11** ¿Qué hacen los dos niños? ______

1. Nadan alegremente en el mar.
2. Están jugando a la pelota.
3. Juegan en la playa.
4. Buscan conchas.

**12** ¿Adónde van los jóvenes? ______

1. Al curso de verano.
2. A una isla tropical.
3. A las montañas.
4. A España.

**13** ¿De qué están hablando estas personas? ______

1. De la dificultad de los cursos.
2. De la necesidad de ganar dinero.
3. De los diferentes tipos de trabajo.
4. Del gran número de universidades.

**14** ¿Qué se sabe de este joven? ______

1. Es muy guapo.
2. Tiene más de veinte años.
3. Sabe hablar varios idiomas.
4. Es un joven ambicioso.

**15** ¿Qué no le gustaba a Francisca? ______

1. El sueldo que le pagan.
2. Las condiciones de su trabajo.
3. La gente que no obedece las reglas.
4. El lugar donde ella trabaja.

**c.** Multiple Choice (Visual) (10 points)

Part 2c consists of 5 questions. For each question, you will hear some background information in English. Then you will hear a passage in Spanish *twice,* followed by a question in English. After you have heard the question, look at the question and four pictures in your book. Choose the picture that best answers the question and circle its number.

**16** Which picture best describes Paco's occupation?

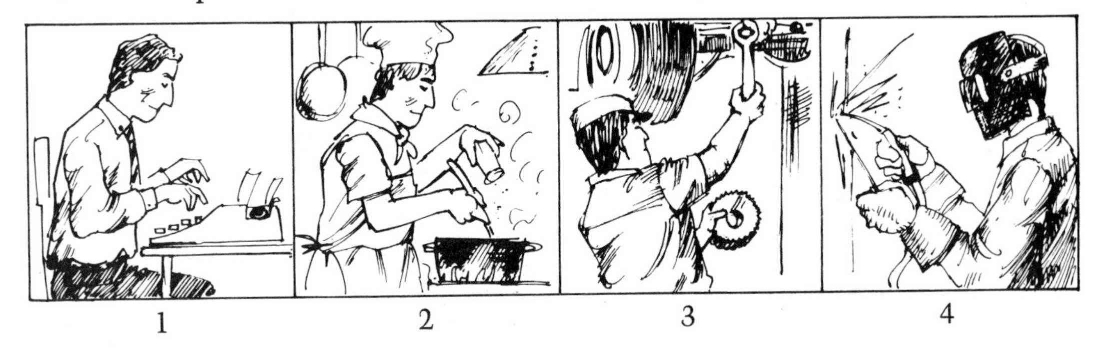

1 2 3 4

**17** What are some of the things bought by the customer?

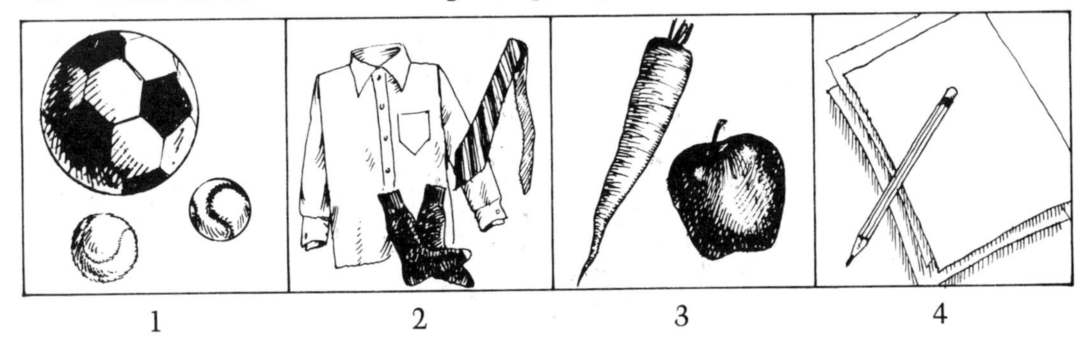

1 2 3 4

**18** Where is Lola going?

1 2 3 4

**19** What is being described?

1 2 3 4

**20** What did the policeman do?

1 2 3 4

## 3. Reading

**a.** Multiple Choice (English) (12 points)

Part 3a consists of 6 questions in English, each based on a reading selection in Spanish. Choose the best answer to each question. Base your choice on the content of the reading selection. Write the number of your answer in the space provided.

**21** Where does the student responding to this ad study a foreign language? ______

**•ALEMÁN**
**• ESPAÑOL**
**• FRANCÉS**
**• INGLÉS**

**EN SÓLO 8 SEMANAS**

Empezamos desde cero (o desde el nivel en que usted se encuentra ahora) y llegamos hasta el nivel universitario. Usted estudia en su propia casa por medio del sistema de instrucción programada, de gran fama mundial.

**INFORMACIÓN AL TELÉFONO**
**• (204) 555-2121 •**

Pregunte por la Dra. Linguadora, obien remítanos el cupón de abajo y recibirá mas información sin ningún compromiso.

**MULTILANGUAGE INSTITUTE**
15 Language Drive, Converse, NJ 08407

**Nombre** ______
**TELÉFONO** ______
**Dirección** ______
**Ciudad** ______ **Estado** ______

1. At the university.
2. At home.
3. At the program center.
4. Throughout the world.

**22** What kinds of students should go to this school? ______

**ESCUELA DE AUTOMOVILISMO**

APRENDA A MANEJAR EL AUTO A LA DEFENSIVA

*NUESTRA REPUTACIÓN HABLA POR SÍ SOLA*

■ ■ ■

- PRINCIPANTES Y ESTUDIANTES ADELANTADOS
- NOS ESPECIALIZAMOS EN ESTUDIANTES NERVIOSOS
- PAGUE SEGÚN APRENDA
- CLASES 7 DÍAS A LA SEMANA
- CLASES DE 3 HORAS EN LA OFICINA
- LE CONSEGUIMOS GRATUITAMENTE EL PERMISO PARA APRENDER A MANEJAR
- LE RECOGEMOS GRATIS EN SU CASA

*SERVIMOS A LA COMUNIDAD DE HABLA ESPAÑOLA*

**(525) 249-6666**

1. Those who are not nervous.
2. Those who want to learn self-defense.
3. Professional drivers.
4. Beginning to advanced students.

**23** What fees do these lawyers charge? ______

DAÑOS GRAVES Y ACCIDENTES

- ACCIDENTES DE AUTOMÓVIL
- ACCIDENTES EN PROPIEDADES PELIGROSAS
- CAÍDAS
- MÁQUINAS Y PRODUCTOS DEFECTUOSOS
- CASOS DE CONSTRUCCIÓN
- Y CUALQUIER OTRO DAÑO
- VISITAS A SU CASA Y AL HOSPITAL

NO COBRAMOS SI NO GANAMOS

*SE HABLA ESPAÑOL*

(102) 556-1000

A·B·O·G·A·D·O·S
ASOCIADOS LTD.

1. Highest fees for auto accidents.
2. Nothing if the injuries are serious.
3. Nothing if they lose the case.
4. Lower fees if the victim is hospitalized.

**24** Who should answer this ad? ______

• SIN EJERCICIOS • SIN MEDICINAS •
• SIN DEJAR DE COMER •

**Remodele su Cuerpo Para el Verano**

¡No deje que la gordura le impida exhibirse!

Deje que nuestras máquinas hagan el trabajo mientras Ud. se relaja.

**Nuestro sistema único le permitirá obtener:**

• Estómago Firme • Tono Muscular •
• Endurecimiento de todo su cuerpo •

**Supervisión Médica Completa**

VIGÍAPESA

1. Those who want to lose weight.
2. Those who want to gain weight.
3. Those who need medical supervision.
4. Those who want to go on a summer vacation.

**25** What are the plans of the orchestra from Argentina? ______

"PRODUCCIONES ARGENTINA"
PRESENTA
Gran Baile
Sabado 20 de agosto
de 10:00 pm a 2:00 am
DESPEDIDA DE LOS ESTADOS UNIDOS
DE LA PRIMERÍSIMA
ORQUESTA DE LA ARGENTINA
"LOS GAUCHOS"
Con sus cantantes internacionales
PACO Y ALEJANDRA
6 HORAS CONTINUAS DE BAILE
Y
LA MEJOR ORQUESTA DE NEW YORK
LOS HERALDOS


1. It is going on an international tour.
2. It is leaving the United States.
3. It is taking the place of "Los Heraldos."
4. It will continue as a dance band.

**26** What happens to people who come by car to this establishment? ______

UNA NUEVA MANERA DE OFRECER COMIDAS EN
NUESTRO LOCAL REDECORADO Y AMPLIADO
4 SALAS DE BANQUETES
(20 A 1000 PERSONAS)
Para su
• BODA • BANQUETE • BAILE
• CEREMONIA DE COMPROMISO
• DESAYUNO DE COMUNIÓN
• ANIVERSARIOS • BAUTIZOS
FUNCIONES SOCIALES Y COMERCIALES
• TODAS CON AIRE ACONDICIONADO
• ESTACIONAMIENTO GRATIS ILIMITADO
• HABITACIÓN PRIVADA PARA LA NOVIA
• MENÚS ESPECIALES DE LUNES A VIERNES
• SERVICIO DE ASCENSOR


1. There is no room for them.
2. They have to pay extra.
3. They have to make their own parking arrangements.
4. They will find ample parking.

**b.** Multiple Choice (Spanish) (8 points)

Part 3b consists of 4 questions in Spanish, each based on a reading selection in Spanish. Choose the best answer to each question. Base your choice on the content of the reading selection. Write the number of your answer in the space provided.

**27** ¿Quiénes necesitan los servicios de este doctor? ______

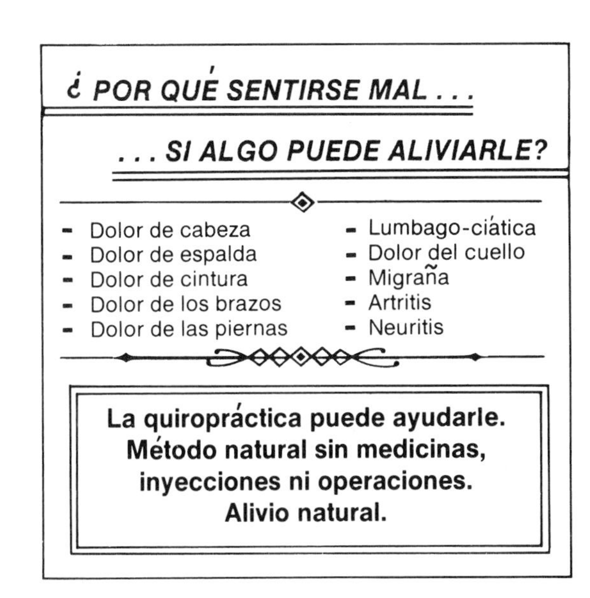

¿ POR QUÉ SENTIRSE MAL . . .
. . . SI ALGO PUEDE ALIVIARLE?
- Dolor de cabeza
- Dolor de espalda
- Dolor de cintura
- Dolor de los brazos
- Dolor de las piernas
- Lumbago-ciática
- Dolor del cuello
- Migraña
- Artritis
- Neuritis
La quiropráctica puede ayudarle.
Método natural sin medicinas,
inyecciones ni operaciones.
Alivio natural.


1. Las personas de edad avanzada.
2. Las que tienen enfermedades contagiosas.
3. Las que tienen mucho dolor.
4. Las que necesitan una operación.

**28** ¿Qué quiere vender o comprar esta compañía? ______

¡ATENCIÓN!

PROPIETARIOS DE EDIFICIOS DE APARTAMENTOS Y DUEÑOS DE CASA

¿ Piensa Ud. Comprar, Vender o Canjear?

*TENEMOS COMPRADORES LISTOS PARA COMPRAR AL CONTADO, EN CUALQUIER CONDICIÓN, EN CUALQUIER ZONA*

- PROPIEDADES COMERCIALES Y RESIDENCIALES
- PERITOS EN FINANCIAMIENTO
- AVALÚOS

**(727) 824-3000**

1. Toda clase de cosas.
2. Cosas en buena condición.
3. Sólo propiedades residenciales.
4. Toda clase de propiedades.

**29** ¿Dónde se usan los servicios de Perillón? ______

1. En un aniversario de boda.
2. En el cumpleaños de un niño.
3. En una fiesta de boda.
4. En una celebración patriótica.

**30** ¿Dónde empaca esta compañía de mudanzas? ______

1. En Puerto Rico.
2. En la casa del cliente.
3. En la calle.
4. En sus camiones.

## 4. Writing

**a.** Notes (6 points)

Write 2 notes in Spanish as directed below. Each note must consist of at least 12 words.

1. You have received a birthday present from a cousin. Write a note in Spanish expressing your thanks.

______________________________

______________________________

______________________________

______________________________

2. You are spending two weeks in Acapulco, Mexico, during your vacation. Write a note in Spanish to a friend telling how you are.

______________________________

______________________________

______________________________

______________________________

**b.** Lists (4 points)

Write 2 lists in Spanish as directed below. Each list must contain 4 items. One-word items must not be proper names.

1. Your class is planning a party. In Spanish, list 4 things you might want to bring to the party.

______________________________

______________________________

______________________________

______________________________

2. You need clothing for the new school year. In Spanish, list 4 articles of clothing you could buy.

________________________________________

________________________________________

________________________________________

________________________________________

# Spanish-English Vocabulary

The Spanish-English Vocabulary is intended to be complete for the contexts of this book.

Nouns are listed in the singular. The gender of nouns is indicated as follows:

*m.* = masculine
*f.* = feminine
*m.* & *f.* = masculine and feminine

Adjectives are listed in the masculine form.

Verbs with spelling changes, stem-changing verbs, and irregular verbs are identified by the type of change as follows: **poder (ue)**; **tener** (*irr.*).

**a** to, at
**abajo** below
**abierto** open
**abogado** *m.*, **abogada** *f.* lawyer; **abogado defensor** defense lawyer
**abrigo** *m.* coat
**abrir** to open
**aburrido** bored, boring
**acabar** to finish; **acabar de** to have just
**aceite** *m.* oil
**acelerador** *m.* accelerator, gas pedal
**acercarse (qu)** to approach, come near
**acompañar** to accompany, go with
**acordarse de (ue)** to remember
**acostar (ue)** to put to bed; **acostarse** to lie down, go to bed
**activo** active
**acto** *m.* act
**actuar** to act
**acuerdo** *m.* agreement; **estar de acuerdo** to agree; **de acuerdo** agreed; yes, of course
**adelante** forward; **de ahora en adelante** from now on
**adelanto** advanced; *m.* advance
**además (de)** besides
**adentro** inside
**adivina** *f.* fortune teller
**adivinar** to guess, foretell
**¿adónde?** where (to)?
**aduana** *f.* customs
**aduanero** *m.* customs official
**aeromozo** *m.*, **aeromoza** *f.* flight attendant
**afeitarse** to shave
**aficionado** *m.*, **aficionada** *f.* fan
**afortunadamente** fortunately, luckily
**afuera** outside; **comer afuera** to eat out
**agresivo** aggressive
**agua** *f.* **(el agua)** water
**aguacate** *m.* avocado
**aguafiestas** *m.* & *f.* partypooper, spoilsport
**agüero** *m.* omen
**ahí** there; **por ahí** that way, over there
**ahora** now; **ahora mismo** right now
**aire acondicionado** *m.* air conditioning
**ahorrar** to save
**ajo** *m.* garlic
**alegre** happy
**alegremente** happily
**alemán** German
**alfabeto** *m.* alphabet
**alfombra** *f.* rug
**algo** something
**algodón** *m.* cotton
**alguien** somebody
**alguno** some, any
**aliento** *m.* breath
**aliviar** to relieve
**alivio** *m.* relief
**allá** there, over there
**allí** there
**almacén** *m.* store; warehouse; department store
**almacenaje** *m.* storage
**almorzar (ue, c)** to eat (have) lunch
**almuerzo** *m.* lunch
**alrededor de** around
**alto** tall, high
**alunizar (c)** to land on the moon
**amable** kind, nice
**amarillento** yellowish
**amarillo** yellow
**ambicioso** ambitious
**amigo** *m.*, **amiga** *f.* friend
**amiguito** *m.* little friend, pal
**amor** *m.* love; **amorcito** my love, my darling
**ampliar** to enlarge
**amuleto** *m.* charm
**ancho** wide
**andar** (*irr.*) to go about, walk

**anillo** *m.* ring
**anoche** last night
**anteayer** the day before yesterday
**antena** *f.* antenna
**antes (de)** before
**antiguo** old, ancient
**antipático** unpleasant
**anunciar** to announce
**anuncio** *m.* announcement, sign; **anuncio clasificado** classified ad; **anuncio comercial** ad
**año** *m.* year
**apagar (gu)** to turn off
**aplauso** *m.* applause, clapping
**aprender** to learn
**aquel, aquella** that
**aquellos, aquellas** those
**aquí** here; **por aquí** this way
**araña** *f.* spider
**árbitro** *m.* umpire
**ardilla** *f.* squirrel
**arena** *f.* sand
**arete** *m.* earring
**armonía** *f.* harmony
**arrancar (qu)** to start (auto)
**arreglar** to fix, repair
**arrogante** arrogant, haughty
**arroz** *m.* rice; **arroz con leche** rice pudding
**artículo** *m.* article; **artículo de fondo** editorial
**ascensor** *m.* elevator
**asegurado** insured
**asegurar** to insure; to assure
**asesino** *m.* murderer
**así** so, thus
**asiento** *m.* chair, seat; **tomar asiento** to take a seat, sit down
**asistir** to attend
**asociación** *f.* society
**aspirina** *f.* aspirin
**astro** *m.* star
**astrología** *f.* astrology
**astronauta** *m.* f. astronaut
**astronave** *f.* space ship
**asunto** *m.* matter, affair
**atención** *f.* attention; **prestar atención** to pay attention
**atento** attentive, polite
**aterrizar (c)** to land
**atractivo** attractive
**atrapar** to trap; to catch
**atrás** back, backwards
**atropellar** to run over
**aún** even
**aunque** even though
**auto** *m.*, **automóvil** *m.* car
**auxilio** *m.* help
**avalúo** *m.* appraisal
**avanzar (c)** to advance
**avenida** *f.* avenue
**avión** *m.* plane
**ayer** yesterday; **anteayer** the day before yesterday
**ayuda** *f.* help
**ayudante** *m.* & *f.* helper, assistant
**ayudar** to help
**azafata** *f.* stewardess
**azul** blue

**bailar** to dance
**baile** *m.* dance
**bajar** to go (come) down
**bajo** short; under, underneath
**balón** *m.* large ball
**baloncesto** *m.* basketball
**ballena** *f.* whale
**banco** *m.* bank
**banda** *f.* band
**bandera** *f.* flag
**bañar** to bathe; **bañarse** to take a bath
**baño** *m.* bathroom; **traje de baño** *m.* bathing suit
**barba** *f.* beard
**barbacoa** *f.* barbecue
**barco** *m.* boat; **barco de vela** sailboat
**barrio** *m.* neighborhood
**basado** based
**básketbol** *m.* basketball
**bastante** enough
**basura** *f.* garbage
**bata** *f.* robe, housecoat
**bate** *m.* bat
**bateador** *m.* batter
**batear** to bat
**batería** *f.* battery
**bautizo** *m.* baptism
**batir** to beat, break a record
**bebé** *m.* baby
**béisbol** *m.* baseball
**beso** *m.* kiss
**biblioteca** *f.* library
**bien** well; **está bien** it's all right; O.K.
**bienvenido** welcome
**bigote** *m.* mustache
**blanco** white
**blando** soft
**blusa** *f.* blouse
**bobo** silly, foolish
**boca** *f.* mouth
**boda** *f.* marriage, wedding
**bola** *f.* ball
**bolera** *f.* bowling alley
**bolo: jugar (ue, gu) a los bolos** to bowl, go bowling
**bolsillo** *m.* pocket
**bolso** *m.* purse
**bombero** *m.* fireman
**bonito** pretty, good-looking
**bota** *f.* boot
**botar** to throw away
**botella** *f.* bottle
**botón** *m.* button
**boxeo** *m.* boxing
**brazalete** *m.* bracelet
**brazo** *m.* arm; **brazo de gitano** sponge cake roll with rum cream filling
**brillante** shiny, brilliant
**brillar** to shine
**brisa** *f.* breeze
**broche** *m.* brooch, pin
**bronceador** tanning
**bruja** *f.* witch
**brujo** *m.* wizard, sorcerer
**buenaventura** *f.* fortune, good luck; **decir** (*irr.*) **la buenaventura** to tell one's fortune
**bueno** good
**bufanda** *f.* scarf
**buscar (qu)** to look for
**butaca** *f.* armchair, easy chair
**buzón** *m.* mailbox

**caballero** *m.* gentleman
**caballo** *m.* horse; **montar a caballo** to go horseback riding
**cabeza** *f.* head
**cada** each, every
**cadena** *f.* chain
**caer(se)** (*irr.*) to fall (down)
**café** *m.* coffee; café
**caída** *f.* fall
**caja** *f.* box; **caja fuerte** safe
**cajero** *m.*, **cajera** *f.* cashier
**calamar** *m.* squid
**caldo** *m.* broth; **caldo gallego** white bean, turnip, and potato soup
**caliente** hot
**calle** *f.* street
**cama** *f.* bed
**camarón** *m.* shrimp
**cambiar** to change, exchange

**caminata** *f.* hike, long walk; **dar** (*irr.*) **una caminata** to go hiking
**caminar** to walk
**camión** *m.* truck
**camisa** *f.* shirt; **camisa de dormir** night gown
**camiseta** *f.* T-shirt
**campamento** *m.* camp
**campeón** *m.*, **campeona** *f.* champion
**campo** *m.* country, field
**canción** *f.* song
**canguro** *m.* kangaroo
**canjear** to exchange
**cansado** tired
**cantante** *m.* & *f.* singer
**cantar** to sing
**capital** *f.* capital
**capítulo** *m.* chapter
**capó** *m.* hood
**cápsula** *f.* capsule
**cara** *f.* face
**cárcel** *f.* jail
**carga** *f.* freight
**carne** *f.* meat
**carnicería** *f.* butchershop
**carnicero** *m.* butcher
**caro** expensive
**carrera** *f.* race
**carretera** *f.* highway
**carro** *m.* car
**carta** *f.* letter
**cartelera** *f.* billboard
**cartera** *f.* purse
**cartón** *m.* carton, cardboard
**casa** *f.* house; **a casa** home; **en casa** at home
**casado** married
**casarse** to get married
**casco** *m.* helmet
**casi** almost
**caso** *m.* case
**castillo** *m.* castle
**catarro** *m.* cold
**causa: a causa de** because of
**cavar** to dig
**celoso** jealous
**cenar** to have dinner
**centro** *m.* center, middle; downtown
**cepillar(se)** to brush
**cepillo** *m.* brush; **cepillo de dientes** toothbrush
**cerca (de)** near
**cerrado** closed
**cerrar (ie)** to close, shut
**certificado** *m.* certificate
**cerveza** *f.* beer
**cesta** *f.* basket
**ciclismo** *m.* cycling
**ciclista** *m.* & *f.* cyclist
**cielo** *m.* sky, heaven; **mi cielo** my love, sweetheart
**ciencia** *f.* science; **ciencia ficción** science fiction
**científico** *m.*, **científica** *f.* scientist
**ciento** (one) hundred; **por ciento** percent
**cierto** certain, sure; **es cierto** it's true
**ciervo** *m.* deer
**cigarrillo** *m.* cigarette
**cine** *m.* movies
**cintura** *f.* waist; lower back
**cinturón** *m.* belt
**cita** *f.* date, appointment
**ciudad** *f.* city
**ciudadano** *m.*, **ciudadana** *f.* citizen
**claro** light; clear; of course!; **claro que no** of course not; **claro que sí** of course!
**clase** *f.* class, kind
**clave** *f.* key (to code)
**clima** *m.* climate, weather
**cobrar** to charge
**cocina** *f.* kitchen
**cocinar** to cook
**cocodrilo** *m.* crocodile
**coche** *m.* car; carriage
**codo** *m.* elbow
**coger (j)** to grasp, grab, catch, take
**cohete** *m.* rocket
**cola** *f.* tail
**colección** *f.* collection
**colocar (qu)** to place, put
**collar** *m.* necklace
**combatir** to combat, fight
**comedor** *m.* dining room
**comenzar (ie, c)** to begin
**comer** to eat
**cometer** to commit
**cómico** funny, amusing, comical
**comida** *f.* food, meal
**como** as, like
**¿cómo?** how?, what?
**cómoda** *f.* dresser
**cómodo** comfortable
**comportamiento** *m.* behavior
**cómplice** *m.* & *f.* accomplice
**compra** *f.* purchase; **de compras** shopping
**comprador** *m.* buyer
**comprar** to buy
**comprender** to understand
**comprensivo** understanding
**comprobar (ue)** to check, verify
**compromiso** *m.* commitment; engagement
**computador** *m.*, **computadora** *f.* computer
**común** common
**comunidad** *f.* community
**con** with
**concierto** *m.* concert; **sala de conciertos** *f.* concert hall
**concursante** *m.* & *f.* contestant
**concurso** *m.* contest
**concha** *f.* (sea)shell
**conejo** *m.* rabbit
**confianza** *f.* confidence, trust
**congelador** *m.* freezer
**conjunto** *m.* set
**conmigo** with me
**conocer** to know, be acquainted with
**conocido** *m.* acquaintance
**conseguir (i, g)** to obtain
**consejero** *m.*, **consejera** *f.* counselor, adviser
**consejo** *m.* advice
**considerar** to consider
**consistir (en)** to consist of
**consultorio** *m.* doctor's office
**contado: al/de contado** cash down, for cash
**contar (ue)** to tell; to count
**contento** happy, satisfied
**contestar** to answer
**contigo** with you (fam.)
**continuación** *f.* continuation; **a continuación** next, as follows
**continuo** continuous
**contra** against
**contrario** opposite; **al contrario, por el contrario** on the contrary
**contrato** *m.* contract
**convencer** to convince
**convertir (ie) en** to turn into
**coñac** *m.* brandy
**copa** *f.* glass, goblet
**coro** *m.* choir
**corregir (i, j)** to correct
**correo** *m.* mail; post office
**correr** to run
**cortar** to cut
**cortés** courteous, polite
**corto** short

**cortina** *f.* curtain
**cosa** *f.* thing; **eso es otra cosa** that's something else
**cosmonauta** *m.* & *f.* cosmonaut
**costar (ue)** to cost; **costar un ojo de la cara** to cost a fortune
**creencia** *f.* belief
**creer** to believe
**crema** *f.* cream
**criminal** *m.* & *f.* criminal
**cristal** *m.* glass, crystal
**crucero** *m.* cruise, crossing; **hacer un crucero** to take a cruise
**crueldad** *f.* cruelty
**cruzar (c)** to cross
**cuadro** *m.* picture, painting; square; **a cuadros** plaid
**cuadrado** square
**¿cuál?** which (one)?, what?
**cualidad** *f.* quality, characteristic
**cualquier** any
**¿cuándo?** when?
**¿cuánto?** how much?; **¿cuántos?** how many?
**cuarto** fourth; *m.* room
**cubierta** *m.* hood
**cubierto** covered
**cubo** *m.* pail
**cubrir** to cover
**cuello** *m.* neck; collar
**cuenta** *f.* bill; count; **cuenta atrás** countdown
**cuerpo** *m.* body
**cuidado** *m.* care; **tener** (*irr.*) **cuidado** to be careful
**cuidadoso** careful
**culebra** *f.* snake
**cumpleaños** *m.* birthday
**cura** *m.* priest
**curso** *m.* course; session

**chaleco** *m.* vest
**chica** *f.* girl
**chico** *m.* boy
**chile** *m.* red pepper; **chile con carne** spiced chopped meat with chili sauce
**chiste** *m.* joke
**chocar (qu)** to crash
**chofer** *m.* driver
**chupar** to suck; **chuparse el dedo** to suck one's finger

**dama** *f.* lady
**daño** *m.* damage
**dar** (*irr.*) to give; **dar un paseo** to take a walk; **me da pena** it makes me sad
**de** of, from
**debajo (de)** underneath, under, below; **por debajo de** underneath
**deber** must
**débil** weak
**decidir** to decide
**décimo** tenth
**decir** (*irr.*) to say; **querer decir** to mean
**declaración** *f.* declaration, statement
**declarar** to declare; to testify
**decorar** to decorate
**dedo** *m.* finger
**defectuoso** defective
**defender (ie)** to defend
**defensa** *f.* defense; **defensa propia** self-defense
**defensivo** defensive; **a la defensiva** defensively
**dejar** to leave; to let, allow; **dejar de** to stop, give up
**delante (de)** in front (of)
**delincuencia** *f.* delinquency
**demás: los demás** the others, the rest
**demasiado** too much
**demostrar (ue)** to demonstrate
**dentro de** inside, in
**deporte** *m.* sport
**deportista** *m.* & *f.* sportsman, sportswoman
**deportivo** sports
**derecho** *m.* right
**derramar** to spill
**desarrollar (se)** to develop
**desarrollo** *m.* development
**desayuno** *m.* breakfast
**descansar** to rest
**descargar (gu)** to unload
**desconocido** unknown; **lo desconocido** the unknown
**describir** to describe
**descubrir** to discover
**desde** since; from
**desempacar** to unpack
**deseo** *m.* desire, wish; **tener deseos de** to feel like
**desesperado** desperate
**desierto** empty, deserted
**desodorante** *m.* deodorant
**desorden** *m.* disorder
**despacho** *m.* office
**despacio** slowly
**despedida** *f.* farewell
**despedir (i)** to dismiss, fire
**despegar (gu)** to take off
**despertar(se) (ie)** to wake up
**después** later, afterwards; **después de** after
**desvestirse (i)** to undress
**detalle** *m.* detail
**detrás (de)** in back of, behind
**devolver (ue)** to return (*an object*)
**día** *m.* day; **al día siguiente** the following day; **del día** of the day; **hoy (en) día** nowadays; **todos los días** every day
**diamante** *m.* diamond
**diario** *m.* newspaper, daily
**diente** *m.* tooth; **cepillo de dientes** toothbrush; **pasta de dientes** toothpaste
**difícil** difficult
**dinámico** dynamic
**dinero** *m.* money
**dirección** *m.* address
**director** *m.*, **directora** *f.* manager; principal
**dirigir (j)** to direct
**disco** *m.* record
**discutir** to discuss, argue
**diseñar** to design
**distancia** *f.* distance
**divertido** entertaining, enjoyable, amusing
**divertir (ie)** to amuse; **divertirse** to have fun (a good time)
**divino** divine, heavenly
**dólar** *m.* dollar
**doler (ue)** to hurt
**dolor** *m.* pain; **dolor de cabeza** headache
**donde** where; at (someone's place); **¿dónde?** where?
**dormido** asleep
**dormir (ue)** to sleep; **dormirse** to fall asleep
**dormitorio** *m.* bedroom
**duda** *f.* doubt
**dueño** *m.*, **dueña** *f.* owner
**dulce** sweet, gentle; *m.* sweet, candy
**durar** to last

**echar** to throw, toss
**edad** *f.* age
**edificio** *m.* building
**efectivo** *m.* cash

**ejemplo** *m.* example; **por ejemplo** for example
**ejercicio** *m.* exercise
**electricista** *m.* & *f.* electrician
**elegir (i, j)** to elect
**empanada** *f.* meat pie
**embarcar (qu)** to sail away, embark
**embargo: sin embargo** however, nonetheless
**empacar** to pack
**empezar (ie, c)** to begin
**empleado** *m.*, **empleada** *f.* employee
**en** in, on
**enamorado** in love
**encaje** *m.* lace
**encantador** charming
**encantar** to enchant, charm; **me encanta** I love it
**encender (ie)** to light; to turn on
**encontrar (ue)** to find; **encontrarse** to find oneself; to meet (each other)
**enchilada** *f.* rolled and stuffed tortilla with chili sauce
**endurecimiento** *m.* hardening
**enemigo** *m.*, **enemiga** *f.* enemy
**enfermedad** *f.* illness
**enfermero** *m.*, **enfermera** *f.* nurse
**enfermo** sick
**enojarse** to get angry
**enorme** enormous, huge
**ensalada** *f.* salad; **ensalada mixta** mixed salad
**ensayar** to try
**enseñar** to teach
**entender (ie)** to understand
**enterarse** to find out
**entero** whole
**entonces** then
**entrada** *f.* entrance; ticket; appetizer
**entrar** to enter, go in
**entre** among, between
**entrenador** *m.* trainer
**entrenar** to train
**entrevista** *f.* interview
**enviar** to send; **enviar de regreso** to return, send back
**envidia** *f.* envy
**equipaje** *m.* luggage
**equipo** *m.* set, equipment; team
**equivalente** equivalent
**equivocado** mistaken, wrong
**equivocarse (qu)** to make a mistake
**error** *m.* mistake, error
**escalera** *f.* stairs; ladder
**escaparse** to get away, run away
**escenario** *m.* stage
**escoger (j)** to choose
**esconder** to hide
**escondido** hidden
**escritorio** *m.* desk
**escribir** to write
**escritor** *m.*, **escritora** *f.* writer
**escuchar** to listen to
**escuela** (*f.*) **de automovilismo** driving school
**esa, ese, eso** that; **ésa, ése** that one; **en eso** just then
**esas, esos** those
**esfuerzo** *m.* effort
**espalda** *f.* back
**espacial** space
**español** Spanish
**especial** special; **en especial** especially
**especialidad** *f.* specialty
**especialisarse** to specialize
**espectáculo** *m.* spectacle, show
**espejo** *m.* mirror; **espejo retrovisor** rearview mirror
**esperar** to wait (for)
**espíritu** *m.* spirit
**esposa** *f.* wife
**esquí** *m.* ski; skiing
**esquiar** to ski
**esquina** *f.* corner
**establecer** to establish
**estación** *f.* station
**estacionado** parked
**estacionamento** *m.* parking
**estadio** *m.* stadium
**estado** *m.* state; **Estados Unidos** United States
**estampilla** *f.* stamp
**estante** *m.* shelf; **estante para libros** bookshelf
**estar** (*irr.*) to be
**esta, este, esto** this; **ésta, éste** this one
**estas, estos** these
**estómago** *m.* stomach, abdomen
**estornudar** to sneeze
**estrecho** narrow
**estrella** *f.* star
**estricto** strict, severe
**estudiar** to study
**estudioso** studious
**estufa** *f.* stove
**estupendo** great, marvelous
**estupidez** *f.* stupidity
**estúpido** stupid
**eternidad** *f.* eternity
**etiqueta** *f.* label, tag
**evitar** to avoid
**exactamente** exactly
**examen** *m.* exam, test
**examinar** to examine
**exhibición** *m.* exhibit
**exhibirse** to show oneself
**existir** to exist
**éxito** *m.* success; **tener** (*irr.*) **éxito** to be successful
**explicar (qu)** to explain
**extranjero** foreign; **al extranjero** abroad
**extraño** strange

**fabada** *f.* thick bean soup with sausages
**fácil** easy
**falda** *f.* skirt
**fama** *f.* fame
**familia** *f.* family
**fantasía** *f.* fantasy
**fantasma** *m.* ghost
**farmacéutico** *m.*, **farmacéutica** *f.* pharmacist
**farmacia** *f.* pharmacy, drugstore
**faro** *m.* headlight
**favor** *m.* favor; **por favor** please
**fecha** *f.* date
**felicitaciones** congratulations
**feo** ugly
**feroz** fierce, savage
**fiebre** *f.* fever
**fiesta** *f.* party, celebration; **día de fiesta** *m.* holiday; **fiesta infantil** children's party
**filmación** *f.* filming
**fin** *m.* end; **por fin** finally
**final** *m.* end; **al final** in the end; **al final de** at the end of
**financiamento** *m.* financing
**firmar** to sign
**fiscal** *m.* & *f.* prosecutor; district attorney
**flaco** skinny, thin
**flan** *m.* caramel custard
**florero** *m.* vase
**flota** *f.* fleet
**foto** *f.* picture; **sacar (qu) fotos** to take pictures
**fotógrafo** *m.*, **fotógrafa** *f.* photographer

**fracaso** *m.* failure
**francés** French
**frase** *f.* sentence
**frecuentemente** frequently, often
**freno** *m.* brake
**frente** *m.* front; **frente a** opposite, in front of
**frijol** *m.* bean
**frío** cold
**frito** fried
**frontera** *f.* border, frontier
**fruta** *f.* fruit
**fuego** *m.* fire
**fuerte** strong
**fuerza** *f.* strength
**fumar** to smoke
**función** *f.* show, performance
**funcionar** to work
**fútbol** *m.* soccer; **fútbol americano** football

**gafas** *f. pl.* glasses; **gafas de sol** sunglasses
**ganador** *m.*, **ganadora** *f.* winner
**ganga** *f.* bargain
**ganar** to win; to earn
**garganta** *f.* throat
**gastar** to spend
**gato** *m.* cat
**gazpacho** *m.* cold, fresh vegetable soup
**general** general; **por lo general** in general
**generalmente** generally
**generoso** generous
**gente** *f.* people
**gerente** *m.* & *f.* manager
**gitana** *f.* Gypsy
**globo** *m.* balloon
**golpe** *m.* blow
**goma** *f.* rubber
**gordo** fat
**gordura** *f.* overweight
**gorra** *f.* cap
**grabar** to record
**gracias** thanks; **dar** (*irr.*) **las gracias** to thank
**grado** *m.* degree; stage
**graduarse** to graduate
**grande** large, big; great
**gratuitamente** free (of charge)
**gripe** *f.* flu
**gritar** to yell, scream, cry out
**grito** *m.* scream, cry
**grupo** *m.* group
**guacamole** *m.* avocado dip
**guante** *m.* glove
**guapo** handsome
**guardafango** *m.* fender
**guardar** to keep
**guía** *m.* & *f.* guide; *f.* guidebook
**guiar** to guide; to drive
**gustar** to like
**gusto** *m.* taste

**haber** (*irr.*) to have
**había** there was, there were
**hábil** skillful
**habitación** *f.* room
**hábito** *m.* habit
**habla** *f.* speech
**hace** ago; **hace poco** a little while ago
**hacer** (*irr.*) to do, make; **hacer calor** to be hot; **hacer caso de** to pay attention to; **hacer pedazos** to break into pieces; **hacer sol** to be sunny; **hacer un viaje** to take a trip; **hacerse** to become
**hacia** towards
**hada** *f.* **(el hada)** fairy
**hasta** until, up to; as far as
**hay** there is, there are; **hay que** it is necessary, one must
**helado** *m.* ice cream
**herencia** *f.* inheritance
**hermana** *f.* sister
**hermano** *m.* brother
**hielo** *m.* ice; **patinar en el hielo** to ice skate
**hija** *f.* daughter
**hijo** *m.* son; *pl.* sons, children
**hipnotismo** *m.* hypnotism
**hipnotista** *m.* hypnotist
**hogar** *m.* home
**hoja** *f.* leaf
**hombre** *m.* man
**hombro** *m.* shoulder
**honesto** honest
**hormiga** *f.* ant
**horno** *m.* oven
**hoy** today; **hoy (en) día** nowadays; **de hoy en ocho días** a week from today; **de hoy en quince días** two weeks from today
**huella** *f.* track, footprint; **huella digital** fingerprint
**huevo** *m.* egg

**idear** to devise, think of
**idioma** *m.* language
**iglesia** *f.* church
**ignorancia** *f.* ignorance
**igual** equal, the same, similar
**ilimitado** unlimited
**impedir** to impede, prevent
**impermeable** *m.* raincoat
**importar** to matter; **¿qué importa?** what difference does it make?
**impuesto** *m.* tax
**impulsivo** impulsive
**incendio** *m.* fire
**inclinarse** to bend over, bend down
**increíble** unbelievable
**indicar (qu)** to indicate, point out
**individuo** *m.* individual
**inesperado** unexpected
**influencia** *f.* influence
**ingeniero** *m.*, **ingeniera** *f.* engineer
**inglés** English
**ingrediente** *m.* ingredient
**iniciar** to start, initiate
**inseguridad** *f.* insecurity
**invierno** *m.* winter
**ir** (*irr.*) to go; **ir bien (a una persona)** to go well; **irse** to go away, leave; **le va bien** it fits you well; **¡qué va!** no way!, nonsense!; **vamos a** let's
**isla** *f.* island
**izquierdo** left

**jabón** *m.* soap
**jamás** never, not ever
**jarabe** *m.* syrup; **jarabe para la tos** cough syrup
**jardín** *m.* garden
**jirafa** *f.* giraffe
**jonrón** *m.* homerun
**joven** young; *m.* young man; *f.* young woman
**joya** *f.* jewel
**joyería** *f.* jewelry store
**juego** *m.* game; set
**juez** *m.* judge
**jugador** *m.*, **jugadora** *f.* player
**jugar (ue, gu)** to play
**jugo** *m.* juice
**juguete** *m.* toy
**juntos** together
**jurar** to swear
**justamente** precisely, exactly
**justo** just, fair
**juvenil** juvenile

**lado** *m.* side; **al lado** next to, beside; **al otro lado** on the other side; **de al lado** next
**ladrar** to bark
**ladrillo** *m.* brick
**ladrón** *m.* thief
**lago** *m.* lake
**lámpara** *f.* lamp
**lana** *f.* wool
**largo** long
**lavadora** *f.* washer
**lavaplatos** *m.* dishwasher
**lavar** to wash; **lavarse** to get washed, wash oneself
**leche** *f.* milk
**legumbre** *f.* vegetable
**lejos** far (away); **a lo lejos** in the distance
**lengua** *f.* tongue; language
**lentamente** slowly
**leopardo** *m.* leopard
**letra** *f.* letter; lyrics
**letrero** *m.* sign
**levantar** to lift, raise; **levantarse** to get up
**libra** *f.* pound
**libre** free
**librero** *m.* bookcase
**libreta** *f.* notebook
**licor** *m.* liquor
**líder** *m.* leader
**liebre** *f.* hare
**liga** *f.* league
**ligero** light
**limpiar** to clean
**listo** ready
**local** *m.* place, quarters
**loción** *f.* lotion
**loco** crazy
**lucha** *f.* fight; **lucha libre** wrestling
**luego** soon, then, later; **hasta luego** see you later
**lugar** *m.* place; **tener** (*irr.*) **lugar** to take place
**lujoso** luxurious
**luna** *f.* moon
**luz** *f.* light

**llamada** *f.* call
**llamar** to call; **llamarse** to be named, be called
**llanta** *f.* tire
**llegar (gu)** to arrive
**llevar** to wear; to carry, take; **llevarse** to take away; **llevarse bien** to get along
**llover (ue)** to rain

**madera** *f.* wood
**maestro** *m.*, **maestra** *f.* teacher; master; **maestro de ceremonias** TV host, master of ceremonies
**magia** *f.* magic
**magnífico** magnificent, wonderful
**mago** *m.* magician
**maíz** *m.* corn
**mal** badly, poorly
**maleducado** ill-mannered, rude
**maleta** *f.* suitcase
**maletero** *m.* trunk
**maletín** *m.* briefcase; small bag
**malo** bad
**manchado** stained
**manejar** to drive
**manera** *f.* manner
**manga** *f.* sleeve
**mano** *f.* hand
**manzana** *f.* apple
**mañana** tomorrow; **pasado mañana** the day after tomorrow
**mapa** *m.* map
**máquina** *f.* machine
**mar** *m.* ocean, sea
**marca** *f.* brand
**marido** *m.* husband
**mariscos** *m. pl.* shellfish; **zarzuela de mariscos** *f.* shellfish stew
**martes** Tuesday
**más** more, most
**matar** to kill
**matemáticas** *f., pl.* mathematics
**matrimonio** *m.* married couple, husband and wife
**mayonesa** *f.* mayonnaise
**mayor** greater, greatest; older, oldest
**medianoche** *f.* midnight
**medio** half
**medio** *m.* means
**medir (i)** to measure
**mejor** better, best
**mejorarse** to get better
**memoria** *f.* memory; **aprender de memoria** to learn by heart; **saber** (*irr.*) **de memoria** to know by heart
**mencionar** to mention, name
**menor** least, slightest; younger, youngest
**menos** less
**mensual** monthly

**mentir (ie)** to lie
**mentira** *f.* lie
**mentiroso** liar
**mes** *m.* month; **al mes** per month
**mesero** *m.* waiter
**mesita** *f.* small table; **mesita de café** coffee table; **mesita de noche** night table
**meter** to place, put in
**método** *m.* method
**mexicano** Mexican
**mi** my
**miedo** *m.* fear; **tener** (*irr.*) **miedo** to be afraid
**miembro** *m.* member
**mientras** while
**mil** a thousand
**milla** *f.* mile
**millón** *m.* a million
**mirar** to look at; **mirarse** to look at oneself
**mismo** same; **lo mismo** the same thing; **ahora mismo** right now; **sí mismo** himself, herself; **ti mismo** yourself
**moda** *f.* fashion, style; **de moda** in fashion
**módulo** *m.* module; **módulo de mando** command module; **módulo lunar** lunar module
**mojado** wet
**moneda** *f.* coin
**monje** *m.* monk
**mono** *m.* monkey
**montaña** *f.* mountain
**montar** to mount; **montar a caballo** to ride a horse; **montar en bicicleta** to ride a bicycle
**morder (ue)** to bite
**morir (ue)** to die
**mosca** *f.* fly
**mostrar (ue)** to show
**motor** *m.* engine, motor
**mover(se) (ue)** to move
**movimiento** *m.* movement
**mucho** much, a lot; **muchos** many
**mudanza** *f.* moving
**mueble** *m.* piece of furniture; *pl.* furniture
**mueblería** *f.* furniture store
**muerto** *m.* dead man
**mujer** *f.* woman
**multa** *f.* ticket, fine; **poner** (*irr.*) **una multa** to issue a ticket
**mundial** world

**mundo** *m.* world; **por todo el mundo** everywhere; **todo el mundo** everybody
**muy** very

**nacer** to be born
**nada** nothing
**nadar** to swim
**nadie** nobody
**naranja** *f.* orange
**natación** *f.* swimming
**natilla** *f.* soft custard
**nave** *f.* ship, vessel; **nave espacial** space ship
**Navidad** *f.* Christmas
**necesitar** to need
**negro** black; **de negro** in black
**nervioso** nervous
**nevar (ie)** to snow
**nevera** *f.* ice box, refrigerator
**ni** neither, nor
**ninguno** no, not any
**niño** *m.*, **niña** *f.* child; **de niño** as a child
**nivel** *m.* level
**noche** *f.* night; **esta noche** tonight; **por la noche** at night
**norteamericano** North American
**nota** *f.* note; grade
**noticia** *f.* news item; *pl.* news
**novela** *f.* novel; **novela policíaca** detective story
**noveno** ninth
**novia** *f.* bride
**nuestro** our
**nuevo** new
**número** *m.* number
**nunca** never, not ever

**obedecer** to obey
**objeto** *m.* object
**obstante: no obstante** nevertheless
**obtener** to obtain
**octavo** eighth
**ocupado** busy
**ocurrir** to happen
**oficina** *f.* office
**ofrecer** to offer
**oído** *m.* ear
**oír** (*irr.*) to hear
**ojo** *m.* eye
**ola** *f.* wave
**onza** *f.* ounce
**opuesto** opposite; opposed
**órbita** *f.* orbit
**orden** *m.* order
**ordinario** ordinary, common
**oreja** *f.* ear
**orilla** *f.* shore, bank
**oro** *m.* gold
**oscuro** dark
**oso** *m.* bear
**otro** other

**paciencia** *f.* patience
**paella** *f.* saffron rice with meat, seafood, and vegetables
**pagar (gu)** to pay
**página** *f.* page
**pago** *m.* payment
**país** *m.* country
**pájaro** *m.* bird
**pala** *f.* shovel
**palabra** *f.* word
**palmera** *f.* palm tree
**pan** *m.* bread
**panadero** *m.*, **panadera** *f.* baker
**pantalones** *m. pl.* pants
**pantera** *f.* panther
**pantufla** *f.* slipper
**pañuelo** *m.* handkerchief; **pañuelo de papel** tissue
**papa** *f.* potato
**papel** *m.* paper; **papel higiénico** toilet paper
**para** for, in order to
**parabrisas** *m.* windshield
**parachoques** *m.* bumper
**parada** *f.* stop
**paraguas** *m.* umbrella
**paraíso** *m.* paradise, heaven
**parar** to stop
**parecer** to seem; **al parecer** apparently; **¿qué le parece?** what do you think?
**parecido** similar
**pareja** *f.* couple, pair
**parte** *f.* part; **en cualquier parte** anywhere; **en todas partes** everywhere
**partida** *f.* certificate; **partida de matrimonio** marriage certificate; **partida de nacimiento** birth certificate
**partido** *m.* game, match
**pasado** *m.* past; **el lunes (mes, verano, año) pasado** last Monday (month, summer, year)
**pasajero** *m.*, **pasajera** *f.* passenger
**pasaporte** *m.* passport
**pasar** to pass; to spend (*time*); to happen; **¿qué pasa?** what's going on?, what's up?; **pase por aquí** come this way
**paseo** *m.* stroll, walk; **dar** (*irr.*) **un paseo** to take a walk
**pasillo** *m.* corridor, lobby, hall
**pasta** *f.* paste; **pasta de dientes** toothpaste
**pastel** *m.* cake, pastry
**pastilla** *f.* tablet; **pastilla para la tos** cough drop
**pata** *f.* animal leg or foot
**patata** *f.* potato
**patín** *m.* skate
**patinar** to skate
**pavo** *m.* turkey
**payaso** *m.* clown
**paz** *f.* peace
**peatón** *m.* pedestrian
**pedir (i)** to order, ask for, request; **pedir prestado** to borrow
**peinar** to comb; **peinarse** to comb one's hair
**peine** *m.* comb
**pelear** to fight
**película** *f.* film
**peligroso** dangerous
**pelo** *m.* hair
**pelota** *f.* ball
**peluquero** *m.*, **peluquera** *f.* hairdresser
**pena** *f.* sorrow; **¡qué pena!** what a shame!
**pensar (ie)** to think
**pequeño** small, little
**perder (ie)** to lose
**periódico** *m.* newspaper
**periodista** *m.* & *f.* reporter, journalist
**perito** *m.* expert
**perla** *f.* pearl
**permiso** *m.* permission; permit
**permitir** to permit
**pero** but
**perro** *m.* dog
**perseguir (i, g)** to pursue
**pesa** *f.* weight; **levantar pesas** weight lifting
**pesadilla** *f.* nightmare
**pesado** heavy
**pesar** to weigh
**pescado** *m.* fish
**pescar (qu)** to fish, go fishing
**peso** *m.* weight
**picante** hot, spicy

**pie** *m.* foot; **pie cuadrado** square foot
**piedra** *f.* stone
**piel** *f.* skin; leather
**pijama** *m.* pajama
**píldora** *f.* pill
**piloto** *m.* pilot
**pirata** *m.* pirate
**piscina** *f.* swimming pool
**piso** *m.* floor
**pistola** *f.* gun
**placa** *f.* license plate
**planear** to plan
**planeta** *m.* planet
**planta** *f.* plant
**plata** *f.* silver
**plato** *m.* dish, plate
**playa** *f.* beach
**plaza** *f.* public square
**plazo** *m.* installment
**poco** little
**poder (ue,** *irr.***)** to be able, can
**poder** *m.* power
**poema** *m.* poem
**policía** *m.* policeman; *f.* police force
**pollo** *m.* chicken
**ponche** *m.* punch
**poner** (*irr.*) to put; **ponerse** to put on
**por** for, by, through, along; **¿por qué?** why?
**porque** because
**poseer** to possess
**posible** possible; **todo lo posible** everything possible
**postre** *m.* dessert
**precio** *m.* price
**precioso** lovely, beautiful
**preferido** favorite
**preferir (ie)** to prefer
**pregunta** *f.* question; **hacer** (*irr.*) **una pregunta** to ask a question
**preguntar** to ask
**premio** *m.* prize
**prenda** *f.* article of clothing
**prendedor** *m.* pin, brooch
**preocupado** worried
**preocuparse** to worry
**preparar** to prepare
**prestado: pedir prestado** to borrow
**prestar** to lend; **prestar atención** to pay attention
**primerismo** foremost
**primero** first
**primo** *m.*, **prima** *f.* cousin
**principio** *m.* beginning; **al principio** at the beginning
**principiante** *m.* & *f.* beginner
**probar (ue)** to try; **probarse** to try on
**problema** *m.* problem
**programa** *m.* program
**programador** *m.*, **programadora** *f.* computer programmer
**promesa** *f.* promise
**pronto** quickly, soon; **por lo pronto** meanwhile
**propiedad** *f.* property
**proprietario** *m.* owner
**propio** own
**proponer** (*irr.*) to propose
**propósito** *m.* purpose; **a propósito** by the way
**proteger (j)** to protect
**próximo** next
**psiquiatra** *m.* & *f.* psychiatrist
**publicar (qu)** to publish
**puerta** *f.* door
**pues** well, then
**puesto** *m.* job, position
**pulsera** *f.* bracelet; **reloj de pulsera** *m.* wristwatch
**punto** *m.* point; period; **en punto** on the dot

**que** that; **más que** more than; **¿qué?** what?
**quedar** to remain; to be (located); **quedarse** to stay, remain; **quedarse con** to keep
**querer (ie,** *irr.***)** to want, wish for; **querer decir** to mean
**querido** dear
**¿quién?** who?; **¿a quién?** whom?; **¿de quién?** whose?
**quinto** fifth
**quiropráctica** *f.* chiropractic
**quitarse** to take off
**quizás** perhaps, maybe

**rápido** fast
**raqueta** *f.* racket
**ratón** *m.* mouse
**raya** *f.* stripe; **a rayas** striped
**razón** *f.* reason; **tener** (*irr.*) **razón** to be right; **no tener razón** to be wrong
**reaccionar** to react
**realizar (c)** to realize, fulfill
**realmente** really
**recibir** to receive; to go and meet
**recientemente** recently
**recoger (j)** to pick up; to gather
**reconocer** to recognize
**recordar (ue)** to remember
**recostado** leaning on; **estar** (*irr.*) **recostado** to be lying down
**refinado** refined
**reflejar** to reflect
**refresco** *m.* soft drink; *pl.* refreshments
**refrigerador** *m.* refrigerator
**refrito** refried
**regalar** to give (away)
**regalo** *m.* present, gift
**regla** *f.* rule; ruler
**regresar** to return
**reír(se) (í)** to laugh
**relajarse** to relax
**reloj** *m.* watch; **reloj de pulsera** wristwatch
**remar** to row
**remitir** to send
**rendido** exhausted
**repente: de repente** suddenly
**repetir (i)** to repeat
**reservado** reserved
**resolver (ue)** to resolve, solve
**respetar** to respect
**respuesta** *f.* answer, response
**restar** to subtract
**restaurante** *m.* restaurant
**resultado** *m.* result
**retraso** *m.* delay
**revelar** to reveal
**revisar** to check, go through
**revista** *f.* magazine
**rey** *m.* king
**ridículo** ridiculous
**rincón** *m.* corner
**río** *m.* river
**robar** to steal
**robo** *m.* theft
**rodear** to surround
**rodilla** *f.* knee
**rojo** red
**romper** to break
**ropa** *f.* clothes
**rubí** *m.* ruby
**rubio** blond
**rueda** *f.* wheel

**sábado** Saturday
**saber** (*irr.*) to know
**sacar (qu)** to take out, remove; to get (grade); **sacar fotos** to take pictures

**saco** *m.* coat, jacket; **saco de sport** sport jacket
**sal** *f.* salt
**sala** *f.* living room; **sala de conciertos** concert hall
**salir** to go out, leave
**salsa** *f.* sauce
**saltar** to jump
**salud** *f.* health
**saludar** to greet, say hello
**salvaje** savage, wild
**salvavidas** *m.* lifeguard
**satélite** *m.* satellite
**secadora** *f.* drier
**sección** *f.* section
**seda** *f.* silk
**seguir (i)** to follow; to continue
**según** according to
**segundo** second; *m.* second
**seguro** sure, certain
**sello** *m.* stamp
**semana** *f.* week; **la semana pasada** last week; **la semana que viene** next week
**señal** *f.* signal
**sentado** seated
**sentar (ie)** to seat; **sentarse** to sit down
**sentido** *m.* sense
**sentimiento** *m.* feeling
**sentir(se) (ie)** to feel; **lo siento** I'm sorry
**señal** *f.* sign
**séptimo** seventh
**sepultado** buried
**ser** (*irr.*) to be; *m.* being
**seriamente** seriously
**serie** *f.* series
**serio** serious, reserved
**serpiente** *f.* snake, serpent
**servir (i)** to serve; to be useful; **¿en qué puedo servirle?** what can I do for you?
**sexto** sixth
**si** if
**siempre** always
**siglo** *m.* century
**significar (qu)** to mean
**siguiente** following
**silla** *f.* chair
**sillón** *m.* armchair
**simpático** nice, pleasant
**sin** without
**sincero** sincere
**siquiera: ni siquiera** not even
**sirena** *f.* siren
**sitio** *m.* place, spot
**sobre** *m.* envelope
**sobre** on, on top of, over; about
**sobrenatural** supernatural
**socorro** *m.* help
**sofá** *m.* sofa, couch
**sofisticado** sophisticated
**sol** *m.* sun; **tomar el sol** to sunbathe
**solamente** only
**soldado** *m.* soldier
**sólo** only, just
**solo** alone
**soltero** single
**sombra** *f.* shadow
**sombrero** *m.* hat
**sombrilla** *f.* umbrella, sunshade
**sonar (ue)** to sound, ring; **sonarse (las narices)** to blow one's nose
**sonido** *m.* sound
**sonreír (í)** to smile
**soñar (ue) con** to dream of
**sopa** *f.* soup
**sorprender** to surprise
**sortija** *f.* ring
**su** his, her, its, your, their
**subir** to climb, to go (come) up
**sucio** dirty
**suegra** *f.* mother-in-law
**sueldo** *m.* salary
**sueño** *m.* sleep; dream; **tener** (*irr.*) **sueño** to be sleepy
**suerte** *f.* luck; **tener suerte** to be lucky
**suéter** *m.* sweater
**suficiente** enough
**sumar** to add (up)
**supuesto: por supuesto** of course, naturally
**suspiro** *m.* sigh; **echar un suspiro** to sigh

**tabla** *f.* board
**tacaño** stingy
**talla** *f.* size
**también** also
**tampoco** neither; **ni yo tampoco** neither do I
**tanque** *m.* tank
**tanto** so much; **tanto como** as much as
**tarde** late; **más tarde** later
**tarde** *f.* afternoon; **por la tarde** in the afternoon
**tarea** *f.* homework
**tarjeta** *f.* card; **tarjeta postal** postcard
**tela** *f.* fabric, material
**telaraña** *f.* spider's web, cobweb
**teléfono** *m.* telephone; **hablar por teléfono** to be on the phone; **llamar por teléfono** to telephone
**televidente** *m.* & *f.* TV viewer
**televisor** *m.* TV set
**temor** *m.* fear, dread
**temprano** early
**tener** (*irr.*) to have; **tener__años** to be__old; **tener cuidado** to be careful; **tener miedo** to be afraid; **tener sueño** to be sleepy
**tercero** third
**terciopelo** *m.* velvet
**terminar** to finish, end
**termómetro** *m.* thermometer
**ternera** *f.* veal
**terrestre** terrestrial, earthly
**tesoro** *m.* treasure
**testigo** *m.* & *f.* witness
**tiburón** *m.* shark
**tiempo** *m.* time; weather
**tienda** *f.* store
**tierno** tender
**tierra** *f.* earth; land
**tímido** shy
**tinta** *f.* ink
**típico** typical, traditional
**tipo** *m.* type
**tirar** to throw
**títere** *m.* puppet
**toalla** *f.* towel
**tocar (qu)** to touch; to knock; to play (musical instrument); **tocar a la puerta** to knock on the door; **tocar madera** to knock on wood
**todavía** yet
**todo** all, everything; **todos** everybody
**tomar** to take; to drink; **tomar asiento** to take a seat; **tomar el sol** to sunbathe
**tontería** *f.* silly thing, foolishness; *pl.* nonsense
**tonto** foolish, silly
**toro** *m.* bull
**torta** *f.* cake
**tortilla** *f.* cornmeal pancake; omelette
**tortuga** *f.* turtle
**tos** *f.* cough
**toser** to cough
**trabajo** *m.* work
**traer** (*irr.*) to bring

**traje** *m.* suit; **traje de baño** bathing suit
**tránsito** *m.* traffic
**transporte** *m.* transportation
**tratar** to treat, to deal with; **tratar de** to try to
**trato** *m.* deal
**través: a través** through
**trébol** *m.* clover
**triste** sad
**truco** *m.* trick
**tubo** *m.* tube

**últimamente** lately
**último** last
**único** original, unique; only
**universitario** university
**usar** to use; to wear
**uso** *m.* use; **de uso** used
**utilizar (c)** to use

**vacaciones** *f. pl.* vacation, holidays
**vacío** empty
**vacunación** *f.* vaccination
**valer** to be worth; **más vale** (it's) better
**valiente** brave
**valor** *m.* value
**variedades** *f. pl.* variety show
**varios** several, some
**vaso** *m.* glass
**vecino** *m.*, **vecina** *f.* neighbor
**vegetal** *m.* vegetable
**vela** *f.* sail
**veloz** fast, quick
**venda** *f.* bandage
**vendado** bandaged; blind-folded
**vendar** to bandage
**vendedor** *m.*, **vendedora** *f.* salesperson
**vender** to sell
**venir** (*irr.*) to come; **el mes que viene** next month
**venta** *f.* sale
**ventaja** *f.* advantage; **llevar ventaja a** to have the advantage over
**ventana** *f.* window
**ventanilla** *f.* small window, car window
**ver** to see
**verano** *m.* summer
**veras: de veras** really, truly
**verdad** *f.* truth; **¿verdad?** isn't that so?
**verde** green
**vestido** *m.* dress
**vestir (i)** to dress; **vestirse** to get dressed
**veterinario** *m.*, **veterinaria** *f.* veterinarian
**vez** *f.* time; **en vez de** instead of; **otra vez** again; **por primera vez** for the first time; **tal vez** perhaps
**viajar** to travel
**viaje** *m.* trip; **viaje espacial** space voyage; **hacer** (*irr.*) **un viaje** to take a trip
**víctima** *f.* victim
**vida** *f.* life; **mi vida** my love
**viejo** old
**viernes** Friday
**visa** *f.* visa
**visita** *f.* visitor; visit
**visitar** to visit
**vitamina** *f.* vitamin
**viviente** living
**vivir** to live
**volante** *m.* steering wheel
**volar (ue)** to fly
**volibol** *m.* volleyball
**volver (ue)** to return, to go (come) back
**vuelta** *f.* turn; **vuelta ciclista** long-distance cycle race

**ya** already

**zapatero** *m.* shoemaker
**zapatilla** *f.* slipper
**zapato** *m.* shoe

# *English-Spanish Vocabulary*

The English-Spanish Vocabulary includes only those words that occur in the English-to-Spanish exercises.

**about** sobre, acerca de
**address** dirección *f.*
**advice** consejo *m.*
**afterwards** después
**ago** hace
**airplane** avión *m.*
**airport** aeropuerto *m.*
**all** todo, todos
**also** también
**always** siempre
**answer** contestar
**any** cualquier; alguno; **not any** ninguno; **any more** más
**anything** algo; **not anything** nada
**appetizer** entrada *f.*
**armchair** butaca *f.*, sillón *m.*
**arrive** llegar (gu)
**ask** preguntar; **ask for** pedir (i)
**asleep** dormido; **to fall asleep** dormirse (ue)
**aspirin** aspirina *f.*

**baby** bebé *m.*
**bad** malo
**baker** panadero *m.*, panadera *f.*
**barbecue** barbacoa *f.*
**baseball** béisbol *m.*
**bath** baño *m.*; **to take a bath** bañarse
**bathroom** cuarto de baño *m.*
**bathing suit** traje de baño *m.*
**be** estar (*irr.*); ser (*irr.*)
**beach** playa *f.*
**bear** oso *m.*
**beautiful** bonito, precioso
**because** porque
**bed** cama *f.*; **to go to bed** acostarse (ue)
**belt** cinturón *m.*
**best** (el, la) mejor
**bicycle** bicicleta *f.*
**body** cuerpo *m.*
**bookcase** librero *m.*
**bookshelf** estante para libros *m.*
**boot** bota *f.*
**brake** freno *m.*
**breakfast** desayuno *m.*
**bring** traer (*irr.*)
**brother** hermano *m.*
**brush** cepillo *m.*; cepillarse
**building** edificio *m.*
**bus** autobús *m.*
**but** pero
**butcher** carnicero *m.*
**buy** comprar

**cafeteria** cafetería *f.*
**call** llamar
**can** poder (ue, *irr.*)
**candidate** candidato *m.*
**careful** cuidadoso; **to be careful** tener (*irr.*) cuidado
**carefully** cuidadosamente
**chain** cadena *f.*
**chair** silla *f.*
**champion** campeón *m.*, campeona *f.*
**choose** escoger (j)
**city** ciudad *f.*
**close** cerrar (ie)
**clothes** ropa *f.*
**coat** abrigo *m.*
**cold** frío; **to be cold** hacer (*irr.*) frío
**comb** peine *m.*; **to comb one's hair** peinarse
**come** venir (*irr.*); **come back** volver (ue), regresar
**comfortable** cómodo
**comfortably** cómodamente
**concert** concierto *m.*
**correct** corregir (i, j)
**cost** costar (ue)
**cough** tos *f.*; toser
**country** país *m.*
**crazily** locamente
**criminal** criminal *m.* & *f.*
**crocodile** cocodrilo *m.*
**cruise** crucero *m.*; **to take a cruise** hacer (*irr.*) un crucero
**curtain** cortina *f.*

**dangerous** peligroso
**day** día *m.*
**deodorant** desodorante *m.*
**dessert** postre *m.*
**dining room** comedor *m.*
**dish** plato *m.*
**dog** perro *m.*
**door** puerta *f.*
**downtown** centro *m.*
**dress** vestido; **to get dressed** vestirse (i)
**dresser** cómoda *f.*
**dressing gown** bata *f.*
**driver** chofer *m.*
**during** durante

**early** temprano
**earn** ganar
**earth** tierra *f.*
**easily** fácilmente
**eat** comer; **eat out** comer afuera
**elect** elegir (i, j)
**embrace** abrazar (c)
**employee** empleado *m.*, empleada *f.*
**English** inglés *m.*
**enough** suficiente
**enter** entrar

**envelope** sobre *m.*
**every** cada; **every day** todos los días; **every morning** todas las mañanas
**example** ejemplo *m.*
**exhibit** exhibición *f.*
**explain** explicar (qu)

**face** cara *f.*
**family** familia *f.*
**fast** rapido, rápidamente
**father** padre *m.*, papá *m.*
**favorite** preferido
**fender** guardafango *m.*
**film** película *f.*
**fingerprint** huella digital *f.*
**fireman** bombero *m.*
**first** primero
**fish** pescar (qu)
**follow** seguir (i, g)
**food** comida *f.*
**football** fútbol *m.*
**freezer** congelador *m.*
**friend** amigo *m.*, amiga *f.*
**fun** diversión *f.*; **to have fun** divertirse (ie)
**furniture** muebles *m. pl.*

**game** partido *m.*; juego *m.*
**gas** gasolina *f.*
**get up** levantarse
**giraffe** jirafa *f.*
**give** dar (*irr.*)
**go** ir (*irr*).; **to go away** irse
**good** bueno
**grandparents** abuelos *m. pl.*

**hair** peló *m.*
**hairdresser** peluquero *m.*, peluquera *f.*
**hand** mano *f.*
**happy** contento
**hat** sombrero *m.*
**have** haber (*irr.*); tener (*irr.*); **to have to** tener que
**headlight** faro *m.*, luz *f.*
**helmet** casco *m.*
**here** aquí
**hike** dar (*irr.*) una caminata
**homework** tarea *f.*
**hood** cubierta *f.*, capó *m.*
**hour** hora *f.*
**house** casa *f.*
**how?** ¿cómo?; **how old are you?** ¿cuántos años tienes?
**hundred** cien

**idea** idea *f.*
**Indian** indio *m.*, india *f.*
**intelligently** inteligentemente
**invite** invitar
**island** isla *f.*

**jacket** chaqueta *f.*; **sports jacket** saco de sport *m.*
**jail** cárcel *f.*
**job** puesto *m.*, trabajo *m.*
**judge** juez *m.*

**knock** (*on the door*) tocar (qu) a la puerta
**know** saber (*irr.*); (*to be acquainted with*) conocer

**land** aterrizar (c)
**large** grande
**last** último; **last summer** el verano pasado
**lawyer** abogado *m.*, abogada *f.*
**learn** aprender
**leave** salir, irse (*irr.*)
**lend** prestar
**leopard** leopardo *m.*
**license plate** placa *f.*
**lie** mentira *f.*
**light** luz *f.*
**like** gustar
**listen** escuchar
**little** pequeño, chico; poco
**live** vivir
**long** largo
**look (at)** mirar; **to look for** buscar (qu)
**lot: a lot** mucho
**lotion** loción *f.*; **suntan lotion** loción bronceadora
**lunch** almuerzo *m.*; **to have lunch** almorzar (ue, c)

**magazine** revista *f.*
**mailbox** buzón *m.*
**mailman** cartero *m.*
**many** muchos; **how many?** ¿cuántos?
**married** casado
**meal** comida *f.*
**meat** carne *f.*
**menu** menú *m.*
**mirror** espejo *m.*; **rear-view mirror** espejo retrovisor
**mistake** error *m.*
**Monday** lunes
**money** dinero *m.*
**moon** luna *f.*
**morning** mañana *f.*
**mother** madre *f.*, mamá *f.*
**movies** cine *m.*
**much** mucho; **how much?** ¿cuánto?

**name** nombre *m.*; **what's your name?** ¿cómo te llamas?
**near** cerca (de)
**need** necesitar
**neighborhood** barrio *m.*
**neither** tampoco; **neither . . . nor** ni . . ni
**never** nunca, jamás
**new** nuevo
**newspaper** periódico *m.*, diario *m.*
**night** noche *f.*
**nobody** nadie
**none** ninguno
**nothing** nada
**now** ahora

**obtain** conseguir (i, g)
**often** a menudo; frecuentemente
**oil** aceite *m.*
**old** viejo; **older, oldest** mayor; **to be__years old** tener (*irr.*)__años; **how old are you?** ¿cuántos años tienes?
**one** un, uno
**only** sólo, solamente
**open** abrir
**outing** excursión *f.*

**pail** cubo *m.*
**pajama** pijama *m.*
**palm tree** palmera *f.*
**pants** pantalones *m. pl.*
**parents** padres *m. pl.*
**party** fiesta *f.*
**people** gente *f.*
**perfectly** perfectamente
**photographer** fotógrafo *m.*, fotógrafa *f.*
**picture** foto *f.*; **to take pictures** sacar (qu) fotos
**pilot** piloto *m.*
**place** lugar; **to take place** tener (*irr.*) lugar
**planet** planeta *m.*
**plate** plato *m.*
**play** jugar (ue, gu)
**player** jugador *m.*, jugadora *f.*
**political** político
**postcard** tarjeta postal *f.*
**prefer** preferir (ie)
**professional** profesional
**programmer** programador *m.*, programadora *f.*

**protect** proteger (j)
**pursue** perseguir (i, g)
**put** poner (*irr.*); **to put on** ponerse
**pyramid** pirámide *f.*

**quickly** rápidamente; pronto
**quietly** en silencio, sin hacer ruido

**rain** llover (ue)
**raincoat** impermeable *m.*, gabardina *f.*
**ready** listo; **to be ready** estar (*irr.*) listo
**really** realmente
**reporter** periodista *m.* & *f.*
**ring** anillo *m.*, sortija *f.*
**river** río *m.*
**robbery** robo *m.*
**room** cuarto *m.*
**row** remar
**rubber** goma *f.*
**rug** alfombra *f.*
**rule** regla *f.*
**ruler** regla *f.*
**run** correr; **to run away** escaparse

**sailboat** barco de vela *m.*
**sand** arena *f.*
**sandcastle** castillo de arena *m.*
**say** decir (*irr.*)
**scream** gritar
**sea** mar *m.*
**seashell** concha *f.*
**see** ver
**seriously** seriamente
**serve** servir (i)
**shark** tiburón *m.*
**shine** brillar
**shirt** camisa *f.*
**shoe** zapato *m.*
**shoemaker** zapatero *m.*
**shovel** pala *f.*
**sister** hermana *f.*
**sit (down)** sentarse (ie)
**ski** esquiar
**sleep** dormir (ue)
**slipper** pantufla *f.*, zapatilla *f.*
**snake** culebra *f.*, serpiente *f.*
**soap** jabón *m.*
**soccer** fútbol *m.*
**sock** calcetín *m.*, media *f.*
**somebody** alguien
**something** algo
**soon** pronto
**sorry** perdón; **I'm sorry** lo siento
**soup** sopa *f.*
**speak** hablar
**spider** araña *f.*
**squirrel** ardilla *f.*
**stamp** estampilla *f.*
**star** estrella *f.*
**station** estación *f.*; **police station** estación de policía
**steering wheel** volante *m.*
**stop** parar; parada *f.*
**store** tienda *f.*
**story** cuento *m.*, historia *f.*
**stove** estufa *f.*
**strong** fuerte
**study** estudiar
**style** moda; **in style** de moda
**summer** verano *m.*
**sun** sol *m.*
**sunbathe** tomar el sol
**Sunday** domingo
**sunglasses** gafas de sol *f. pl.*
**sweater** suéter *m.*
**swim** nadar
**swimming pool** piscina *f.*
**syrup** jarabe *m.*; **cough syrup** jarabe para la tos

**table** mesa *f.*; **coffee table** mesita de café; **night table** mesita de noche
**take** tomar; llevar; **to take away** llevarse; **to take off** quitarse
**tank** tanque *m.*
**team** equipo *m.*
**tell** decir (*irr.*); contar (ue)
**thermometer** termómetro *m.*
**there** ahí, allí
**thief** ladrón *m.*
**thing** cosa *f.*
**tie** corbata *f.*
**tiger** tigre *m.*
**time** tiempo *m.*; vez *f.*; **at what time?** ¿a qué hora?; **on time** a tiempo
**tire** llanta *f.*
**tissue** pañuelo de papel *m.*
**today** hoy
**toilet paper** papel higiénico *m.*
**tomorrow** mañana
**too** también
**toothbrush** cepillo de dientes *m.*
**toothpaste** pasta de dientes *f.*
**towel** toalla *f.*
**train** tren *m.*
**travel** viajar
**tree** árbol *m.*
**trip** viaje *m.*
**trunk** maletero *m.*
**T-shirt** camiseta *f.*
**Tuesday** martes
**turkey** pavo *m.*
**turtle** tortuga *f.*

**umbrella** paraguas *m.*; sombrilla *f.*
**underneath** debajo de
**understand** comprender, entender (ie)
**undress** desvestirse (i)
**use** usar, utilizar

**vacation** vacaciones *f. pl.*
**vase** florero *m.*
**very** muy
**vest** chaleco *m.*
**veterinarian** veterinario *m.*, veterinaria *f.*
**victim** víctima *f.*
**visit** visitar

**waiter** mesero *m.*; camarero *m.*
**wake up** despertarse (ie)
**wall** pared *f.*
**want** querer (ie, *irr.*)
**wash** lavar; **to wash oneself** lavarse
**watch** mirar
**wear** llevar, usar
**weekend** fin de semana *m.*
**well** bien
**whale** ballena *f.*
**what?** ¿qué?
**wheel** rueda *f.*
**when** cuando; **when?** ¿cuándo?
**where?** ¿dónde?; **where (to)?** ¿adónde?
**which?** ¿cuál? ¿qué?
**who?** ¿quién?
**whole** entero, todo
**whom** ¿a quién?
**whose?** ¿de quién?
**why?** ¿por qué?
**window** ventana *f.*
**with** con
**word** palabra *f.*
**work** funcionar; trabajar
**write** escribir

**year** año *m.*
**yesterday** ayer
**young** joven; **younger, youngest** menor, más pequeño; **young man** joven *m.*; **young woman** joven *f.*

**zoo** (parque) zoológico *m.*

# Grammatical Index

# Topical Index